PEACE IN TATTERS

PEACE IN TATTERS

Israel, Palestine, and
the Middle East

Yoram Meital

LYNNE
RIENNER
PUBLISHERS

BOULDER
LONDON

Published in the United States of America in 2006 by
Lynne Rienner Publishers, Inc.
1800 30th Street, Boulder, Colorado 80301
www.rienner.com

and in the United Kingdom by
Lynne Rienner Publishers, Inc.
3 Henrietta Street, Covent Garden, London WC2E 8LU

Excerpt from "A State of Siege," by Mahmoud Darwish, translated by Yoram Meital,
reprinted by permission from Riyad al-Rayyis lil-Kutub wa-al-Nashr, 2002.

Library of Congress Cataloging-in-Publication Data
Meital, Yoram.
    Peace in tatters : Israel, Palestine, and the Middle East / Yoram Meital.
      p. cm.
    Includes bibliographical references and index.
    ISBN 1-58826-362-2 (hardcover : alk. paper) — ISBN 1-58826-387-8 (pbk. : alk. paper)
      1. Arab-Israeli conflict—1993—Peace.   2. Israel—Politics and government—1993-   3.
Palestinian Arabs—Politics and government—1993-   4. Al-Aqsa Intifada, 2000-   5. United
States—Politics and government—1993-2001.   6. United States—Politics and government—
2001-   I. Title.
DS119.76.M444   2005
956.05'4—dc22
                                                                          2005011009

British Cataloguing in Publication Data
A Cataloguing in Publication record for this book
is available from the British Library.

Printed and bound in the United States of America

The paper used in this publication meets the requirements
∞ of the American National Standard for Permanence of
Paper for Printed Library Materials Z39.48-1992.

5   4   3   2   1

For Ronit

These are the times of chaos; opinions are a scramble; parties are a jumble; the language of new ideas has not been created; nothing is more difficult than to give a good definition of oneself in religion, in philosophy, in politics. One feels, one knows, one lives and at need, one dies for one's cause, but one cannot name it. It is the problem of the times to classify things and men. . . . The world has jumbled its catalog.

—Alphonse de Lamartine

Contents

Acknowledgments

It is my pleasant duty to express my gratitude to a number of colleagues and friends who helped with the preparation of this treatise. I would like to thank Gabi Sheffer, who challenged me to write a book on so loaded and knotty a subject. My appreciation goes to Lynne Rienner, head of the publishing house that has lent its patronage to the English version of the book. Special gratitude goes to friends and colleagues at Ben-Gurion University—Amnon Raz-Krakotzkin; Haggai Ram; Zvi Barel, who read the complete manuscript; and Benny Morris, who read Chapter 7. The crucial comments, suggestions, and questions raised by these experienced, critical readers were a welcome contribution to the book's final form. Odelia Naamani, Oren Steinitz, and Hussein al-Ghul proved to be exceptional research assistants, for which they have my thanks and appreciation. I thank Evelyn Abel for her outstanding translation of the Hebrew text. Last but not least, I would like to thank my wife, Ronit, who during the book's incubation was an interested, encouraging audience and at its completion was, as usual, its first reader. It goes without saying that the responsibility for any errors and for all formulations is mine alone.

—*Yoram Meital*

1

Introduction

In the summer of 2000, the cards of the Israeli-Palestinian conflict were completely reshuffled. A brand-new game began. The ambitious attempt to resolve all outstanding issues between the parties at Camp David (11–25 July) had come to nothing, and violence, terror, and incitement became the daily fare of the peoples dwelling in the disputed land. In both societies, mainstream and fringe alike succumbed to despair, rage, and loathing. The Oslo political process, often referred to as "Oslo" or the "peace process," appeared to be bankrupt. This backslide into bloodshed raised many questions: What caused the Israeli-Palestinian "peace process" to collapse? How were the hegemonic narratives about the political process and the resumption of violence molded in both societies? How do the changes in US policy in the Middle East affect the Israeli-Palestinian conflict? What conditions might help mend the tattered peace? In Israeli and Palestinian eyes, can the adoption of unilateral measures (a separation fence and disengagement) pose an alternative to a two-state solution? This book is the result of my attempt to understand the perplexing new situation.

The first part of the book ("The Goal: An End to Conflict") is devoted to the historicization of the political process from the 1948 war to the failed summit held by Ehud Barak, Yasser Arafat, and Bill Clinton at Camp David. In this part, the emphasis is on the repercussions of agreements signed between Israel, Egypt, and the United States at the end of the 1970s for the Arab-Israeli conflict in general and the Israeli-Palestinian conflict in particular. The launching of the Oslo process is described as a crossroads marked by both continuity and change. With regard to continuity, a number of basic guidelines first raised in the Camp David Accords (17 September 1978) made their way into the Declaration of Principles (DOP, 13 September 1993). With regard to change, the foremost development was mutual recognition by Israel and the

1

Palestine Liberation Organization (PLO) and their adoption of the assumption that the conflict's resolution would be based on partitioning the disputed land into two states. As in the 1978 Camp David blueprint, so in the DOP it was agreed that final status would be discussed only after a lengthy interim stage. Oslo's architects hoped that the new dynamics would so alter relations between the two peoples as to allow the sides to make the far-reaching compromises and take the risks necessary to seal a much-desired peace. In the Middle East and beyond, expectations for the "peace process" skyrocketed. Today, more than a decade after the breakthrough of Oslo, it is all too clear that the sides managed to put in place a "process" reflecting numerous agreements and arrangements but very little "peace." In discussing the disparity between the "peace process" and the facts on the ground, I make two chief arguments. First, I consider the problems with the Oslo blueprint itself and the simplistic way that the formulators sought not only to create something out of nothing—a "peace process"—but also politically and publicly to avoid dealing with the basic questions of the Israeli-Palestinian conflict. Second, the internal political and national contexts in both Israeli and Palestinian society did and do exercise a decisive influence on the policies adopted by the leaders and their approach to the other side.

The Israeli and Palestinian leaders both attributed great weight to domestic political constraints yet found it very difficult to appreciate the constraints on the other side. Nor did either side waste much energy considering the effects of their deeds and declarations on the opposite camp and its leaders. While each side scrutinized the statements of the other with a fine-toothed comb, the spokespeople on each side did not bother to examine the impact of their own pronouncements on the other. In many instances, the assertions of the other side were cited piecemeal, with little attention paid to the context in which they had been made. In principle, each side showed an inflated indulgence for all manner of scathing proclamations emanating from its own society, a measure of lenience that suddenly evaporated when it came to like remarks made in the opposite camp. Examples are countless. Thus, there was no straightforward, official condemnation of Minister Avigdor Lieberman's repeated comments (from January 2001 on) that, in certain circumstances, he, as minister of National Infrastructure, would support the burning of Lebanon's capital and the bombing of Egypt's Aswan Dam. Racist, inflammatory, anti-Arab remarks voiced by such Israeli politicians as Benny Eilon, Michael Kleiner, and many others were left to hang in the air without triggering the rejoinder they deserved. Sometimes, even ostensibly pertinent comments had an unfortunate effect, such as Prime Minister Ariel Sharon's declaration in a press interview (13 April 2001) that "The War of Independence has not ended" to this day. The Palestinian side saw this as an unveiled threat showing Israel's intentions to conquer the West Bank and Gaza Strip and transfer the Palestinians out of the territories. By the same token, Arafat's speech at a Johannesburg mosque (10 May 1994) left the bleak impression that he had adopted the Oslo blueprint and accords with Israel solely as a tactical move. He likened his conduct toward Israel to that of the Prophet Muhammad, who in 628 had signed a cease-fire with the Quraish tribe, only to later attack and quell his foes on the battlefield and conquer Mecca by storm. Many in Israel took the analogy as evidence of Arafat's true motives and demanded a halt to the political negotiations with the Palestinian Authority (PA) that he headed. Arafat's occasional public slurs also helped chip away Israeli trust. When in June 2001, twenty-five Israeli teenagers were murdered at the Dolphinarium discotheque on the Tel Aviv–Jaffa seam, Arafat remarked that he suspected Israel to have been behind the terror attack; the perpetrator was a young Palestinian from Hamas who had donned a belt of explosives and blown himself up near the doorway. Members of militant Islamic groups like Hamas, Islamic Jihad, Hizbollah, and al-Qaeda frequently made similar arrogant and insulting comments about Israel and even just about Jews.

In Israel, different political parties and, of course, the settler public and their supporters thoroughly opposed the Oslo blueprint and took various steps to thwart its implementation. The Oslo process also met with strong criticism in the governing parties (in both Labor and, to a larger extent, in Likud). Nevertheless, the accords with the Palestinians had been signed in the name of the state of Israel, and its leaders were obliged to honor them regardless of political considerations or ideological commitment. Despite their different party affiliations, prime ministers such as Benjamin Netanyahu and Ehud Barak were bound by the Oslo course, although neither man made any bones about his dissatisfaction with and reservations concerning the agreements concluded by their predecessors. Their words and actions seemed to imply at times that to proceed along this road was to jeopardize the vital interests of the state of Israel. In Chapters 3 and 4, I show how they introduced into signed agreements and commitments "amendments" designed to reduce the risks to Israel. In the Palestinian camp as well, the Oslo blueprint was condemned and opposed by organizations, movements, and personalities from the whole spectrum of political opinion. Hamas, the Islamic Resistance Movement, posed an alternative, advocating religious (Islamic) resistance (*al-muqawama*) à la the Muslim Brotherhood. Islamic Jihad shared a similar platform on the anti-Israel struggle but dressed it (and a whole slew of internal affairs) in a more radical interpretation. In the post-1993 Palestinian climate of increasingly bitter disappointment, the two movements firmed up their postures and filled their ranks with activists and supporters. The mission was to torpedo the political process. Members did not shrink from acts of terror against Israelis per se, and perpetrators were portrayed as heroes ready to sacrifice themselves for their country and beliefs. What's more, national organizations on the left, such as the Popular Front for the Liberation of Palestine (PFLP) and the Popular Democratic Front for the Liberation of Palestine (PDFLP), lambasted the political process and the Palestinian leadership that had embraced it. They described the accords as a charade; their activists called for continued armed struggle and the meaningful representation of all political streams in the Palestinian administration and government. The PA leadership, with Arafat at its head, was also slammed by public figures and intellectuals whose pointed pens and sharp tongues found expression in books, articles, and media interviews. The latter included the recently deceased Edward Said, the most prominent Palestinian intellectual of our times, who produced a number of articles on the subject. In mid-August 2001, he referred to the Palestinian leadership as a corrupt band of "fat, cigar-chomping bureaucrats who want their business deals preserved and their VIP passes renewed, and who have lost all trace of decency or credibility," as a group leading the Palestinian people from bad to worse, instead of conducting the struggle for liberation and looking out for their true interests.[1]

Since its failure, numerous articles and statements have addressed the July 2000 Camp David summit. It was undoubtedly an event of enormous import. A discussion of its implications comprises the lion's share of this book. Chapter 5, "Camp David: The Great Charade," examines the positions and measures taken by Israel and the PA in the months preceding the Camp David summit and the course of the negotiations. In contrast to the common tendency to concentrate on results (i.e., the failed negotiations) and Arafat's sole responsibility for them, I have tried to bring out the sequence of events on both sides prior to the decisive conclave. In particular, I looked at the effects in both arenas of internal, political developments on the policy lines and stances espoused by the leaders with respect to a permanent settlement. I examined Barak's decision to embark on pivotal negotiations even though he had lost his Knesset majority, when the government "of all" that he had formed was left with only a handful of supporters. In discussing the path to the summit, I considered the lack of preparation in the months leading up to the negotiations. Its negative effects had palpable consequences at the final-status talks, primarily on the extremely complex issue of dividing sovereignty in Jerusalem and control of the holy sites. Not only did the delegations approach the most sensitive issues of the Israeli-Palestinian conflict without any prior understandings, but both senior and junior negotiators were fuzzy about a whole range of final positions. I attempted, without any embellishment, to examine the "generous offer" that Israel placed on the table, the response of the Palestinian negotiators, and the way that the Americans convened and managed the summit. This review resulted in a totally different picture from that widely held, particularly in Israel and the United States. It is my conclusion that the blueprint for final settlement proposed by Barak months in advance of and during the summit itself was based on faulty premises and that the Clinton administration should not have convoked a crucial summit at this problematic juncture when they knew full well that the preparations were raw and the chances slim of bridging the gulf and burying the conflict once and for all. In addition, US management of the negotiating agenda and teamwork was disorganized and lacked the sort of imaginative thinking that might have spared unnecessary crises, most of which were predictable. The US negotiators displayed a clear empathy for Barak and the political risks he was taking, and largely ignored the constraints of the Palestinian leadership. The bridging proposals presented by the Americans were closer to Israel's maximal positions than to the Palestinian's minimal demands. At various stages during the summit, the Palestinian leadership, notably Arafat, failed to counter proposals with their own ideas, leaving the impression that they were not ready for true compromise.

Chapters 6, 7, and 8 deal with the two separate major events that reshuffled the cards of the Arab-Israeli conflict: the second intifada and the September 11 attack in the United States. Against the backdrop of failed final-status negotiations, a wave of violence and terror began between Israelis and Palestinians at the end of September 2000. For many Israelis and Palestinians, the intifada spelled the collapse of the Oslo process. The Palestinians and others, following suit, called the struggle against Israel "the al-Aqsa intifada"; in Israel, the struggle against the Palestinians was dressed in military terms (*Homat Maggen*, or "defensive shield"; *Derekh Nehusha*, or "resolve") or more generally denoted as *Milhemet Kiyum* ("a war for survival"). A year later, on 11 September 2001, the al-Qaeda organization committed the worst act of terror ever. The fateful convergence between Osama bin Laden's 9/11 act of terror and the neoconservative Bush administration resulted in dramatic changes in US policy in countless spheres. The worldwide campaign against terror led by the United States, particularly the wars in Afghanistan and Iraq, have had visible consequences for the societies and regimes of the Middle East.

Within no time, these two events, despite their different contexts, markedly affected the Israeli-Palestinian confrontation. They toppled the lighthouses that for years had guided Israeli and Palestinian helmsmen. The one lighthouse was the peace process and the commitments undertaken by both parties to abide by signed agreements. The other was US policy in the Middle East and its commitment to see that the Arab-Israeli conflict reached a peaceful settlement.

The collapse of the political process significantly shaped consensus in Israeli and Palestinian societies regarding the responsibility for the failure of the final-status negotiations and the eruption of violence and terror. Chapters 6 and 7 consider the construction of the hegemonic narratives about the causes of the severe deterioration, their media dissemination, and their reception by various Israeli and Palestinian groups. On both sides, a sense of emergency caused the populations to close ranks. As the acts of hostility continued, there seemed to be no way out, and any real differences between left and right, religious and secular, the regime and its critics virtually vanished. Israel's dominant narrative, embraced to varying degrees across the political spectrum (with the exception of

Arab and non-Zionist political parties), centered on the following arguments: at Camp David, Israel made the Palestinians a most generous, unprecedented offer for the resolution of final-status issues, including Israel's withdrawal from the Gaza Strip and most of the West Bank and a Palestinian foothold in East Jerusalem. The negotiations collapsed once it became clear that Arafat and his aides were not interested in peace or in settling the conflict but in arrangements inimical to the very existence of Israel as the state of the Jewish people. After failing to achieve their goals at the negotiating table, the Palestinians resorted to violence and terror in the belief that Israeli society would not be able to take the heat and that its leadership would have to back down from their legitimate positions. The renewal of bloodshed in September 2000 was an "existential war" on Israel that had been masterminded in advance by the PA. Arafat blatantly controlled the violence and terror against Israeli targets, civilian and military alike. This being the case, "there is no one to talk to and nothing to talk about." Only after the Palestinians elect a new, peace-seeking leadership will it be possible to resume the peace process.

Quite often, Israeli spokespeople pinned the collapse of the final-status dialogue and the ensuing rash of violence also on the character and conduct of "the Arabs," on Islam's hostility towards Jews, and on the lack of democracy in Arab lands. These generalizations rested on the simplistic premise that religious and cultural affiliation exerts a definite, self-evident influence on the national public agenda in Arab society, including policy toward Israel. Hamstrung by Arabic culture and Islamic religion, Arabs do not know the meaning of public opinion or political opposition. The ultimate proof, so to speak, is that no Arab state has sprouted a democratic regime based on the rule of law and open to free competition for government. In the absence of such governments, there is little likelihood of concluding durable peace agreements.[2] The argument is vacuous and deserves short shrift. If the lack of democracy is the nub, how is it that Israel signed peace treaties with Egypt and Jordan? Most responses take the line that Egypt was ruled by Sadat and Jordan by King Hussein. How simple, the riddle is solved: the leader is all. For better or for worse. Time and time again, Israeli spokespeople lamented the absence in Syrian or Palestinian society of a leader cut from the same cloth as Egypt's former president or Jordan's previous king. President Sadat's eloquence and etiquette and even more so King Hussein's captured Israeli hearts. What the same Israelis ignored is that all the pretty speeches made by the two about the right to live together in peace and their public gestures for the most part had *followed* the signing of treaties based on the principle of land for peace, in other words, in an entirely different historical and political context.

The hyperfocus on leaders and wistfulness for a "new" Sadat or Hussein colored Israel's public discourse on the confrontation with the Palestinians. For decades, nearly everything concerning the Palestinians had been viewed through the prism of Arafat's personality. To be sure, Arafat had left his imprint on the Palestinian national struggle. Yet to regard him as the be-all and end-all of the whole situation is highly problematic; since the summer of 2000, this attitude has led to a pat conception of the conflict between the two peoples and a distorted narrative on the aborted Israeli-Palestinian political process. In effect, Israelis dismissed all public discussion of the factors leading up to the crisis and the conditions sustaining it; most spokespeople pushed aside the political, social, and economic setting of the bulk of the Palestinian population, who for years have lived under occupation. Moreover, undue concentration on Arafat boosted the groundless impression that Palestinians constitute a monolithic society, free of party or organizational political feuding over the national agenda.

In the public discourse on the Arab and Palestinian side, the dominant narrative as to the failure of final-status negotiations and the eruption of violence was totally different from Israel's. The Palestinians were presented as victims, and their leadership was showered with praise for standing fast against the intolerable dictates of Israel and the United States at Camp David. According to this version, there is no truth to the pervasive claim that it was Israel who came up with offers to resolve final-status issues and who displayed a readiness for far-reaching concessions both at Camp David and subsequent deliberations, whereas the Palestinians made no counterproposals and in fact missed an opportunity for real peace. Barak's "generous offer"—the argument continues—was a mere attempt to force on the Palestinians conditions that were too remote from their minimal demands for settling the conflict. They are the establishment of a Palestinian state in the West Bank and the Gaza Strip according to the 4 June 1967 borders; recognition of al-Quds as the capital of the Palestinian state, which will include the Arab neighborhoods of East Jerusalem and al-Haram al-Sharif compound (the Temple Mount); and a just solution to the refugee problem (the "right of return") on the basis of UN General Assembly Resolution 194 (11 December 1948). Only Israel's agreement in principle to these stipulations (the "rights") would have allowed the Palestinians to weigh minimal border modifications—based on an equivalent territorial "exchange"—or take into account Israel's demographic concerns with respect to the number of refugees it would permit to return to its jurisdiction. The proposal that Israel put on the table at Camp David was a "trap" to dupe the Palestinian leadership and obtain their consent to the establishment of a Palestinian entity unworthy of being called a viable, independent, and sovereign state. Such a state would consist of semi-independent cantons, a patchwork of sovereign territories, at best connected by access roads and remaining under full Israeli control. For all intents and purposes, Palestinian acceptance of the security arrangements that Barak and his people sought to force on them would have stripped their independent, sovereign entity of all meaning as a state. The main goal of the Israeli negotiators at Camp David was not a serious search for a permanent settlement or a readiness for true compromise; it was a pretext to saddle their Palestinian counterparts with the responsibility for failing to reach an agreement, while taking cynical advantage of the United States and its president. The al-Aqsa intifada was the reaction of the Palestinian people with all its factions and organizations to the impossible situation that Israel sought to perpetuate in the Occupied Territories.

Palestinian public discussion of this dominant narrative often included a simplistic approach to Israeli social processes. Israel's political pluralism, for example, was said to be a sham, there being no significant differences between the Zionist parties: both Likud-led and Labor-led governments had undeniably encouraged the establishment of settlements in the occupied territories and granted the Israel Defense Forces (IDF) a virtually free hand to act against the Palestinian civilian population. Such a focus on the bottom line ignored the long-standing political, social, and security contexts of life in Israel. On top of this, it was evident from the discourse that extensive sectors of the Arab and Palestinian publics had little or no knowledge of Israel's political system, power struggles, and conflicts of interest. (The tendency to make light of Israeli democracy and its political constraints is gradually being eroded. Leading Arab media channels—primarily TV stations such as al-Jazeera, Abu Dhabi, al-Arabiyya, MBC, and LBC and newspapers such as *al-Hayat* [Arabic] and *al-Ahram Weekly* [English]—now report directly from Israel, providing political coverage as well as occasional interviews with spokespeople all across the board. Arab leaders, too, have been referring more and more to internal Israeli politics, a plain sign of its added weight.)

Israelis and Palestinians related to the dominant narrative each had cultivated on the failure of negotiations and the eruption of violence as if it were fact, brightly illuminating the irrefutable justice of its own stance. In the wake of Camp David, it was the vigorous opponents of the two-state solution who began to set the tone of the public discourse. These included individuals and groups who had striven to undermine the Oslo process from its inception, and they viewed its collapse as just reward for their toil, indeed, a sign from heaven. The stepped-up violence and sense of despair provided oppositionists with a golden opportunity to expound their arguments or to make do with a simple "we told you so." Those who disagreed with the increasingly dominant narrative were to be heard only on the fringes of the public debate, their voices mostly drowned out in the flood of reports on the growing violence. The concerted embedding of the dominant narrative in each society marginalized the discussion of the conflict's historical, political, and diplomatic contexts.

Chapters 9 through 11 review the attempts made in 2002–2004 to rehabilitate the Israeli-Palestinian political process. They outline various proposals and the reactions to the Saudi initiative adopted by the Arab League convening in Beirut at the end of March 2002, the Bush vision of a resolution to the Israeli-Palestinian conflict publicized some three months later, the Roadmap formulated within the Quartet (the United States, the European

Union, the UN, and Russia) and formally made public in April 2003, and the Geneva Initiative presented on the first day of December 2003. Separate discussion is devoted to the "separation fence" Israel is building and its disengagement plan. Chapter 11—"High Fences Make Good Neighbors?"—sheds light on the problematic conception of unilateral measures on which these programs thrive. A good part of the aforementioned initiatives and plans rested on the assumption of there being "no partner" in the Palestinian leadership. Few initiatives took issue with this claim but instead sought to neutralize Arafat's involvement in a renewed political process. The decisive influence of the problematic narrative as to sole Palestinian responsibility for the failure of the peace process thus becomes readily apparent. It is an enlightening illustration of the terrific impact of widely held public conceptions on decision- and policymaking.

I chose to end the book with what was defined at the end of 2004 as a "window of opportunity." A series of events induced many commentators and politicians to conclude that the Israeli-Palestinian conflict was on the verge of dramatic change. Arafat's death and Mahmoud Abbas's (Abu Mazen's) election as his successor, Bush's reelection for a second term of office and his declaration that the US government would accord top priority to settling the conflict, Ariel Sharon's resolve to forge ahead with the disengagement plan, and Egypt's growing involvement—all these strengthened the impression that the Middle East was on the threshold of a new era. In Chapter 12, I added my own assessment of this forecast. Mainly, I sought to drive home the recognition that, unless the basic questions of the Israeli-Palestinian conflict are met head-on, a durable peace cannot be achieved. Answering these questions calls for a political and public discussion that has not even begun. Without a thorough revamping of rampant misconceptions, there is no chance of settling the conflict by peaceful means. The two sides still have a long way to go before they can reach calm and security.

Notes

1. Said, *The End of the Peace Process*, p. 368. Said reiterated the claim that, ultimately, Arafat and his aides had bowed to the dictates imposed on them during the Oslo process, for all practical purposes harming the chances of establishing an independent, sovereign Palestinian state.

2. In an article published by Benjamin Netanyahu on the topic, he claimed: "Since the chances of real democratization of the Arab world are slim, stable peace in the Middle East must be based on the force of deterrence. . . . What has prevented an Arab attack on the state of Israel in the past 20 years is our control of the Golan and of the hills of Judea and Samaria. . . . Any relinquishment of these lands in the framework of a peace treaty would harm Israel's deterrent capability, endanger its security and invite

additional attack." Thus, for reasons of morality (democracy) and security Netanyahu spurned the formula of "land for peace." *Haaretz*, 21 June 1993. It goes without saying that the regard for democratization as a prior condition for peace did not characterize only spokespeople of Israel's right. In an article written during the deliberations of the Palestinian leadership after Arafat's passing ("Ha-tnai le-hesder: Democratizatzya" [The condition for a settlement: Democratization]), senior journalist Ari Shavit argued that Israel should now adopt a "new paradigm" focused on the demand to establish a democratic regime in Palestinian society. "No Israeli-Palestinian agreement will survive the test of time without such a transformation, since no unilateral Israeli measure will be of sustainable stability in the absence of such change and because, unlike in the past, such change is possible." *Haaretz*, 18 November 2004. The interrelations of freedom to people and foreign policy were the main theme in Natan Sharansky's book (*The Case for Democracy*). The book circulated around the globe following President Bush's statement that this text reflects his perceptions on foreign policy.

Part 1

The Goal:
An End to Conflict

2

From War to Peace

In the years 1947–1948, the seeds of the greatest controversy of the Arab-Israeli conflict were sown, sprouting the prevailing Israeli and Arab narratives on the events of this period. On one point, however, the descriptions agree: the war of 1948 was a war of "no choice." Zionism, which took its first hesitant steps as the national movement of Jewish people toward the close of the nineteenth century, soon became a worldwide organization, its leaders assiduously creating the institutions of the state-in-the-making. The Balfour Declaration (November 1917) issued by the British government, as well as some of the measures of the British Mandate government in the country from the early 1920s, were regarded by the Zionist leadership as congruous with its desire to establish a Jewish state.[1] Mainly, however, the partitioning of the mandatory land area in Palestine won international backing because of World War II and specifically the Holocaust against European Jewry. The bitter war against Nazi Germany, along with the struggle of Jewish and Arab movements and organizations against the Mandate, induced Britain to relinquish its hold on the disputed land in 1948 and leave its political future to the UN. In parallel, there was a swelling stream of Jewish immigrants to the country, providing an unprecedented boost for the two hallmarks of practical Zionism: *'aliya* (Jewish immigration or "ascent" to the land of Israel) and *hityashvut* (settling the land).

These developments contrasted sharply with how the Arabs and especially the Palestinians viewed the essence of the conflict with Zionism and the possibility of resolving it by consent. The Palestinian leadership, though seriously divided, nevertheless concurred on one basic principle: resolute opposition to the establishment of a Jewish state. They saw the widening international support for the idea of a Jewish state based on partition as an attempt to right the evil done to European Jewry in the Holocaust by doing the Arabs, particularly the Palestinians, another evil. To them, the immigration to and settlement of Jews in Palestine reflected Zionism's colonial nature. But they lacked the wherewithal to thwart these developments, being plagued by serious shortcomings: the absence of a consolidated leadership acceptable to most of Palestinian society, reliance on support from Arab states that were themselves enmeshed in rivalry, a dearth of material resources, and an inability to organize governmental institutions and a military force.

Against this background, the UN General Assembly adopted Resolution 181 (29 November 1947). The "partition resolution," as it became known, provided for the conclusion of the British Mandate and the establishment of two states in the area west of the Jordan River. The proposed territorial partition, the internationalization of Jerusalem, and Jewish-Arab cooperation at the state level were contingent on the two sides agreeing to the partition principle and each recognizing the right of the other to self-determination. Mutual recognition was, in fact, the major obstacle. In both societies, the majority of the population aspired to a state of their own in the entire territory of Palestine/the land of Israel; for both, mutual recognition meant giving up this hope. The Arab peoples, particularly the Palestinians, on principle rejected the idea of a Jewish state in any part of the land of Palestine. Moreover, they objected to the partition borders, which left control over most of the country's territory (55 percent) in the hands of the demographically smaller group—the Jews (estimated at 620,000 to 650,000, as opposed to 1.3 million Palestinians).[2] In diplomatic messages and public statements, Arab leaders remonstrated against the partition proposal, indeed declaring that they would resort to force to block the establishment of a Jewish state. As far as they were concerned, Israel's proclamation of independence would be a casus belli—an act of aggression endangering paramount Arab interests. To a large extent, the Arab spokespeople ensnared themselves in commitments and promises. Few decisionmakers or army personnel really examined the readiness and fitness of Arab armies to wage a full-fledged war. The reservations of those who did were a drop in the ocean of muscle-flexing rhetoric supplied by leaders in echo of public demands. The leaders of the Jewish *yishuv* (the prestate Jewish community in Palestine) also deliberated over the UN's partition proposal. Not all were prepared to yield areas that they considered integral to the homeland and Israel's historical patrimony to the earmarked Arab state. Nonetheless, the national mainstream under David Ben-Gurion managed to get the Zionist national institutions to agree to partition. The recognition accorded by the nations of the world to the Jewish state was regarded by most of the leadership as Zionism's crowning achievement. Another important consideration for partition advocates was the possibility of opening up the state's borders to millions of *'olim* (Jewish immigrants), along with the assessment that the Arabs would in any case reject the partition proposal, making it impossible to predict the Jewish state's future and final borders.

In mid-May 1948, the Zionist leadership proclaimed the independence of the state of Israel. The violence that had been escalating between the two sides since the UN vote soon turned into all-out war. The armies of Egypt, Transjordan (which became the Hashemite Kingdom of Jordan in April 1949), Syria, and Iraq and the Palestinian militias launched an attack on the state of Israel, their actions marked above all by the absence of political and military coordination. Playing against the aggressors were a lack of preparedness for a drawn-out, overall campaign; faulty military planning; mistaken assumptions about enemy forces; the absence of a chain of command; the poor condition of the fighting forces; long, inadequate supply lines; reliance on unreliable intelligence; and a baleful mutual distrust among Arab leaders. On the other side, the Zionist leadership had shown an impressive ability to recruit most of its manpower; numerous domestic and foreign resources had been harnessed to the war effort; the sense of emergency and fear of catastrophe contributed to the general response; the political and military levels cooperated efficiently; and reliable intelligence made it possible to exploit the weaknesses of the Arab forces. All these factors helped Israel chalk up gains in the campaign.

The long months of war ended in Israel signing armistice agreements with Egypt, Lebanon, Jordan, and Syria between February and July 1949. The overriding Israeli spirit was well captured in popular songs and literary works: a sense of profound loss for the thousands of casualties who fell in the campaign, mingled with a new optimism. The war left the nascent state holding far more extensive territory than it had been allotted by the partition plan. By far, most of the population within the 1949 ceasefire lines was now Jewish. The "departure" of hundreds of thousands of Palestinians from their homes in the course of battle was exploited for a rapid takeover of hundreds of villages and tens of thousands of houses, soon to be placed at the disposal of the new inhabitants of the Promised Land. The Palestinian minority (more than 150,000 in 1949) that remained within the new borders of the state of Israel was placed under strict military rule that lasted seventeen years.[3] From the point of view of Israelis, this was the price the Arabs had to pay for their aggression and refusal to recognize the state of Israel's right to exist. Concomitant with the continued state of belligerence with the Arabs, a highly complex domestic task now faced Israeli society: the absorption of more than a million Jewish immigrants who arrived on Israel's shores within a very short space of time.

Their resounding defeat did not dent the implacable refusal of the Arab public to recognize the state of Israel and enter into political talks with it. Many continued to treat the establishment of the Jewish state as a sin and its expanding cooperation with Western states as a sure sign that it was a pawn designed to further the interests of Western powers. In several Arab states, the presence of hundreds of thousands of Palestinian refugees had significant consequences.[4] On the eve of and especially during the 1948 war, the roads were filled with columns of Palestinians, most of whom had abandoned their homes for fear of hostilities; a minority of unclear numbers was expelled. More than 150,000 sought shelter in Lebanon and Syria, flocking to towns and being housed in refugee camps. A far higher figure (about 550,000) made their way to the West Bank (of the Jordan River) and the Gaza Strip, which as a result of the war fell into Jordanian and Egyptian hands, respectively. Jordan's decision to annex the West Bank and grant citizenship to more than 350,000 Palestinians altered the kingdom's social, political, geographic, and demographic realities. The Palestinians soon made up the majority of Jordan's population. Their representation in governmental institutions and the business sector grew increasingly, though the royal house and the social sectors that backed it strove to preserve the realm's Hashemite-Jordanian character. According to numerous Arab spokespeople, keeping the Palestinians in refugee camps was to be preferred over integrating them into permanent communities in Arab states. The most common explanation given for this was the fear that their full integration would primarily serve Israel's claim that the Palestinians had a choice of some twenty countries in which to be absorbed, whereas Israel was the only Jewish state, and it would therefore resist the demand to repatriate the refugees.

The serious consequences of the 1948 war unleashed sharp public debate in Arab societies. While the ruling elites resorted to excuses, pretexts, and conspiracy theories to explain the fiasco, there was also unadorned criticism of the decisionmakers. In this climate, the prominent Arab intellectual, Constantine Zureik, gave the name *al-Nakba* (loosely, the catastrophe) to the 1948 war. Born in Syria but having spent most of his active life in Beirut, Zureik wrote and published a book in which he leveled most of his criticism at the Arab regimes that had waged the losing battle and incisively examined Arab weakness as a nation called upon to meet the complex challenges posed by various forms of Western imperialism.[5] Like many other Arab nationalists, he was quick to express his support for the revolutionary regimes ensconced in Egypt, Syria, and Iraq since the 1950s. Following Egypt's accomplishments in the Suez campaign and the establishment of the Egyptian-Syrian union, many Arabs had looked in hope and admiration to Gamal Abdul Nasser. His enormous popularity with tens of millions of Arabs from Morocco in the west to Iraq in the east blurred his title as president of Egypt and sharpened his image as the ultimate pan-Arab leader. In Arab eyes, the failure of the British-French-Israeli incursion into Egyptian territory in the autumn of 1956 and the withdrawal of their forces a few months later had been a watershed. After decades of foreign rule, the true independence they longed for had seemed closer than ever. In many Arab hearts, the statements made by Egypt's revolutionary leadership, that Egypt was committed to the Palestinian cause and would struggle uncompromisingly against Israel, planted a sure sense that another confrontation was merely a question of time.

The 1967 Crisis and Its Repercussions

No one had foreseen the outbreak of war in early June 1967 nor, certainly, its results and repercussions. The battles that began with a massive air raid by Israel sounded the opening note for one of the shortest wars in history. The fighting lasted a total of 132 hours. The campaign on the southern front was, in fact, decided on the first morning of June 5 with the destruction of most of Egypt's air power. The Israeli Defense Forces (IDF) quickly gained control of the Sinai Peninsula and took the Gaza Strip by storm. The conquest of the West Bank, including the neighborhoods and villages of East Jerusalem, saw fierce battles between the IDF and the Jordanian Legion. At a crucial point in the fighting, a decision was taken to conquer the Golan Heights. Thus, after six days of warfare, Israel had conquered Arab areas more than three times the size of its territory on the eve of the war. The Arabs were drubbed. And once more, processions of Palestinian refugees plied the roads, most of them from the West Bank inland into the kingdom of Jordan.[6]

The June 1967 war dealt a new hand in the Israeli-Arab conflict. Its aftermath imprinted the adversaries with the telltale signs of victory and defeat that continue to linger on, nearly forty years later. Such was its impact that, in many respects, most of the parties concerned have lived in its shadow ever since. When the cannons fell silent, the muses began to roar. In Israel, the triumph of the Six Day War was celebrated with glossy albums, medallions, stamps, and textbooks. "Liberation" and "return" to the ancient patrimony were eulogized in songs and featured in literature, the theater, and the arts. Naomi Shemer's "Jerusalem of Gold," which had debuted at an annual song festival some three weeks before the war, poignantly described Jerusalem as a city "that dwells apart with a wall through its heart," whose sites are in a woeful state:

> The cisterns are dry, the market square empty
> The Temple Mount desolate—this, the Old City
> Through caverns in the rock, how the winds squeal,
> Jericho Road is blocked off, down to the Dead Sea.[7]

Right after the Six Day War, the poet added a new verse to the original three. The gist was the contrast between the city described above and its new state. In words that bored into Israel's collective consciousness, she stressed the motif of the Jewish people's return to the sites of Jerusalem:

> We've returned to the cisterns, marketplace, and square
> A shofar calls on Temple Mount—this, the Old City
> In caverns in the rock, myriad suns gleam
> Jericho Road is open, down to the Dead Sea.

"It's a lot easier to change a song than a city," the prolific songwriter told paratroopers at a performance of the new version. The song was a hit. Thirty years later, on the fiftieth anniversary of Israel's independence in 1998, it was voted the most popular Israeli song of all time. Also thirty years later, Palestinian poet Mahmoud Darwish wrote to his friend, Samih al-Qasim: "Will we repossess Jerusalem's beauty as they repossessed it with that song of theirs which destroyed us: 'Jerusalem of gold and of copper and of light?. . .' There's no question about it, Samikh," he added, "it truly cuts the flesh."[8]

In town and country, the victory was commemorated with the naming of public streets and squares after the Six Day War. The prewar anxiety was replaced by a rare euphoria. At school, pupils were taught to sketch the homeland's new borders. Classroom walls were graced by new maps flanked by pictures of war heroes, all IDF's generals. Visitors thronged to freshly liberated homeland sites, especially the Western Wall, Rachel's Tomb, and the Tomb of the Patriarchs. Israeli television, which was only just beginning to broadcast then, brought the land of Israel into the homes of the people of Israel, and the West Bank's early Jewish settlers featured as the pioneers of the era as they set down stakes in the new homeland soil.

The reunion with parts of the ancestral land that had been outside the state boundaries was bathed in awe. But the inhabitants were another story. There was no lack of disdain and disrespect for the Arab populace, whom few in this period referred to as Palestinians. For many Israelis, it was easy enough to distinguish between the numerous residents of Judea, Samaria, and the Gaza Strip and the fact that their national aspirations enjoyed no legitimacy. At most, they were regarded as temporary residents of an Israeli homeland that was now welcoming back its original sons and daughters—the generation of rebirth, valor, and victory. The Israeli image of the Arab was confined to men sporting kaffiyehs, women wearing embroidered robes and head covers, and children hawking sweets or soft drinks. Only gradually did the frosty gazes sink in, along with a demonstrative avoidance and, above all, a heavy silence. The silence of the vanquished in the thunder of the victorious. A new public discourse solidified in Israel, planting in Israeli minds a sense of the transience of the "locals." Israel soon assumed the administration of the occupied territories and population, retaining the "Jordanian order" (that had prevailed in the West Bank since the Hashemite Kingdom of Jordan annexed these territories in April 1950), and incorporating it into the "Israeli order," whose mechanisms of control invaded all walks of life in the West Bank and Gaza Strip.

Though the defeat did not lead to regime changes in Egypt, Syria, or Jordan, the seeds of change had been sown and were soon plain to see. As the days passed, more and more writers, poets, intellectuals, artists, political columnists, and spokespeople began to address the significance of the war, widely referred to as *al-Naksa*—a recurrent blow—and reminiscent of the *al-*

Nakba of twenty years back. The pan-Arab agenda was radically revamped. Gone was the "Arab Cold War," as Malcolm Kerr aptly defined relations between the revolutionary and conservative camps.[9] In the changed circumstances, the hopes pinned on Nasser's revolutionary training and leadership gave way to despair. Thrashed on the battlefield, Arab heads of state turned their attention to reconditioning their regimes and their armies. More and more, the public discourse showed signs of soul-searching. The new situation was widely described as a new stage in the history of the Arab nation, especially in the conflict with the Zionists. Like a long shadow, the sense of having lost one's way, of frustration and helplessness, was to stalk broad sectors of Arab states for years to come. Harsh self-criticism was voiced by intellectuals and artists in their works. Concomitantly, groups and organizations with a religious agenda grew significantly stronger. The leaders tried to broadcast an optimistic message: the damage could be undone; domestic and foreign challenges could be met. But few people were buying it.

The June 1967 war was a critical juncture in the history of the Palestinian people and leadership. Once the battle dust settled, the Palestinians found themselves in territories occupied by Israeli forces, a new and unfamiliar state of affairs. There was no way of knowing how it would affect daily life or how long Israel's grip on the West Bank and Gaza Strip would last. Change also came to the Palestine Liberation Organization (PLO) leadership. Since its inception in 1964, the organization had functioned under Egyptian patronage and the chairmanship of Ahmad Shuqayri, whose policies and modus operandi now came under attack. Led by Yasser Arafat, a group of young activists took over the reins of the largest Palestinian organization and took up the goal of armed struggle against Israel. Concomitantly, Arafat worked relentlessly to raise international awareness of the Palestinian national liberation struggle. With Egypt's help, the PLO formed initial contacts with the Soviet Union and many members of the bloc of nonaligned states.[10]

The first months after the June 1967 war hummed with diplomatic activity, most of it outside the Middle East. There was universal concern about the new status quo and the chances of changing it as local, regional, and global interests hung in the balance. It was not long before the dramatic transformation in the Middle East knocked on the doors of key international players, notably the two superpowers. In the summer and autumn of 1967, leaders and diplomats inside and outside the region had their hands full. With the support of the United States and Britain, Israel robustly opposed the attempts of the (Soviet-backed) Arab states to repeat the precedent of the 1956 Suez War and force on it a diplomatic agreement to withdraw from the occupied territories in exchange for security arrangements under UN supervision. After all, the unbelievable ease with which the UN forces had evacuated the Sinai Peninsula at the end of May 1967 and the closure of the Straits of Tiran were seen by Israel as proof of the impotence of the international organization in times of crisis. Israel considered withdrawing from Sinai, the Golan Heights, and significant portions of the West Bank and Gaza in exchange for full peace treaties with Egypt, Syria, and Jordan. They, however, demanded Israel's full withdrawal and rejected the idea of signing peace treaties with it in exchange for its readiness to withdraw from the conquered areas. The UN grappled with a formula for ceasefire and a peaceful accommodation to bring stability to a Middle East riddled with crisis and conflict. On 22 November 1967 these efforts culminated in the adoption of Security Council Resolution 242. Aptly termed by Henry Kissinger "constructive ambiguity," it was a carefully worded framework for a political settlement between the parties to the Arab-Israeli conflict, which lent itself to different readings. That is what made it unanimously acceptable to the permanent members of the Security Council, as well as to some of the rival camps—first to Egypt and Jordan, then to Israel, and years later, to Syria, Lebanon, and the PLO.

The adoption of UN Resolution 242 raised a sigh of relief from the many statesmen and diplomats seeking deliverance for the Middle East. But it did not alter the facts on the ground or abate the violence and flare-ups. Israel's military hastened to install security arrangements in the extensive areas now in its hands, while Arab heads of state explored ideas to stymie Israel's increasing hold on the territories it had conquered. Egypt and Jordan considered both diplomatic and military measures to retrieve the territories lost in June 1967. The contrast between the crushing blow suffered by their armed forces and the entrenchment of Israeli forces in the Sinai Peninsula, the West Bank, and the Gaza Strip posed a serious dilemma for Egyptian president Nasser and Jordan's King Hussein: how to achieve Israeli withdrawal in view of their limited military resources and the inaction in the political arena? Nasser may have declared that "what was taken by force would be regained only by force," but Egyptian officials—and more explicitly, Jordanian ones—indicated that they were prepared to resolve the crisis with Israel by peaceful means.[11] They, however, set rigid conditions: they would consent to a settlement if the parties did not have to recognize the state of Israel or negotiate directly with it or its representatives or sign a peace treaty with it. As hamstrung as it was, the very readiness of Egypt and Jordan to embark on political measures and focus the Arab conflict on the return of the territories lost in June 1967 was castigated in various Arab quarters, notably Syria, Iraq, and the PLO. Just as they had done before the June 1967 War, the latter continued to call for armed struggle over all of Palestine, summarily rejecting political means in the belief that they would lead to further pressure for Arab concessions. Thus, Egyptian and Jordanian acceptance of Resolution 242 actually exacerbated Arab polarization with regard to the management of the conflict with Israel. Concomitantly, following the defeat, Egypt and Saudi Arabia adopted a series of measures that led to the end of the Arab Cold War.

First and foremost, Egypt consented to the conditions the Saudis set for ending the war in Yemen. A decade of hostility between Arab "revolutionary" and "conservative" regimes drew to a close.

Apart from diplomatic lobbying, Egypt also took military steps to thwart Israeli efforts to maintain the status quo, at least on the Suez Canal. On top of local skirmishes, from March 1968 to August 1970 Egyptian and Israeli forces locked horns in a bloody war of attrition that brought Egypt's civilians and civilian infrastructure into the fray as well. Israel, too, paid a heavy toll, though in military casualties; its civilians and communities were far away from the front. The longer the war lasted, the more vividly it showed up UN impotence to restore calm and launch a political process based on Resolution 242. Special UN envoy Gunnar Jarring was dispatched to the region and, for all his intensive work, could only come up with a document summarizing the opposing positions. The United States, meanwhile, had stepped up its involvement in the Middle East conflict, even if most of its attention at the time was devoted to quitting Vietnam and dealing with the collateral domestic and foreign challenges posed by that aimless war. US priorities changed somewhat in the first half of the 1970s, when Egypt and the Soviet Union tightened their military cooperation. In view of the superpower standoff, President Richard Nixon did not look kindly on the stationing of advanced Soviet weapons systems and personnel on Egyptian soil.

These developments gave birth to the Rogers initiative (19 June 1970), whereby the parties were to declare a ceasefire for a defined period and resume diplomatic efforts toward a peaceful settlement based on UN Resolution 242. Egypt consented to the diplomatic endeavor, provoking the ire of the Soviet Union, which in the three years since the drubbing of the Egyptian army had fattened its aid to that country.[12] The Soviets nevertheless opted for restraint rather than upset the applecart at this stage. King Hussein and his government stood by Egypt. Saudi Arabia and the Persian Gulf states sat on the sidelines. Syria, Iraq, and the PLO let their barbs fly. Israel, too, found itself split over the Rogers initiative, both vis-à-vis the Americans and within the government. Gahal, the Herut-Liberal bloc (led by Menachem Begin and Yosef Sapir), resigned from the coalition. In the summer of 1970, not a few ministers in Golda Meir's cabinet considered the Rogers initiative dangerous to Israel's vital interests. In the search for an accommodation to bring stability to the Middle East, it was the most significant US undertaking up to that time, and both its public tabling and its acceptance by Israel and Egypt marked a US achievement. The three-month ceasefire on the Suez front put an end to the War of Attrition and made it possible for UN envoy Gunnar Jarring to renew the diplomatic battle. Everyone waited to see what the United States would do next. But the administration took its time. The adversaries who had tried to wear each other down were evidently relieved by the interval in mutual bloodletting along the Suez Canal.

At virtually the same time, Jordan was facing the worst crisis in the history of the Hashemite Kingdom: Black September, as the Jordanian-Palestinian showdown came to be known, drenched the land in blood. The entire crisis went back to the June 1967 war, when the Palestinians living in Jordanian refugee camps and towns since the 1948 war were now joined by the hundreds of thousands of newly displaced refugees. Jordan's rush to annex the West Bank following the 1948 war had made it difficult to force a separate status on the growing proportion of Palestinians in the kingdom, and it had granted them Jordanian citizenship. At the end of the 1960s, as Israel tightened its grip on the West Bank, most of the Palestinian organizations moved their headquarters eastward across the Jordan River. The support of the Palestinians who had settled along the East Bank of the Jordan River and the proximity to the battleground with Israel soon encouraged the PLO to step up its activities in Jordan and set up numerous bases and offices that provided a variety of services to their people. Jordan's large Palestinian population was an inexhaustible fount for recruiting activists.

But the separate agendas of the Hashemite Kingdom and the Palestinian organizations sparked no few differences. The attempts of the Jordanian security forces to maintain order, especially in the large cities, the refugee camps, and on the long border with Israel entailed endless confrontation with Palestinian organizations. The crisis that erupted in September 1970 soon threatened the kingdom's stability. King Hussein was determined to quell the armed Palestinian militias who posed a challenge to his rule. There was also danger of the clashes snowballing into a regional crisis. Many Palestinians and Jordanians were killed during the fighting, and rumors that Israel meant to exploit the situation troubled Arab publics throughout the Middle East. Disconcerted by reports of Syrian troops on the move and the raising of Israel's level of alert, the kingdom appealed to the United States. Egypt convened an emergency summit of Arab leaders, including King Hussein and PLO chief Yasser Arafat. Apart from the carnage in Jordan and the threat to Jordanian stability, Black September bore a recurring message: the Israeli-Palestinian conflict had significant local, regional, and international implications. The Palestinian issue was inextricably interwoven with the interests of most of the states in the Middle East and found constant expression in their policies. The Arab summit convening in Cairo to discuss the Jordanian-Palestinian crisis closed with an agreement that put a stop both to the bloodletting and soon enough also to the armed presence of Palestinian organizations in the Hashemite Kingdom.

After the last of the Arab leaders left Cairo, the Egyptian president, fifty-two, suddenly took ill. Nasser's failing health had been the talk for years, but that day his condition became critical, and he died within hours of parting from the last summit guests. The news broke like a bolt from the blue. Nasser had led the military coup (23 July 1952) that removed King Farouk and ended the monarchy, consolidating his position as both Egypt's omnipotent ruler and the era's most prominent Arab leader. He had made many foes at home and abroad, but he and his policies had also earned the admiration of wide sectors of the public in Egypt and other Arab societies.

The office of presidency was filled by Muhammad Anwar al-Sadat amid widespread doubt that the gray second-in-command could fill Nasser's shoes. Sadat, it soon appeared, had every intention of both remaining in office and re-thinking overall Egyptian policy. The status quo of "neither peace nor war" that Israel sought to force on the Arabs was seen by Egypt's decisionmakers in a stark light. Furthermore, economic indices showed the country's limited re-sources falling behind population growth as the burden on infrastructure and services grew heavier from year to year. To find a way out of these difficulties, Sadat adopted a new political-security policy that was to characterize his be-havior in the coming years: he used surprise tactics to reshuffle the cards and create new momentum. The first time he used the tactic, it failed him, which may have taught him that the success or failure of the best of initiatives de-pends on the response of rivals as well as partners. On 4 February 1971, amid talks on extending the ceasefire for another three months, Sadat put before the People's Council a peace proposal to be choreographed in stages.[13] It was the first time that the leader of a key Arab state in the conflict with Israel overtly stated that he was prepared to make peace. Other Egyptian leaders since the very end of the June 1967 war had said they were willing to settle the Middle East crisis by peaceful means. But they had rejected any solution that involved either direct dealing or the signing of a peace treaty with Israel. Sadat's Febru-ary initiative accelerated confidential diplomatic channels between Egypt and the United States. In Israel, Golda Meir's government invoked an array of ar-guments to reject and, effectively, bury it.

In view of the rife despair in the country, Sadat and his confidants now re-solved to overturn the status quo by military means: Egypt's campuses whirred with student demonstrations, and its intellectuals signed petitions against what they saw as the regime's powerlessness. The country's top brass decided to ac-cord war preparations top priority and make available the necessary funds. The war plan was again based on the element of surprise. It began with a simulta-neous attack by the armies of Egypt and Syria on Israel—a massive assault, al-beit with limited goals in keeping with the Egyptian army's resources and ca-pabilities. The two Arab armies succeeded in chalking up gains in the first week of the war, although they were subsequently largely eroded, particularly on the Golan Heights. On the Egyptian front, the campaign had been more complex. Egypt's army achieved the key goals it had set itself, including cross-ing the Suez Canal, overrunning Israel's entrenched Bar-Lev Line, and par-tially advancing eastward into Sinai. But at the same time, its Third Army fighting in Sinai found itself cut off as the IDF crossed the canal westwards, taking over areas around the town of Suez.

By the time the guns died down, the war had drastically altered the post-1967 status quo and balance of power. Egypt extolled the achievements of the October 1973 war and inaugurated an anniversary for the unprecedented victory. The link between victory on the battlefield and the start of the political process was frequently cited by its state leaders. In Israel, the fact of having been taken by surprise by the Yom Kippur war became known as *hamehdal* (the debacle), and it rocked society. That by the war's end the IDF had partially recouped major losses in Sinai and on the Golan Heights provided some consolation. But it could not erase the wrath turned both on the political establishment and later on the arrogance of the security conception sown by the Six Day War.[14] Israel's self-examination stopped short at the political level, however. As the months passed, only a minority demanded an accounting of Israeli policy toward the Arabs and withdrawal from the Occupied Territories in exchange for peace agreements.

Israel, Egypt, and Syria signed interim agreements, but basically they were local security provisions. Egypt was disillusioned by its inability to translate the achievements of the October War into meaningful political gains that would see Israel's retreat from large portions of the occupied territories. When the seeds of change began to ripen, they did so in Egypt's internal affairs. A series of declarations, laws, and amendments marked the adoption of an economic policy to reshape Egyptian society. *Al-Infitah* (opening) hinged on creating the right conditions to gradually transform Egypt from a centralized economy resting on the public sector to a market economy emphasizing the private sector and encouraging the investment of (local and foreign) private capital. But the more committed the administration became to *al-Infitah*, the more apparent it was that its success was inescapably bound up with stability and security. For Cairo, the cornerstone of the new program was thus to forge closer ties with the United States and actively involve it in settling the conflict with Israel.

Camp David: The First Time Around

Within two years of the October 1973 war, there were obvious indications that Israel sought to consolidate the familiar situation of "neither peace nor war." The war's momentum subsided. Regime changes in the United States and in Israel in the first half of 1977 brought encouraging as well as worrisome signs. The thirty-ninth US president, Jimmy Carter, showed a great interest in the Middle East from the very start and announced that his government would work toward an overall settlement of the Arab-Israeli conflict. Endorsing a peace plan prepared by the Brookings Institution, he co-opted some of its authors to his advisory staff—a sure sign of a new orientation in US policy on the Middle East. This was immediately plain to Sadat on his visit to Washington (4 April 1977) and in his meeting with the president. The two men, according to Carter's diary, shared a similar outlook from the very first. Carter was enthusiastic. He remarked to his wife, Rosalynn (and later wrote in his diary), that this had been his "best day as president."[15] In the next four years, the ties between the two were to grow stronger, only to be severed by Sadat's assassination. In Israel, general elections saw a sea change. After three decades of Mapai rule, Menachem Begin led the right-wing Likud to a historic victory. The clamors for change by various sectors of Israeli society bore fruit. Hopes for a new agenda skyrocketed. Israel deposited the reins of state in the hands of a man who had come by his reputation of political hawk honestly, and in Arab states, as in the West Bank and the Gaza Strip, people wondered what to make of it. But blasting the government from the opposition benches is one thing and bearing the onus of government another, as Begin and some of his ministers learned within a few months.

A true turning point in the history of the Arab-Israeli conflict came on 9 November 1977, with a speech delivered by Sadat before a special session of the People's Council. The move was aimed at rearranging the political chessboard, and yet again, he had planned it with care. Invited guests included PLO chairman Yasser Arafat as well as the local and international media. Sadat, on the basis of covert and overt contacts, had decided that the time had come for a daring political initiative, though few people in the audience were aware of this. No sooner had he finished speaking than his words were subjected to close scrutiny. But there was no mistaking what he had said: he was ready to travel to Jerusalem to address Israel's Knesset and embark on peace negotiations with Israel's government. All eyes now turned on Begin and Carter. Would they do their bit to facilitate the gambit? Or would it die the same death as Sadat's February 1971 proposal, made on the very same podium at the People's Council? The answer was soon in coming. The United States was busy convening an international conclave on overall peace in the Middle East and found Sadat's move a trifle inconvenient. Israel was apprehensive about Sadat's action and the sincerity of his intentions. Nevertheless, with Carter's encouragement, Begin decided to pick up the gauntlet. A formal invitation was sent out, and the countdown began. On 19 November, after the close of the Sabbath, the aircraft of the president of the Arab Republic of Egypt landed at Ben-Gurion Airport in the state of Israel. Live TV broadcasts brought the extraordinary sights and sounds into the homes of hundreds of millions of viewers across the world and in the Middle East and engraved them on their minds forever: Sadat standing in the doorway of the Boeing and waving in greeting, Sadat shaking hands with dozens of Israeli leaders and representatives, Sadat reviewing the honor guard, and the orchestra striking up the two national anthems.

The following day, Sadat addressed a festive session of Israel's parliament, and media coverage ensured that this event, too, would be widely remembered. Sadat read out his speech, composed by a close associate with obvious attention to detail.[16] It gave expression to the common linkage in the national discourse between territory, sanctity, and historical-cultural heritage. He may have chosen the motif because of Zionism's linkage between the Jewish people and the sanctity of the Promised Land. What he emphasized was this: "To us, the national soil is equal to the holy valley where God Almighty spoke to Moses—peace be upon him. None of us can, or accept to, cede one inch of it, or accept the principle of debating or bargaining over it." In fact, he presented his vision for a peaceful settlement of the Arab-Israeli conflict, the Egyptian-Israeli dispute being only a part of it. It was a speech filled with hope for a better future in which peace would reign between Israelis and Arabs, but it was also a clear statement about the present and the price of peace. In his words:

> There are facts that should be faced with all courage and clarity. There are Arab territories that Israel has occupied by armed force. We insist on complete withdrawal from these territories, including Arab Jerusalem. . . . As for the Palestinians' cause, nobody could deny that it is the crux of the entire problem. . . . In all sincerity, I tell you that there can be no peace without the Palestinians. It is a grave error of unpredictable consequences to overlook or brush aside this cause. Direct confrontation concerning the Palestinian problem, and tackling it in one single language with a view to achieving a durable and just peace, lie in the establishment of their state. . . . With all the guarantees you demand, there should be no fear of a newly born state that needs the assistance of all countries of the world. When the bells of peace ring, there will be no hands to beat the drums of war. Even if they existed, they would be soundless.

That, hereafter, was what supporters of the political process in Egypt meant by the formula of "land-for-peace": complete Israeli withdrawal from the Arab territories occupied since June 1967 in exchange for peace with Egypt, Jordan, Syria, and Lebanon and the establishment of a Palestinian state in the West Bank and Gaza Strip. Peace guaranteed stability, prosperity, and security. In their speeches, Prime Minister Menachem Begin and opposition leader Shimon Peres emphasized Israel's desire for peace, security, and normalization with the Arabs; both, however, refrained from relating directly to Sadat's words about the Palestinian issue and his proposal for a solution. Begin delivered a message that enabled the parties to open political negotiations. With characteristic pathos, he began by reviewing the link "between our People and this Land" and reminded Egypt's president of what he had seen for himself only hours before at the Yad VaShem Holocaust Martyrs and Heroes Remembrance Authority: ("With your own eyes you saw what the fate of our People was when this

Homeland was taken from it.") Then he spelled out the main message he wished to convey:

> President Sadat knows, as he knew from us before he came to Jerusalem, that our position concerning permanent borders between our neighbors and us differs from his. . . . I propose, in the name of the overwhelming majority of this parliament, that everything will be negotiable. . . . No side shall present prior conditions. We will conduct the negotiations with respect. . . . We shall conduct the negotiations as equals. There are no vanquished and there are no victors.[17]

The differences of opinion could not be masked by the festive ambience and were equally apparent in the informal talks held by Israelis and Egyptians. But the public diplomacy and public handshakes of the two men, like the pivotal interests each wished to advance, soon created the necessary momentum for Egypt, Israel, and the United States to set out in earnest on a political course. Sadat's visit to Israel sparked varied reactions. In Israel and Egypt broad sectors of the public applauded the exceptional step he had taken and the welcome he had been given. Many states expressed strong support, notably most of Europe and, naturally, the United States. Arab states and the Palestinians, however, denounced it in anger because they feared that a major Arab country intended to sign a separate peace with Israel. Only the leaders of Sudan and Oman explicitly backed the initiative. Jordan did not live up to expectations and would not lend its support. In most Arab capitals, there were demonstrations against Sadat's visit and a good deal of censure and outrage in the national media. In Egypt, too, there was a rising tide of criticism, primarily from the Muslim Brotherhood and the Nasserites, that the authorities found hard to stem. The criticism increased with the frequency of political contacts between Egypt and Israel, which were maintained with US mediation.

Israeli-Egyptian negotiations were conducted in countless meetings at various levels, a course riddled with crises that often seemed doomed to failure. Complex issues were put on the bargaining table in the full consciousness that a peace treaty between these two key states would set off significant change throughout the region, not just for Egyptians and Israelis. The negotiations climaxed with the thirteen-day Camp David summit (5–17 September 1978), where the most controversial aspects of the Israeli-Egyptian dispute were discussed, along with issues relating to the Arab-Israeli conflict as a whole. One of the thorniest points was the linkage between the Israeli-Egyptian peace treaty and future peace agreements to be reached with Arab states and the Palestinian leadership. The United States assumed a cardinal role with regard to both the management of the parley and the part played by President Carter. Carter remained personally involved beyond the summit's successful conclusion and through the acute stage of political tussling prior to the treaty's signing.

The Camp David negotiations and the agreements signed in their wake were the cornerstone of the US position in the Middle East. From the end of the 1970s, the United States increasingly emerged as the lighthouse for leaders navigating their way out of the Arab-Israeli conflict. Peace with Israel was part of a package deal consisting of economic, military, and political components. "Pax Americana" in the Middle East was to serve both the interests of the parties seeking a political settlement and those of the United States. Apart from its sincere endeavors to achieve peace between Arabs and Israelis, US policy in the Middle East at the time of the Camp David Accords was affected also by its duel with the Soviet Union, which President Ronald Reagan was to dub the Evil Empire. The collapse of the Soviet Union in the late 1980s had far-reaching repercussions for the status of the United States: the US lighthouse now began to beckon also Arab leaders who previously had spurned the format of the Camp David Accords.

The framework agreement concluded at Camp David was followed by tough haggling that resulted in Israel and Egypt signing a peace treaty on 26 March 1979.[18] There were efforts to persuade other Arab states, notably Jordan, to adopt the same framework, but to no avail. Innumerable deliberations held by Israeli, Egyptian, and US delegates on the question of autonomy in the West Bank and the Gaza Strip met with a fainthearted response. The Palestinian issue had little chance of being resolved because the PLO rejected the Camp David blueprint, and Israel and the United States would not deal with the PLO because it refused to recognize Israel and embraced terror in the struggle against it. Yet despite all these obstacles, it was soon clear that the Camp David Accords were a watershed in the history of the Arab-Israeli conflict, including the Zionist-Palestinian aspect. They had shattered one of the most deep-seated assumptions shared by Arabs and Israelis, that it was impossible to reach a political accommodation based on painful concessions by the two national communities. For dozens of years, both sides had made much of "zero sum" rhetoric and abundant explanations, the bottom line of which was "there is no one to talk to and nothing to talk about." Camp David charted both the model for resolving the conflict with Israel and the cost in the present for attaining peace in the future. The package deal was the meat of the accommodation: unqualified mutual recognition, the scope of Israel's withdrawal from Arab land occupied in the June 1967 war, security arrangements and normalization, and implementation schedules and guidelines.

Camp David planted the seeds for Israel's decolonization of the occupied territories and its relinquishment of settlements it had established there. In the international arena and particularly among large sectors of the Arab public, there was increasing awareness that the conflict's resolution would oblige the Arabs to recognize the existence of the state of Israel and its right to live securely within the borders of June 1967 and oblige Israel to cede its control of the Arab territories it had occupied in the Six Day War and agree to an accommodation for the national aspirations of the Palestinians. In many respects, Camp David laid down the basic approach that a future Palestinian entity could, at most, extend over 22 percent of mandatory Palestine. Above all, the political significance of the Camp David Accords was the ability of the negotiators to translate Security Council Resolution 242 of November 1967 into consensual frameworks to facilitate future arrangements between Israel and the Arabs, including the Palestinians. The state of Israel was established following the adoption of UN Resolution 181 on 29 November 1947, which was based on partitioning the country into Jewish and Arab states. This plan had not been implemented. Over the next twenty years, war and animosity between Arabs and Jews peaked in the Six Day War. Two decades after UN Resolution 181, Resolution 242 defined a new framework for settling the Arab-Israeli conflict by peaceful means.

The Camp David Accords were the first breach made by key parties in the wall of Arab-Israeli hostility, a wall erected chiefly by the adversaries. Their deeds and declarations laid its solid, divisive bricks. Decades of war, terror, incitement, and enmity raised and bolstered it. The crucial developments between Sadat's visit to Israel and the conclusion of the Camp David Accords pointed the way to tearing down a hefty chunk of it, but agreements alone cannot dismantle a wall, nor the stroke of a pen dissolve cement. The actions of Israeli and Egyptian leaders were needed to remove more and more bricks, bit by bit, even though at the same time other actions of theirs set new bricks in place. For neither side could ignore events taking place in its adjacent portions of the wall. Egypt was and is a major Arab state, and Israel was and is engaged in ongoing confrontation with most of the Arab peoples, notably the Palestinians, Syrians, and Lebanese.

Even as the Egyptian-Israeli agreement made a breakthrough, counterforces were equally evident: continuing violence and antagonism between Israel and Arabs, mainly the Palestinians, steadily eroded the agreements. All along, Arab and Israeli detractors slammed the Camp David formula on a variety of grounds, reinforcing the uncorroborated impression that only the governments were committed to the signed agreements, whereas the peoples remained skeptical. A certain disillusionment was also apparent among the leaders and ruling elites who had put their names to the groundbreaking accords. Inevitably, Sadat's and Begin's naive proclamations soon encountered reality. Sadat, who had been in the habit of remarking that the lion's share of the conflict was psychological, learned how real—not fanciful—was the vision of a Greater Israel and the part it played in Israeli policy. Begin realized how wrong he had been to think that Egypt's one and only interest was to regain the Sinai Peninsula or that, as far as its government and people were concerned, the Palestinian question was a mere fig leaf for the naked step it had taken of finalizing a separate peace with Israel.

Notes

1. The League of Nations assigned the United Kingdom the task of administering the territory of Palestine on August 12, 1922. The mandate defines its terms as follows: The Mandatory shall have full powers of legislation and of administration. The Mandatory shall be responsible for placing the country under such political, administrative, and economic conditions as will secure the establishment of the Jewish national home, as laid down in the preamble, and the development of self-governing institutions, and also for safeguarding the civil and religious rights of all the inhabitants of Palestine, irrespective of race and religion. The British Mandate came to an end on May 15, 1948.

2. Morris, *Righteous Victims*, p. 192.

3. Morris, *Righteous Victims*, p. 259.

4. The number of Palestinian refugees remains a controversial issue. Official figures published by Israel (520,000–550,000) and by the Palestinians (900,000–1,000,000) reflect the gulf in the estimates. In his groundbreaking work on the subject, historian Benny Morris put the figure at about 700,000. See Morris, *Birth*, p. 604. For a sociological analysis of the various refugee communities, see Kimmerling and Migdal, *Palestinian People*, pp. 135–239.

5. The book *Ma'ane al-Nakba* [The meanings of the *Nakba*] was incorporated in the first volume of his complete works. See Zureiq, *al-A'mal al-fikriyya al-'amma lil-duktur Qustantine Zureik* [The complete works of Qustantine Zureik], pp. 195–260.

6. About 250,000 Palestinian refugees sought shelter in the East Bank (of the Jordan River), in Jordan. Estimates of the number of refugees who fled from their communities on the Golan Heights into Syria range from 50,000 to 100,000. For a detailed summary of the course of the 1967 war, see Oren, *Six Days of War*.

7. Author's translations.

8. Darwish and al-Qasim, *Bein shnei hatsa'ei ha-tapuz* [Between the orange's two halves], p. 35. Shemer's quote can be found at this website: www.snunit.k12.il/sachlav/noar/main/upload/docs/sade9.doc.

9. Kerr, *Arab Cold War*.

10. Sayigh, *Armed Struggle and the Search for State*.

11. Meital, "Khartoum conference."

12. Soviet leader Leonid Brezhnev applied pressure on Nasser and with undisguised criticism wondered how he could accept an initiative that "had an American flag on it." According to Muhammad Hasanayn Heikal, Nasser's confidant, who was present during the conversation, the Egyptian president replied that the plan's whole advantage was that it flew the US flag. Heikal, *Sphinx and Commissar*, p. 201. On Egyptian-Soviet relations, Heikal contended that, at this stage, Nasser believed that consenting to the Rogers plan would open up new opportunities for Egypt.

13. Arab Republic of Egypt, *White Paper*; Sadat, *In Search of Identity*, pp. 280–281.

14. Morris, *Righteous Victims*, Chapter 9.

15. Carter, *Keeping Faith*, pp. 282–284.

16. The link to Sadat's speech in English is http://www.knesset.gov.il/process/docs/sadatspeech_eng.htm/

17. The link to Begin's speech in English is http://www.knesset.gov.il/process/docs/beginspeech_eng.htm.

18. Quandt, *Camp David*; Ali, *Muharibun wa—mufawidun* [Warriors and peacemakers]; Dayan, *Breakthrough*.

3

Oslo: The "Peace" "Process"

The Declaration of Principles (DOP) on Interim Self-Government (13 September 1993), aimed at resolving the Israeli-Palestinian dispute, was signed fifteen years after the Camp David Accords. The venue for wrapping up the negotiations between Israel and the Arab side was once more the White House grounds, and the ceremony was laden with symbolism as Yitzhak Rabin and Yasser Arafat affixed their signatures to a historic document between Israel and the PLO, the representative of the Palestinian people. Like Carter before him, US president Bill Clinton too added his signature, noting that "at this place and upon this desk, three men of great vision signed their names to the Camp David accords. Today, we honor the memories of Menachem Begin and Anwar Sadat, and we salute the wise leadership of President Jimmy Carter."[1] The live broadcast on the whole provided favorable coverage. Detractors and opponents, both Israeli and Arab, received marginal exposure. Nevertheless, there was no hiding the apprehensions and uncertainties, even within the camp that had set the historic measure in motion. Rabin responded to Arafat with a weak handshake. His doubts never left him.

Israel's government under Rabin behaved as if it had entered stormy waters but had not yet resolved to cross the Rubicon. The Palestinian leadership was also plagued by indecision about its own Rubicon. As a strategic goal, it had publicly endorsed the idea of two states between the Mediterranean Sea and the Jordan River at the end of 1988. But it had not done so either in a single day or all at once. For it, the Oslo process was an ideological, political turnabout, as summed up by Yezid Sayigh, a scholar at the Center of International Studies at Cambridge University: "the Palestinian national movement, established with the express aim of liberating Palestine in armed struggle, had proved unable in the intervening years to liberate any part of its national soil by force and had finally accepted the Oslo negotiated compromise, whose

31

terms ran counter to virtually all the principles and aims it had espoused for so long."[2]

The DOP was the minimalist title for the historic agreement signed by the leaders of Israel and the PLO; most people referred to it as the Oslo Accords or just Oslo. More than ten years have passed since its signing, and a host of interpretations have been published on its significance. Basically, it consists of three chief elements: recognition of the state of Israel by the PLO and vice versa, the institution of a "peace process" in the transitional period, and a commitment to achieve a permanent status agreement where most entangled issues will be solved. The recognition Israel earned by virtue of the Camp David Accords and the peace with Egypt were a breakthrough in the Arab-Israeli conflict. Nevertheless, the heart of the conflict was and remains the Israeli-Palestinian dispute. The earliest Israelis strove to obtain recognition for Israel as the independent sovereign state of the Jewish people. Resolution 242 and the accords signed between Israel and the Arab governments promised formal recognition. It was a vital step on the long road to recognition, to be consolidated upon the resolution of all the major issues of the Arab-Israeli conflict and the instatement of peace. The Palestinian national movement under the PLO had struggled long years for recognition of its legitimate right to an independent sovereign state. The question of recognition is crucial because it is tied up with other issues, such as borders and the nature of the sovereign independence of each people. It is also complex because considerable slices of both populations oppose mutual recognition on religious, historical, and national grounds, although their numbers and their ability to disrupt the mutual agreements and recognition vary.

On the Israeli side, the first major manifestation of mutual recognition was the Knesset's passing of an amendment to the Ordinance for the Prevention of Terror, Number Three (19 January 1993), which had made it illegal for Israelis to meet with PLO officials. This was briskly followed by clandestine talks in the Norwegian capital—later known as the Oslo channel.[3] As Israeli personnel became more deeply involved, they more and more forcefully demanded the annulment of the Palestinian National Charter (the latest version of which dates back to 17 July 1968). Many of the charter's articles oppose Israel's existence in no uncertain terms. Article 19 states: "The partition of Palestine in 1947 and the establishment of the state of Israel are entirely illegal." Armed struggle against Israel is defined as "the only way to liberate Palestine. Thus it is the overall strategy, not merely a tactical phase" (Article 9). Palestinian negotiators referred their counterparts to documents and declarations of Israeli organizations and even political parties that not only rejected Palestinian national rights but denied the existence of a Palestinian people. They also directed Israel's attention to the decisions of the Palestinian leadership that had stripped the charter of all meaning. Thus, the Palestinian Declaration of Independence promulgated in 15 November 1988 recognized the partition of the country between the two peoples and accepted both Resolution 242 as the basis for negotiating with Israel and the fact that the Palestinian state would be established on only 22 percent of the territory of historical Palestine.[4] The parties were obviously aware of the political and symbolic difficulty for Palestinians in revoking outright the much-publicized national charter. The charter was equally symbolic for most Israelis, however, who wished to see it annulled as a sign that the Palestinians had abandoned their intent to destroy the Jewish state.

The progression of the talks in the Oslo channel and upping of the level of negotiators led them to link mutual recognition with changes in the Palestinian charter. Statements contradicting the letter and spirit of the DOP were to be excised from the charter. Four days before the DOP was signed, Arafat and Rabin exchanged letters on the subject. Arafat wrote:

> The PLO recognizes the right of the state of Israel to exist in peace and security. . . . The PLO considers that the signing of the Declaration of Principles constitutes a historic event, inaugurating a new epoch of peaceful coexistence, free from violence and all other acts which endanger peace and stability. Accordingly, the PLO renounces the use of terrorism and other acts of violence and will assume responsibility over all PLO elements and personnel in order to assure their compliance, prevent violations, and discipline violators. In view of the promise of a new era, . . . the PLO affirms that those articles of the Palestinian Covenant which deny Israel's right to exist, and the provisions of the Covenant which are inconsistent with the commitments of this letter are now inoperative and no longer valid.[5]

Arafat closed with a commitment to see to it that the Palestinian National Council (PNC) would ratify the necessary amendments to the charter. Rabin's reply was curt, no more than a sentence, asserting that "in light of the PLO commitments included in your letter, the Government of Israel has decided to recognize the PLO as the representative of the Palestinian people and commence negotiations with the PLO within the Middle East peace process." The commitments of the two leaders were of both practical and symbolic import and made it possible for the DOP to be signed. The DOP itself opened with the dramatic statement that the government of Israel and the PLO "agree that it is time to put an end to decades of confrontation and conflict."[6]

The DOP's seventeen articles related to a wide range of topics, with the parties evidently adopting a number of key principles from the framework for peace in the Middle East approved by Israel, Egypt, and the United States at Camp David fifteen years earlier, in 1978. Notably, these principles included the provision for a transitional period leading to permanent-status negotiations, during which time the most controversial issues would be tackled: Jerusalem, Palestinian refugees, settlements in the Occupied Territories, security arrangements, and borders. Both the Camp David framework and the DOP stipulated a transitional period "not exceeding five years," with permanent-status negotiations to commence as soon as possible but not later than the beginning of the third year of the interim period. There were also several major differences between the framework and the DOP. The September 1978 agreement was concluded without Palestinian representation. The objective was that "Egypt, Israel, Jordan and the representatives of the Palestinian people should participate in negotiations on the resolution of the Palestinian problem in all its aspects." It was further agreed that a "self-governing authority in the West Bank and Gaza" would be established, although its nature and powers were not adequately defined.[7] In contrast, the preamble to the September 1993 DOP stated that Israel and the PLO "recognize their mutual legitimate and political rights" and strive "to live in peaceful coexistence and mutual dignity and security" and "to achieve a just, lasting and comprehensive peace settlement and historic reconciliation through the agreed political process." The DOP outlined the steps leading to the establishment of a Palestinian Authority (PA) that would have sovereign powers, a political entity whose future essence would be determined in permanent-status negotiations. Most observers concurred that the parties to the DOP had in fact endorsed a blueprint for the two-state solution. No longer mere autonomy.

The establishment of a Palestinian Self-Government Authority was one of the key goals of the interim stage. It was agreed that "free and general political elections" would be held for the Palestinian Council. The powers of the elected Palestinian Council, however, were a source of disagreement both during the negotiations and at the start of the interim stage. The divergent interpretations stem from two statements of principle in Article IV of the DOP:

> Jurisdiction of the Council will cover West Bank and Gaza Strip territory, except for issues that will be negotiated in the permanent status negotiations. The two sides view the West Bank and the Gaza Strip as a single territorial unit, whose integrity will be preserved during the interim period.

In this article, the Palestinian negotiators lodged the hope that the Oslo process could lead to the establishment of an independent Palestinian entity in all of the West Bank and the Gaza Strip, a territorially contiguous entity in light of the stipulation that both regions constitute "a single territorial unit" of safeguarded integrity. The Israelis interpreted the article altogether differently. Not camouflaging their intent, they sought to limit the jurisdiction of the elected council to the autonomous administration of internal affairs in the physical areas to be transferred to its control. For the first two years after the declaration's signing, Israeli representatives waged a desperate battle against Palestinian efforts to endow the PA with the trappings of national sovereignty. The vague formulations incorporated in the DOP and some of the later agreements are what made their signing possible, but they also opened the door for wrangling over the extent of Palestinian sovereignty and independence. Israel wished to see a minimalist Palestinian Authority in terms of political sovereignty. The Palestinians, of course, wished the opposite.

As soon as the fact of the Oslo channel became public knowledge, both Israeli and Palestinian society found cause to condemn the political process. Doubters and detractors raised their voices even before the DOP was signed and the seal of approval stamped on mutual recognition. In both societies, the DOP glaringly highlighted the dissension between the government and opposition groups. In both, the most biting criticism emanated from national-religious groups who regarded Oslo as a recipe for disaster, an accommodation of intolerable religious and historical concessions that posed a real threat to the respective national interests of the two peoples. As opposed as their agendas were, these groups shared a common goal—to wipe out the Oslo Agreement. How they set about achieving that goal, however, differed according to the nature of the regimes and political realities in the two societies.

Israel's public discussion of the DOP and Oslo blueprint opened with a three-day (21–23 September 1993) fiery debate in the Knesset, with all members of Knesset (MKs) in attendance.[8] The deliberations ended, symbolically enough, on the eve of Yom Kippur—the twentieth anniversary of the October 1973 war—with many speakers having cited a connection between the events of the past and the present. Everyone had drawn a historical lesson from that war, and everyone invoked the sheer logic of that lesson in support of differing positions on the agreements with the Palestinians. Prime Minister Yitzhak Rabin began by saying that "The Yom Kippur War taught us as well as our enemies both the limits of military force and the latent potentials of a political solution." He stressed that his government would remain committed to the "security and welfare" of the settlers. On the question of Jerusalem, he reiterated the consensual stand: "There is no argument in this House as to Jerusalem being Israel's eternal capital. Jerusalem, one and united, is not open to negotiation; it was and ever will remain the capital of the Jewish people under Israeli sovereignty." The opposition's main objections were laid out by Benjamin Netanyahu, then head of the Likud. The DOP, he said, harbored Israel's consent to the establishment of a Palestinian state, the division of Jerusalem, and even a Palestinian right of return. Netanyahu accused Rabin of burying his head in the sand, at which point Rabin rose and left the hall. This line continued to be pursued by Netanyahu and his colleagues, the heads of the Tzomet Party (Raphael Eitan) and the Mafdal Party (Zebulon Hammer), who also claimed that the parties to the agreement had concluded secret understandings on sensitive issues.

In a chorus of predictable viewpoints, the words of MK Aryeh Der'i stood out. Der'i was head of the religious Sephardi Shas Party and had resigned his position as minister of the interior a week earlier. He began by citing the party's spiritual leader, Rabbi 'Ovadia Yosef, who had ruled on the complex question of "the sanctity of the land of Israel versus the sanctity of man—which takes precedence?"[9] By underscoring the sanctity of man as the supreme value, Shas conspicuously set itself apart from the outlook of other religious adjudicators who served as authorities for other Orthodox and national-religious parties. Der'i was among the very few to situate the DOP in its correct historical context. He considered several of its features that made it an agreement whose "skeleton was the Camp David Accords—with extras." He finished by noting that his party would have found it easier to adopt a distinct position "had this been a completed peace treaty stating plainly the sacrifice asked of the Jewish people—even if the price were the return of territories or parts of the land of Israel—with us knowing what sort of peace we were getting . . . and, above all, what sort of hedge against loss of life we were setting." The Knesset marathon doubled as a test of confidence in Rabin's government. The vote split down the middle. The DOP and Rabin's government won the support of sixty-one members out of a total of 120. Fifty were opposed. Eight, mostly from Shas, abstained. One chose to be absent during the voting.

The Knesset debate was Israel's internal opening volley for an endless marathon of public contests and disputations on the subject. The barricades went up, with the "peace camp" ranged on one side and the "national camp" on the other. The former supported the Oslo process and Rabin's policy (often without having digested all the implications); the latter pointed to the shortcomings of the agreements, resisting the price Israel would be called on to pay in "the assets it had acquired." Both camps soon showed themselves unable to view the situation soberly. Both, for the most part, became locked into slogans, evident in reams of words. The only real alternative posed to government policy and the sterile discourse conducted by the main political camps was the activity of right-wing extraparliamentary bodies, chiefly the various settler organizations. Enlisting all their talents and energy, they depicted the Oslo blueprint as an assault "on [their] home" and, on the whole, resorted to means that the Israeli public and legal establishment considered legitimate. With the blessing of the authorities, construction was stepped up inside the settlements. State coffers allocated enormous public funds for infrastructure that served mostly the settlers and settler security. Israeli governments (under Labor as well as Likud) upheld the right of the settlers to expand according to natural increase and security needs. From the start of the 1990s through all the years of the Oslo process, investment in infrastructure and services for settlements, like the number of residents, spiraled. According to Israel's Central Bureau of Statistics, in 1990 there were 78,600 settlers; in September 2004, there were 239,800 residents of settlements, about 8,000 in the Gaza Strip. The number of settlements in this period grew minimally, from 118 in 1990 to 123.[10] Critics of government policy held their tongues. On this issue, too, many were spellbound by the "peace process." Official spokespeople emphasized that Israel's measures were consistent with the substance of the agreements signed with the Palestinians and that the future of the settlements would be determined only in negotiations on permanent status.

Rather than attenuating the problem, leaving the settlers and settlements in place only exacerbated it. Israel's settlement policy could not hide the Israeli government's basic contentions with the settlers and their backers at home and abroad. On occasion, in defiance of a government action or in response to Palestinian attacks, the settlers reacted with a fitting "Zionist response." This slogan usually translated into activities aimed at taking over additional West Bank lands and establishing further settlements. In some cases, the settlers targeted Palestinian residents and property. As a rule, these acts did not elicit the censure or punishment they deserved. Right-wingers went to bat to garner public support. There was a flurry of political lobbying in the corridors of power, in the work of pressure groups, and in innumerable public and media discussions. Nor did extremists shrink from illegitimate measures. The assassination of Prime Minister Yitzhak Rabin (4 November 1995) was the climax of this activity, but it had been preceded—and was followed—by threats and assaults on politicians and violent language against opponents in the media discourse. Offenses by right-wing extremists against Palestinian residents in the occupied territories became a daily occurrence, ending, in no few cases, in bodily harm and damage to property.

The Palestinian and Arab camp opposing Oslo also grew stronger as the "peace process" progressed. Made up of groups with various goals and agendas, its most vociferous agents were Hamas, the Islamic Jihad, the PFLP, and the PDFLP, along with unaligned intellectuals and public figures, bound by their negative perception of the agreements that the Palestinian administration had signed with Israel. From the start of the Oslo process, the internal Palestinian debate over the two-state solution had become more focused.[11] When it came to defining the goals of the Palestinian people, the priorities for achieving them, and the steps to be taken at one stage or another, there were wide differences. Often enough, because of old and new rivalries, it looked as if hawks were going to bring matters to a violent head. In the background, there were sporadic warnings of civil war and reminders to the different parties of the heavy price Palestinian society had paid for rabid factionalism.

The Hamas movement, the salient Palestinian oppositionist group, had organized around the beginning of the first intifada (8 December 1987). It presented an alternative to the PLO platform that garnered increasing public support. According to its spokespeople, its explicit goal is to establish a single—Palestinian and Islamic—state in all the territory between the Jordan River and the Mediterranean Sea. It champions armed struggle against the Zionist enemy everywhere. Clearly part of the Muslim Brotherhood, Hamas's goals and values are formulated chiefly in Islamic terms. Its charter describes Palestinian soil as a sacred Islamic endowment (*waqf*), ruling out compromise over possession or control of any part of it.[12] It is not one of the organizations in the PLO, and it strenuously objected to the DOP. Its members were most upset that the Palestinian executive had consented to leaving overall security to Israel and the settlements in place. They portrayed the deferred discussion on the fate of al-Quds, the al-Haram al-Sharif mosques, and the Palestinian refugees not merely as immoral but as an opening for far-reaching concessions to be demanded by Israel. In terms of substance, they pointed out that the basis of any agreement with Israel was Security Council Resolution 242, that is, that the approach to the Israeli-Palestinian conflict was based on a resolution anchored in the status quo of the 1967 war, which does not permit discussion of issues unresolved from 1947/8–1967. Hamas was adept at winning over adherents to its diverse activities—both armed struggle against Israel and social services for the Palestinian population. Whether its broad support represented a commitment to an Islamic state is hard to say. The debate over the Palestinian state's religious character was marginal to the public discourse. Everyone, at this stage, was preoccupied with the struggle, political and armed, against Israel. It is noteworthy that the doubts about the intentions of the Israeli "partner" were shared by non-Palestinian Arab critics, as evidenced by the Arab media. Shortly after the signing of the DOP, the *Al-Ahram Weekly* (Egypt) gave these doubts graphic expression in a cartoon showing Rabin and Arafat holding an olive leaf; Rabin's left hand, however, was controlling a settlerlike puppet about to stick a knife in Arafat's back.[13]

Palestinian oppositionist groups and factions had a greater impact once the euphoric carnival of "liberation" bumped into the dual reality of "liberated" Occupied Territories. The effect on Palestinian daily life was restricted movement on the roads, the humiliating requirement to present passes, the hardship caused by IDF-imposed closures and blockades, and the drastic drop in income and standard of living. Both Palestinians and Israelis stoked the cycle of violence without end. On 25 February 1994 Baruch Goldstein massacred thirty-five Palestinian worshipers and wounded another two hundred at the al-Ibrahimi Mosque in the Tomb of the Patriarchs. With one single act of terror, a fanatic doctor reignited the brute force and hatred that he had not begun but certainly aggravated. All the Palestinian organizations vowed to avenge the blood of the innocent, murdered at prayer. In the following months, Hamas carried out a series of terror attacks in 'Afula, Hadera, Ramle, Jerusalem, and Tel Aviv, murdering dozens of Israelis and wounding hundreds.

A variety of motives drove Palestinians and Israelis to hurt one another badly. Every group had its own individual agenda. Peace proclamations and speeches soon made way for cries of grief, despair, and frustration. The "holes" in the Oslo process grew ever larger and blacker. In the two years between the DOP and the signing of the Interim Agreement, Oslo's weak points had surfaced with a bang. Chiefly, they were insufficient attention to how the two sides envisaged permanent status, fuzzy thinking on mechanisms of control to ensure that commitments would be honored during the long interim stage, and a lack of provision for the constraints plaguing Palestinian and Israeli administrations that were caused by domestic groups bent on sabotaging the blueprint. It was also mistakenly assumed that during the relatively long transitional period (five years), the advocates of political settlement would grow stronger and a dynamic would be generated to sap oppositionists in both societies. Because of political and national considerations, neither administration took a tough stand against saboteurs during this period. This passivity left the field free for oppositionists to disrupt the implementation of interim arrangements and torpedo the possibility of true compromise in permanent-status negotiations.

Amid practical discussion of the essence of the Palestinian entity emerging next to the state of Israel, the leaders of the two peoples had to shape policy with a nod to the stance and mood of bitter domestic rivals. Thus, Arafat and his associates portrayed the legislative council as a sovereign parliament in word and deed, squeezing to the last drop the DOP specification of "free and general political elections." International supervision of the elections was seen as an additional device to gain global legitimation of the parliament and PA leadership. The right of participation of Palestinian residents of East Jerusalem (al-Quds) in the elections was taken as a symbolic victory over Israel's long-standing contrary position. The results assured the PLO of most of the council seats (sixty-five out of the eighty-eight seats). Domestically, the PLO grew significantly stronger vis-à-vis its political rivals. Arafat, unsurprisingly, was elected president, winning 88 percent of the vote. Samiha Khalil, head of al-Bireh's family welfare organization, who had contested Arafat's historical leadership, received 9.3 percent.[14]

Elections for the legislative council were a new experience for the PLO. From the opening of the Oslo channel, the leaders of the political process had agreed that the PLO would act for the Palestinian people ("the Partner") and negotiate on their behalf. The PLO leadership conducted the talks with Israel and signed the DOP, and it continued to do so even after the PA was established and the council elected. The Sharm al-Sheikh Memorandum (4 September 1999), signed by Ehud Barak and Arafat, begins with the words: "The Government of the state of Israel (GOI) and the Palestine Liberation Organization (PLO) commit themselves to. . . ." Arafat and his people carried on cultivating the PLO and nurturing ties of loyalty that they had woven over decades. The PLO leadership wanted to entrust its faithful with the establishment of an independent Palestinian state. Other forces in Palestinian society, particularly the local leadership that sprang up in the occupied territories, were cast in minor roles. Inevitably, the friction mounted between the leadership that had come to the territories with Arafat from the "outside" in the wake of agreements with Israel and the "insider" power loci and key figures that had solidified their positions since the first intifada.

Internal friction compounded the task of instituting a new regime, which was in any case slow and largely dependent on Israeli goodwill. PLO senior officials took over many of the PA positions and power loci, while the locals simmered with resentment. From the start, the fledgling PA embraced the management modes and norms that had long characterized the PLO and were tailored to Arafat's style of leadership, drawing much fire for the absence of democratic government and its blows to human rights and freedom of expression (mainly press restrictions). There were material ramifications to the filling of top PA positions with people in the PLO network. With the blessing of the *ra'is* (president), officials seized control of various branches in the Palestinian economy, handsomely lining their bulging pockets via a system of monopolies (mainly over petroleum, cement, cigarettes, and wheat). Homegrown criticism of leadership corruption and the nouveau riche swelled.[15] Israel and the United States were well aware of all that, but they turned a blind eye. At times, it seemed as if they believed that, by financially and politically strengthening the heads of the security mechanisms and the "buddies" of the ruling elite, the monopolies "ensured" their support for the new order.

Much to Israel's chagrin, after the elections to the PA legislative council, the signs of independent Palestinian rule multiplied. The new trappings of self-government in the West Bank and the Gaza Strip included a bureaucracy and police and security forces; systems and administrations for education, health, welfare, direct taxation and value-added tax (VAT), tourism, commerce, agriculture, archaeology, transportation, postage, religion, and the environment; electricity, water, and land boards as well as a Gaza Port Authority; courts and Palestinian development banks; and official, semiofficial, and private (press and electronic) media. Over all these, the PA Council consolidated its standing as the elected national institution of the Palestinian people. Leaders donned titles of sovereignty: Arafat was proclaimed "president" and his associates were awarded ministerial jobs and titles. Regional and international bodies welcomed the PA into their ranks as a member. Arafat, who had been a frequent visitor to state capitals, was now received in most with all the pomp and circumstance generally reserved for heads of state. In this festive climate, the baton demonstratively passed from Israeli to PA hands. The IDF's departure and the transfer of authority from Israel's civil and military administration to the Palestinians brimmed with symbolism. On buildings and in bases from which the IDF and Israel's General Security Services (Shin Bet) had governed the lives of millions of Palestinians in the occupied territories, the Israeli flag came down and the Palestinian flag went up, bearing the semblance of freedom and independence.

The Palestinian media and education system extolled the "liberation" motif. Intellectuals, artists, and performers gave it immortal expression in their works. Pupils memorized texts to its glory that had just rolled off the press. Arab and especially Palestinian media gave broad coverage of the liberation stage in words and pictures. After decades of occupation, anything that smacked of freedom and self-rule was plainly cherished. The Palestinian leadership portrayed the "peace process" to its people as the fast lane to a certain goal: full Palestinian independence over all of the West Bank and Gaza, with al-Quds and its mosques as the recognized capital. It depicted the PA and its administration as a well-oiled machine in the right hands. The DOP had led to Israeli withdrawal from the Gaza Strip and Jericho—this was the half-full cup; the remaining half would no doubt come when a permanent settlement was achieved. The agreements stipulated that after the withdrawal of its forces from certain areas, "Israel will continue to be responsible for external security, and for internal security and public order of settlements and Israelis." But this caveat was played down.

One of the effects of adopting Oslo was immediately apparent in the web of Israeli-Palestinian-Jordanian relations. Jordan and Israel in fact embarked on the road to a peace treaty as soon as Israel signed the DOP with the PLO. The eventuality of a Palestinian state arising in the West Bank and the Gaza Strip undeniably upped their interest in political, military, and economic cooperation. The day after the DOP was signed, Jordan's crown prince Hassan, Israel's foreign minister Shimon Peres, and US president Bill Clinton agreed to create a tripartite economic committee for cooperation and development. On 25 July 1994 Israel's Prime Minister Yitzhak Rabin and Jordan's King Hussein ibn Talal held their first public meeting in Washington, D.C., under Clinton's White House patronage. It resulted in the Washington Declaration, the first signed document of its kind, which affirmed the following: "The long conflict between the two states is now coming to an end" (Article C). The two peoples shared a common goal: "Jordan and Israel aim at the achievement of just, lasting and comprehensive peace between Israel and its neighbors and at the conclusion of a Treaty of Peace between both countries" (Article B.1). Both leaders noted the potential benefits of bringing peace to an additional segment of the Arab-Israeli conflict. Rabin, with uncharacteristic optimism, proclaimed that he felt "at this moment in Jerusalem and Amman, perhaps all over the Middle East, a new era is dawning." Hussein, an old hand at oratory, sounded more optimistic than ever:

This is a dream that those before me had—my dead grandfather, and now I. And to feel that we are close to fulfilling that dream and presenting future generations in our region with a legacy of hope and openness where normality is that which replaces the abnormal in our lives—which, unfortunately, over the years, has become normal—where neighbors meet; where people meet; where human relations thrive; where all seek with their tremendous talents a better future and a better tomorrow. This day is a day of commitment, and this day is a day of hope and vision. We must admit— Prime Minister and for myself—that we owe President Clinton and our American friends much in having made this possible. You are our partners as we seek to construct and build a new future in our region for all our peoples and for all mankind.[16]

Three months later (26 October 1994), Israel and Jordan signed a peace treaty. Beyond the obligatory wording on an end to the state of war and a commitment to good neighborliness, the two parties were noticeably eager to promote contact and normalize relations. The US president witnessed the document and, in exchange for Jordan's joining the Camp David coalition (for which the ground had been laid in the Israeli-Egyptian peace treaty), the United States undertook to help the kingdom meet its foreign debt and provide civilian and military assistance. It was a boost for Pax Americana in the Middle East.

Israeli expectations soared as the public discourse filled with the anticipated "warmth" of the peace with the neighbor to the east. Political spokespeople from all across the board envisaged Israeli-Jordanian relations as radically different from the "cold" peace with Egypt. In the days prior to the treaty's signing, the vision penetrated the political discourse. At the Knesset debate on the subject (24 October 1994), Rabin presented the government's position:

> The peace treaty [with Jordan] is not merely of political significance, but a basic, essential change in our very existence here—no more: "a people that shall dwell alone." This is a profound, thorough change, a change that will affect every walk of our lives: from the trucks that leave Haifa with cargo for Amman to the airplane taking off from Sde Dov and landing 30 minutes later in Amman. Business people who will fly out in the morning to close deals and return in the evening to Jerusalem, and families who will travel to Petra with their children, a three-hour trip from Tel Aviv. The change will affect each and every one of us in our daily lives. . . . the peace treaty to be signed tomorrow elevates relations to the maximal level—full peace.[17]

In Jordan, however, the peace with Israel aroused public controversy that only grew sharper. The unreserved support for the political process shown by King Hussein and his confidants naturally influenced some of the public and the official line. But the glitches in the implementation of the Oslo draft and, in particular, the escalation of Israeli-Palestinian hostilities had a far greater impact on Jordan's population. As violence, terror, and suppressive measures accelerated in the Occupied Territories and in Israel, the public clamored for Jordan to review its policy toward Israel and to take practical steps such as breaking off diplomatic and other relations. Supporters of the peace with Israel stressed its expediency for the kingdom and Jordan's population, and looked hopefully for any sign of the process being put back on course. Opponents of the peace (who grew stronger since the late 1990s) argued that the agreements with Israel were detrimental to pan-Arab interests, undermined political stability at home, and had no economic value. Their frequent claim was that the peace treaties with Jordan and Egypt enabled Israel to act more freely against Arabs, particularly against Palestinians.[18]

The Interminable Transitional State

On 28 September 1995 Israeli and PLO leaders signed the Israeli-Palestinian Interim Agreement on the West Bank and the Gaza Strip. Once more, the White House grounds served as the stage for an important Arab-Israeli political agreement. In more than 300 pages and seven appendices it elaborated the expansion of Palestinian self-government and stipulated the establishment of the "Palestinian Council," its election, and its powers; the redeployment of IDF forces and security arrangements; and arrangements for "safe passage" to facilitate free Palestinian movement between the West Bank and the Gaza Strip. On the Israeli side, troops were to withdraw from six cities and hundreds of villages in the West Bank, and for purposes of transferring control and responsibility during the interim stage, the West Bank was to be subdivided into categories denoted as A, B, and C. Permanent-status negotiations, according to the agreement, were to begin as soon as possible "but not later than May 4, 1996." In an attempt to prevent either side from resorting to unilateral measures, it was further fixed that "Neither side shall initiate or take any step that will change the status of the West Bank and the Gaza Strip pending the outcome of the permanent status negotiations."[19]

The Palestinian leadership regarded the agreement as a major milestone on the road to independent statehood according to the borders of 4 June 1967. Israel preferred not to deal in predictions on the future of the Palestinian entity. Chiefly, it regarded the agreement as a guarantee for maximal security for its population, both in Israel and the settlements. It saw the fight against terror and Oslo oppositionists as a necessary component and a measure of the PA's intentions to abide by its major commitments, as specified in binding agreements. It fully expected the Palestinian security forces to restrain the opposition and take a firm stand against Hamas and Islamic Jihad activists in the areas under PA jurisdiction. The Palestinian leadership did take steps against internal opponents, though the scope and pace of the measures were affected by two factors: the fear of civil war and PA impotence in the face of actions taken by Israeli security forces and settlers in the Occupied Territories.

Israel's political arena was torn by strife at the time of the negotiations and initial execution of the Interim Agreement. The two main blocs faced off again, with the "peace camp," led by Rabin, intent on pursuing the political process, and the "right-wing camp," under Netanyahu, demanding that it be reviewed; in other words, that the Oslo Accords be scrapped. Netanyahu's bloc named itself the "national camp." Both camps were made up of sundry groups that did not always see eye to eye but were held together by a shared hostility for the opposite camp. In the autumn of 1995, following the signing of the Interim Agreement, the protest of the right grew more strident. Large demonstrations were held all over Israel. The media discourse was shot through with gloomy forecasts about the very pursuit of the political process and the existential dangers that the agreements ostensibly presaged for the Jewish state. At the close of the Sabbath on 4 November 1995, "peace camp" filled Tel Aviv's Malchei Yisrael Square. A variety of performers had come to show their support for state leaders, particularly for Yitzhak Rabin, who had been asked to briefly address the tens of thousands of demonstrators spilling out of the square. This was the scene as Israel saw its first political assassination of a prime minister. Rabin instantly became the martyr of Israel's peace camp. The bullets of assailant Yigal 'Amir achieved their goal: the political process was put on ice.

Shimon Peres, Rabin's successor, was obliged to make a number of crucial decisions, mainly about honoring Israel's commitments in the Interim Agreement and apropos the elections that were to be held a year later. At this stage, a series of incidents and decisions on both the Israeli and Palestinian sides ignited the cinders. Peres decided to carry out Israel's commitments almost fully, directing five West Bank cities to be transferred to PA control but holding back on Hebron. Hebron had long been one of the most explosive friction points between Israelis and Palestinians, and given the tensions between rival factions in Israel, the PM chose not to become embroiled in a confrontation with its dozens of "hard-core" settlers and their supporters. The necessary explanations were provided the Palestinian leadership and the United States, while the fanatic settlers of the city of the Patriarchs noted with satisfaction that they had won this round and paraded their success as auspicious for the future. Most Israelis, at the time, seemed absorbed in the various implications of Rabin's murder, and Israeli society swathed itself in a thin veil of soul-searching. Public figures, rabbis, and just plain folk took to breast-beating. The assassin and his patrons were widely depicted as "wild weeds." As the months passed, there were increasing signs that the flowerbeds of Israeli society contained entire patches not unlike the one that had sprouted the assassin and that no few people, like him, regarded the agreement with the Palestinians as treasonous.

Israel's general and political circumstances induced Peres to move up the elections. Simultaneous with this controversial decision, he approved a recommendation from the security services to assassinate Palestinian "engineer" Yehiya 'Ayash (5 January 1996), the reputed mind behind several gruesome suicide attacks. 'Ayash's death dealt Hamas a severe blow, and its leaders publicly vowed revenge and reprisal. This dynamic, known in Israel as "targeted assassination," and the reactions it unleashed soon became routine. Assassinations or suicide bombings led to retaliation, and the wheel of violence went on spinning. Reciprocal killings in January–March 1996 enraged Israelis and Palestinians, obviously doing little to enhance trust. Often, to appease an irate public, the Israeli government would impose closures, blockades, and curfews on the Palestinian residents of the West Bank and the Gaza Strip. Both societies soon learned just how fragile the "peace process" was. The Palestinian leadership was powerless against Israel's very quick way of taking unilateral decisions or steps with a single purpose: collective punishment.

This was the atmosphere in which Israelis went to the polls. Spokespeople across the political spectrum both rued and cited the bloodshed to explain their attitudes toward the Palestinians. The public discourse filled up with simplistic assertions. Newspaper headlines shrieked in red ink. TV talk shows granted politicians of both blocs airtime as long as eternity. This was also the atmosphere in which Arafat instructed his security forces to move against Hamas. The rampant armed struggle of Hamas and Islamic Jihad threatened both the political process and the hard-won Palestinian government, and the Palestinian leadership had reached the conclusion that drastic measures were warranted. An unprecedented number of top brass and activists were arrested and hundreds interrogated. Many were put on trial, convicted, and sentenced to imprisonment in PA jails. The PA wanted to make sure Hamas got the message: Hamas actions harmed Palestinian national interests, and the PA, as the governing authority, would not flinch from using any means at its disposal against them. It was precisely the sort of confrontation that Arafat and his people had feared. The image of the PA leadership was at an all-time low. Palestinian spokespeople on all sides depicted Arafat and his people as a self-serving crew with narrow interests who had sold the Palestinians down the river. Reports of corruption in the PA apparatus, especially among the leaders, spread like wildfire. Arafat and company became the butt of jokes and biting criticism. At the same time, the Palestinian leadership fended off Israeli and US pressure to totally disarm Hamas and Islamic Jihad and disable obstructionists. The Palestinian public discussion rumbled with threat of civil war. This situation, said the word on the street, was exactly what Israel wanted, under the guise of fighting terrorism.

Meanwhile, Israel's northern border heated up. The IDF and Hizbollah (literally, the Party of God) locked horns more and more, and in April 1996, Peres's government approved the Grapes of Wrath operation. The military campaign, as often happens, went awry. As a consequence of IDF shelling of the village of Kafr Kana, 102 civilians were killed—mostly women and children. The Arab world was outraged. Arab and numerous international media channels portrayed Israel as an inhuman predator. Israel's apologies for the error were spurned. Censure and international pressure forced its government to cut short the operation before it had achieved all its goals, and the agreement concluded by the parties to the fray compelled Israel to curtail its military actions on Lebanese territory. One unforeseen consequence was the conduct of many of Israel's Arab citizens. They decided to "punish" the Labor Party and the man who headed it in the forthcoming elections.

The Likud's close election victory under Benjamin Netanyahu (28 May 1996) tested the political process with the Palestinians. For the first—but not last—time, the helm of state was placed in the hands of a man who considered

Oslo to be a serious historical blunder and its implementation inimical to Israel's vital national interests. Since the signing of the DOP, Netanyahu had incessantly attacked the political policies of the Rabin and Peres governments. In the Knesset discussion some two weeks before the signing, he had said that he would lead the opposition "to stop the foolhardy process that endangered the state's very future."[20] He portrayed the PLO's acceptance of the blueprint as part of the organization's program of stages—which it had adopted at its inception and to which it remained committed—aiming at a single goal: Israel's destruction. Like many others in the Likud and on the right, he contended that the PLO had merely changed its tactics, not its strategy. These assumptions rested on assessments made by individuals in Israel's security establishment. Netanyahu's statements, his two books (*A Durable Peace* and *Fighting Terrorism*), and particularly his media appearances marked him as the most fluent spokesman for the Oslo oppositionists. His rebukes of the Palestinian leadership, especially of Arafat, whom he continued to regard as a liar and terrorist, caused people to wonder how a prime minister with such views would act in the political arena, especially when, during his term, the parties were to conclude the transitional stage as well as negotiate and settle permanent-status issues.

Momentous interests hung in the balance. The new prime minister and his cabinet quickly learned how difficult it would be to scrap international commitments or change facts that had emerged on the West Bank and Gaza ground since the autumn of 1993. From the day that his government was sworn into office, Netanyahu reiterated that Israel would honor signed agreements. At the same time, he and his cabinet concluded from their reading of the agreements that there was a great deal of room for maneuvering. They quoted the signatory himself, Yitzhak Rabin, who had remarked that no implementation dates were holy and that implementation would depend on the Palestinians abiding by their undertakings. Netanyahu made these understandings the central axis of his government's policies. He took the principle of "reciprocity" to new heights and marketed it with consummate salesmanship. The failure of the Palestinian leadership to meet its commitments, even on a secondary matter, furnished immediate grounds to postpone implementing the entire agreement. Everything was examined from an Israeli perspective and couched in an Israeli interpretation, taking full advantage of one of Oslo's weak points: the absence of an external watchdog to oversee implementation, with the power to arbitrate disputes. Needless to say, the principle of reciprocity—cherished by Netanyahu as if it were an eminent award—ignored the fact that Israel, too, had failed to carry out many of its commitments to the Palestinians.

In the first year of Netanyahu's government, relations with the Palestinians severely deteriorated. The affair that perhaps best symbolized the escalation and lurking dangers was the opening to visitors of the Hasmonean Tunnel (24 September 1996). Since the conquest of Jerusalem's Old City in the Six Day War, governmental and nongovernmental bodies had conducted archaeological excavations in the area of the Western Wall. Impressive, valuable finds unearthed in the Old City took their place alongside discoveries made by archaeologists since the mid-nineteenth century. Israeli efforts aimed at exposing as much as possible of Jerusalem's Jewish past, particularly in the area of the First and Second Temples. On the whole, these efforts met with a good deal of suspicion and opposition from Muslims and Arabs, especially Palestinians. The latter charged Israel with unilaterally trying to change the status quo governing Jerusalem's most sensitive site and undermining, with the tunnel works, the foundations of the al-Haram al-Sharif compound. These protests could not in themselves halt the work.

One of the main digs at the site was the preparation of the Western Wall Tunnel: an underground passageway from the Western Wall Plaza to the area of the Sisters of Zion Convent (near the end of the Via Dolorosa), an almost 500-meter excavated stretch exposing the full length of the Western Wall. After years of ongoing work, this tunnel had been opened to visitors in 1991. Another key project nearby was the cleaning out and opening of the Hasmonean Tunnel, a canal that, according to archaeologists, conducted water in the Hasmonean era (the first and second centuries BCE) from the north to the Temple Mount (beneath the route of what is today the Via Dolorosa). At the end of the Hasmonean Tunnel, project initiators opened a new 15-meter-long section to facilitate a visitor exit onto the end of the Via Dolorosa.[21]

Beyond the general dispute on the question of excavating so sensitive a site, near the Western Wall and the al-Haram al-Sharif compound, the decision to open the Hasmonean Tunnel was taken amid mounting Israeli-Palestinian tensions. Furthermore, Netanyahu decided to open the tunnel without coordinating with the Palestinian authorities and despite the warnings of Shin Bet head Ami Ayalon that the ongoing crisis with the Palestinians could snowball into violence. The tunnel opening was presented as a sovereign decision, a natural expression of Israeli control of Jerusalem. Mayor Ehud Olmert had strong words for anyone who dared to criticize the government decision. Is it at all thinkable, he asked, that Israelis should not be able to visit Jewish sites in their own capital?[22] The entry of the first Israeli visitors into the site touted as the "Bedrock of our Existence" was documented by Israeli Television (Channel One). Viewers had long been conditioned to the virtual expeditions of correspondents wallowing in burial chambers and relishing archaeological finds that connected Israelis here and now to the nation's roots in antiquity: pottery, coins, sarcophagi, ossuaries, and ancient inscriptions had become the glue meant to bond Israelis to the sites of historical Israel. But the pictures of visitors to the Hasmonean Tunnel were almost instantly replaced by footage of violent protests. The symbol-laden clashes for control of the Old City and the sanctified compound provided further cause for severe escalation. For the first time, too, some of the PA forces were involved in exchanges of fire with Israeli forces.

Violence and frustration amplified Palestinian public criticism of both the "peace process" and Arafat's leadership. Incendiary statements by Israeli cabinet members and aggressive actions by settlers were cited as concrete proof that the political process was a failure. Many inferred that the right under Netanyahu preferred the existing situation of "neither peace nor war" to any other and that it would strive to perpetuate it. For the Palestinians, this situation meant increasing economic hardship due to frequent closures of the territories and the drastically reduced numbers permitted to enter Israel to work. The regression saw the vigorous comeback of several armed Palestinian groups whose actions, from here on in, were to have more and more of an impact. One of these was al-Tanzim, a paramilitary organization set up in the early1980s, which was to withstand PA attempts in 1998 to disarm it. It was headed by Marwan Bargouti, a prominent, authentic voice of the young leadership cadre that had sprung up in the West Bank and Gaza, and derived its status and most of its strength from the first intifada. Bargouti and his followers belonged to the nationalist camp and subscribed to PLO mainstream views. But they wanted to play a part in the leadership, which was a source of discord with the veteran administration. The popular Hamas, too, soon resumed both its armed struggle against Israel and its social work as the PA relaxed its grip.[23]

The escalation also affected the diplomatic sphere. The governments of Egypt and Jordan, who had signed peace treaties with Israel, minced no words in blaming Netanyahu's government for the deterioration. Arab and Islamic states that did not have peace treaties with Israel undid ties that had been cultivated. Morocco shut the liaison office it had opened in Tel Aviv. Tunisia, Oman, Qatar, and Mauritania drastically curtailed relations. The regional economic forum, an annual event since the Casablanca Convention in 1994, ground to a halt. The situation came up for discussion in the Arab League and in the public discourse, and the ensuing consensus was translated into a hostile attitude toward Israel. Arab states committed to the political process rejected demands to void the peace agreements and step up armed conflict. But that alone could not soften the swelling anti-Israel rage that swept through the Middle East. Meanwhile, Israel's leadership sought to convey a message of "business as usual" even at the height of the remonstrations. Construction in the settlements proceeded with zest, and building permits were issued for Jewish neighborhoods in Palestinian areas, particularly around Jerusalem: the controversial development of the Har Homa quarter and residential building permits for Ras al-'Amud were given the green light. In terms of extending the city limits, Ehud Olmert, the capital's relentless mayor, and his colleagues in government seemed to be aiming at a new record.

During Netanyahu's reign, the barometer of Palestinian armed actions and acts of terror shot up. Ghastly suicide missions in the heart of Tel Aviv and Jerusalem tallied up scores of innocent victims, mostly civilians. Israeli and Palestinian mutual frustrations soared. The large number of casualties and the resort to weapons prompted US president Bill Clinton to bring his weight to bear to rein in the two sides. This resulted in a ceasefire, the resumption of cooperation on security matters, and the Hebron Protocol (17 January 1997). On the basis of this agreement, the IDF withdrew from Hebron and the dispute over control of al-Shuhda (The Martyrs) Road was resolved. But the respite could be only temporary because of the presence of Jewish families devoutly committed to the settlement effort and the IDF's overall control of the approach roads to the city.[24] As a byproduct of the protocol and much to Israel's annoyance, the Clinton administration and the PA leadership tightened up relations.

Constant regional (mainly Egyptian), European, and of course US pressure led to negotiations at the Wye River plantation near Washington (15–23 October 1998), a two-week summit with the active involvement of President Clinton. It saw the signing of the Wye Memorandum (23 October 1998), whereby Israel was to complete its redeployment according to the Interim Agreement in three "phases." It was also to release a large number of Palestinian prisoners, sparking renewed public debate over freeing prisoners "with blood on their hands."[25] The Palestinians claimed that the said prisoners had taken part in armed struggle during warfare and should thus be released in the framework of a "peace process." Their efforts were doomed to failure. The violence, however, subsided due to the pressure Netanyahu's government put on the PA and the growing trust and cooperation between the United States and the Palestinians. Slowly, Israeli and Palestinian supporters of the peace process seemed to be recovering from the effects of the incitement, aggression, and terror that had taken so many lives.

Netanyahu's three years of government were a nonstop campaign to derail the implementation of the Oslo blueprint. To a man, cabinet members did all they could to promote the cause, each adding his own ministerial share. In political deliberations, in cabinet and government decisions, and even in Knesset votes the government remained true to the cause, playing havoc with implementation schedules, adopting unilateral decisions, and exploiting the Palestinian leadership's inability to stanch violence and terror. In consequence, Israel's commitment to redeploy in phases became meaningless and was not carried out. Similarly, there was a delay in starting the permanent-status talks; according to the Interim Agreement, a permanent-status agreement should have been signed by 4 May 1999. Netanyahu could note with satisfaction that a large part of his aims had been achieved. The political process was stymied, the blame was not put solely on his government, and the continuing violence had raised doubts about the "peace process" among broad segments of the Israeli public. But under US pressure, Netanyahu's government had also been faced with tough choices. Much to its distress, it had been compelled to resume talks with the PA, to sign the Hebron Protocol as well as the Wye Memorandum, and to order the IDF to redeploy in parts of the West Bank.

Notes

1. US Department of State dispatch, http://usinfo.state.gov/products/pdq/pdq.htm.

2. Sayigh, "Armed Struggle and State Formation," p. 17.

3. State of Israel, *Knesset Proceedings* 128, no. 13: 2582–2655.

4. For the Palestinian Declaration of Independence (1988), see www.palestine center.org/cpap/documents/independence.html; for the Palestinian National Charter (July 1968), see www.mideastweb.org/plocha.htm.

5. "Israel-PLO Recognition: Exchange of Letters Between PM Rabin and Chairman Arafat," September 9, 1993. The complete text is on the US Department of State website, www.state.gov/p/nea/rls/22579.htm.

6. The complete text of the DOP is on the website of the US Department of State: http://www.state.gov/p/nea/rls/22602.htm.

7. The Camp David Agreement (17 September 1978) can be found at www.mfa.gov.il/mfa/go.asp?MFAH00pz0.

8. For the protocol (in Hebrew) of the three-day debate, see State of Israel, *Knesset Proceedings* 131, no. 43 (21–23 September 1993): 7675–8008.

9. Ibid., pp. 7967–7971.

10. The figures do not include outposts and are a matter of dispute among the parties involved. I have used the data appearing in Israel's statistics annual. See www .cbs.gov.il/population/new_2004/tab_1.pdf. On 24 July 2003 Israel Radio reported that the number of settlers is 231,443 (of these, 7,700 live in settlements in the Gaza Strip). For a detailed report on the settlement infrastructure, its enormous costs, and the continuous support for it furnished by all Israeli governments, see *Haaretz*, 26 September 2003.

11. Alongside the two main streams reflected by the positions of the PLO and Hamas, some spokespeople in the Palestinian public discourse supported the establishment of a single secular and democratic state with full equality between Jews and Arabs. This format of "a state of all its citizens" was to be an ideological and practical alternative to both the PLO and Hamas. Its advocates argued that only this type of solution could serve moral and historical justice and lead to the end of conflict between the two peoples sharing the same piece of land that contained deeply embedded roots of their past and beliefs. Another political notion worth mentioning here is the solution based on a binational format. This is a political solution to the conflict that held the assumption that the two states for two peoples option is fading, and the goal of a Palestinian state should be exchanged for the establishment of a binational state where Israelis and Palestinians enjoy full rights. See Meron Benvenisti, "The Binational Option," *Haaretz*, 27 May 2005. The article can be found at http://www.haaretzdaily .com/hasen/pages/ShArt.jhtml?itemNo=227850&contrassID=2&subContrassID=4& sbSubContrassID=0&listSrc=Y. Advocates of this type of solution became more audible after the failure to reach a final-status agreement at Camp David. Political support for these platforms remained marginal.

12. See the Hamas Charter, www.palestinecenter.org/cpap/documents/charter.html.

13. *Al-Ahram Weekly*, 11 November 1993. This motif mirrors Israeli cartoons on Arafat and the Palestinians, waving an olive branch in one hand and holding a bomb in the other.

14. For the elections results, see www.pna.gov.ps/Government/gov/Elections_ in_Palestine.asp. Palestinians living outside the occupied territories were not permitted to take part in these "general elections." Millions of Palestinian refugees were thus denied all possibility of participating in the elections for the national institutions and leadership. Public opinion polls showed that many Palestinian refugees objected to the Oslo blueprint.

15. This found expression in public opinion surveys conducted by Palestinian research institutes. On the whole, the respondents ascribed the absence of democracy and freedoms in the occupied territories to the Israeli occupation and the conduct of the PA. See Multaqa Peace Process Opinion Polls Chart, in www.multaqa.org/ programs/peace-process/peace-process-polls-chart-right.html.

16. For the text of both the Washington Declaration and the leaders' words, see: U.S Department of State, http://usinfo.state.gov/products/pdq/pdq.htm.

17. *Knesset Proceedings*, 4 (24 October 1994): 752–755.

18. Before the Washington Summit even began, eight Jordanian oppositionist parties publicized objections to the Israeli-Jordanian Peace Treaty, specifically to the clauses on normalization and economic cooperation. They claimed that since the basic issues of the Arab-Israeli conflict were far from being solved in a just manner, there was no reason to implement these clauses. In their eyes, any progress in the Israeli-Jordanian peace process thus meant bowing to the dictates of the United States and Israel. See *Al-Hadaf* [Damascus] 1197 (31 July 1994), p. 24. This view was shared by numerous intellectuals, trade unions, opposition parties, and the Muslim Brotherhood. See *Al-Dirasat al-Filastiniyya* 19 (Summer 1994): 160–162.

19. "The Israeli-Palestinian Interim Agreement on the West Bank and the Gaza Strip," Washington, D.C., September 28, 1995. For the text, see http://www.state.gov/ p/nea/rls/22678.htm.

20. *Knesset Proceedings* 131 (30 August 1993): 7558.

21. This opening, according to project directors, was meant to permit the passage of a larger number of visitors at the site. Israel Antiquity Authority experts repeatedly maintained that there was no truth to the claim that Western Wall Tunnel excavations were being carried out beneath the al-Haram al-Sharif compound and that there was no fear of the compound plaza collapsing as a result of archaeological digs outside the area on which the mosques stand.

22. For Olmert's statements in Israeli media, see *Haaretz*, 25 September 1996; and an interview with Israel's television, Channel Two, 28 September 1996.

23. On 15 April 2002, Marwan Bargouti was arrested by Israel's security forces. He was convicted on 20 May 2002 and was given five cumulative life sentences and an additional forty years for involvement in the murder of Israelis and membership in a terror organization. His trial and sentencing increased the popularity of Palestinian prisoner "Number One."

24. See "Protocol Concerning the Redeployment in Hebron," http://www.mfa.gov .il/MFA/Peace+Process/Guide+to+the+Peace+Process/Protocol+Concerning+the+ Redeployment+in+Hebron.htm. For a detailed account on the protocol's negotiations, see Ross, *The Missing Peace*, pp. 269–322.

25. For the Wye Memorandum, see http://www.mfa.gov.il/mfa/go.asp? MFAH00pz0; for a discussion of the negotiations, see Ross, *The Missing Peace*, pp. 415–459.

4

Barak's Blueprint
and Its Failure

On 17 May 1999 Ehud Barak won an overwhelming victory in Israel's prime ministerial race. His meteoric rise from chief of general staff of the Israeli Defense Forces to chief politician was due to a number of circumstances. Netanyahu had managed to alienate many people in different camps, including within Likud, and voters punished him. Large portions of the public believed that Barak offered a real alternative. He seemed to present a coherent, convincing picture of the future and looked as if he had a good idea of where he was going in both the socioeconomic sphere and the conflict with the Palestinians. He spoke of the "painful concessions" the two sides would have to make to reach a permanent settlement, a stage he wished to get to without delay. He promised to withdraw the IDF from southern Lebanon within a year and proffered an equally ambitious social platform: he would institute civil and constitutional reform to revamp the Orthodox-secular status quo and put it on a new footing. In the previous elections, the Israeli public had bought the ocean of vain promises and magic solutions scattered by Netanyahu. In the 1999 elections, they seemed eager to repeat the experience with Barak.

Barak enjoyed widespread respect both as chief of general staff and fledgling politician. Rabin had paved the way for him to the political forefront and party leadership, though the two men had had their disagreements. Barak, throughout his command of the IDF and as MK and Labor Party minister, had never hidden his reservations about Oslo. Both in the Knesset and at the cabinet table he had pointed out its shortcomings, notably the transfer of territory to the Palestinians without any fair "exchange" in return, and he had abstained in the vote on the Interim Agreement. None of this dented his self-perception as Rabin's political successor, and that is how he was packaged in the election campaign. He presented himself as the leader imperative for the fateful decisions at hand, the sort of decisions David Ben-Gurion had made on the eve of the establishment of the state of Israel. The Labor Party campaign highlighted his stock as a fearless warrior capable of executing special missions that called for imagination, daring, and precise planning.[1] Israeli society had long regarded senior commanders as endowed with the necessary talents and mettle for political leadership, a fact Barak's campaign managers were well aware of. It was an assessment drawn from long years of battle, conflict, and war. It was not unusual for political hacks to try to recruit officers to their parties even before they had stripped off their uniforms. Like many of his colleagues in Israel's security elite, Barak, too, was conscious of the advantages he enjoyed because of his army career. Embarking on a second career, especially in politics, was common. The public was receptive to it, and few people knew just how uncommon it was in democratic regimes.[2]

Years of army service train senior officers to manage complex military systems based on extensive manpower and advanced technologies. Liberal, Western political regimes are not built like that. There is a world of difference between the considerations and constraints of the two. Barak, like all Israeli officers, was educated and educated others on the premise that no mission is impossible. Careful planning and faith in oneself are a recipe for success. Barak's goal-oriented focus as chief of general staff could not prepare him for the wide range of considerations that Israeli prime ministers must take into account in deciding crucial issues. True, senior officers rub shoulders with elected leaders, getting a glimpse of the workings of the political and diplomatic arenas. They also (especially the chief of general staff and IDF generals) play an active role in the leadership's decisionmaking on security and state issues. They do so in a professional capacity, advising the government on matters that come within their sphere of responsibility and translating political decisions into operational military plans. As a result, it may look as if the senior command has close knowledge of the influences at the political level. But the officers are not, in fact, exposed to all the political, diplomatic, economic, media, and public opinion factors swaying state leaders. Nor do they bear the responsibility for carrying out policy.

Israeli expectations of the general-turned-prime-minister knew no bounds. To garner as broad public support as possible for his future moves in both the peace process and domestic reforms, Barak put together a government representing seven political parties. A vain illusion of national unity in which hawks and doves could coexist. A wall-to-wall coalition. Almost. The prime minister "of everyone" chose to exclude two important political groups from his government: Likud and the Arab parties. Israel's Arab citizens, who had by and large voted for Barak, found themselves outside his coalition. Barak entered office seemingly convinced that his term could set Israel on a new road in both external and internal affairs. He voiced his commitment to renewing the political process, although he intended to steer it along a new course. He was well aware that the implementation of the Interim Agreement was behind schedule and, like others, judged that there would be no choice but to enter into negotiations on permanent status during his term of office. The hourglass was fast running out. The two sides had agreed that the interim stage would come to an end in 1999 and that all their commitments would be met by that year, including IDF redeployment (withdrawal).

It soon transpired that Barak meant to take the bull by the horns, but in a way that no one in Israel, the PA, or the United States had expected. In his eyes, to complete the agreed redeployment in the West Bank was a bad mistake. Israel could well find itself at the permanent-status negotiations in an irrevocable position if the most valuable assets had already been handed over to the Palestinians. "The implementation of redeployment as stipulated in the Wye Memorandum schedule was potentially harmful to the political and security interests of the state of Israel," Barak announced at a Knesset debate some months following his election (8 September 1999), after the Sharm al-Sheikh Memorandum was signed.[3] What he sought, then, was an alternative blueprint to the tactic on which Oslo was based: the parties would conduct direct negotiations on permanent status, concluding them within twelve to fifteen months. The permanent-status settlement would finalize all pending issues between the sides and put an end to the Israeli-Palestinian conflict.

From the first, in fact, Barak had plainly labored under the assumption that the two sides might not be able to resolve all the issues in dispute. After his first official visit to Washington, when the Knesset convened on a confidence motion tabled by the Likud, Shinui (Change), and Ihud Leumi (National Unity) parties (27 July 1999), Barak presented the anticipated negotiations as a "window of opportunity," "at the close of which we will know where we stand."[4] The permanent-status negotiations were to be preceded by a framework agreement summarizing the commitments of the two sides until the signing of a permanent-status settlement. The proposal had a twofold significance: Israel would not at that stage execute the third phase of redeployment it had agreed to at Wye, and the United States would not be directly involved in the negotiations other than to guarantee that the agreement would be reached and to assist in its implementation. Barak had reason to fear that the US position was close to that of the Palestinians on several basic issues, which could mean heavy US pressure on his government. He may also have assumed that direct negotiations would restrict Palestinian and expand Israeli maneuverability, seeing as Israel had total control of the territories.

In the diplomatic and security spheres, Barak's first year in office was very busy. As opposed to most of his predecessors, he gave the immediate impression that he was the right man at the right time in the right place to make the historical decisions that would bring the Israeli-Palestinian conflict to safe harbor. PA, Egyptian, and US leaders were prepared to grant him the credit he sought after their frustration with Netanyahu's government. Expectations for him were enormous, as he could sense in a meeting with Arab and western leaders headed by Husni Mubarak, Arafat, and Clinton. They, too, assumed that he was political heir to Rabin, symbol of Israel's historic decision to settle the Israeli-Arab conflict by peaceful means. According to one of Barak's associates, during their first White House meeting (19 July 1999), Clinton promised the prime minister that "America will walk at your side." Although this wording was not included in any of the official statements, the latter, along with the White House press release, hint at the special atmosphere and, more importantly, at the meaningful concord achieved at the meeting. The two leaders reached "a broad new understanding," the White House press release stated, bringing the special relationship between the two countries "to an even higher level of strategic partnership."[5] In their dealings with Barak, the Americans had become convinced that, more concretely than previous incumbents, he subscribed to a vision of overall peace in the Middle East, including a permanent settlement with the Palestinians. The US administration thus showed that it was prepared to do all it could to help allay Israeli fears, signing a memorandum of understanding on massive assistance. In his Knesset address on 26 July 1999, Barak promised "to leave no stone unturned and to open all avenues [to ensure] Israel's security, to achieve peace, and to prevent unnecessary war."[6]

Having become an ardent fan of public opinion polls, Barak knew that a solid Israeli majority (an average of 65 percent in the early months of his term) was in favor of resuming the political process with the Palestinians and was ready to make major concessions for a permanent peace settlement.[7] In general, however, most polls suffer from a similar weakness: they regard the definitions they use as self-evident, not bothering to examine how familiar different groups were with the topics they were asked about. Most of the surveys did not check how the respondents understood the terms used in the questions. "Peace process," "readiness for concessions," and "refugee problem" were bandied about as if they meant exactly the same thing to all pollees. Nor did the public and media discourse really address the expectations, demands, and positions of key Palestinian sectors vis-à-vis Israel and the possibilities of settling the conflict.

More than anything else, Israeli consensus reflected a total disregard for what most Palestinians expected and demanded: the establishment of an independent sovereign Palestinian state according to the borders of 4 June 1967. The word *state* featured prominently in Israel's public discourse, but what it really meant hardly crept into the media discourse. Official and nonofficial spokespeople frequently alluded to Palestinian statehood, but it was so hedged in as to clip its sovereignty and independence. Just how hollow and meaningless the term *Palestinian state* was can be seen from the national hobby of political discussion, like a one-sided simulation game. Many Israelis, including those who supported a historical compromise with the Palestinians, erroneously assumed that the latter would be prepared to accept a "lesser state."

Many listed the "red lines" that must not be crossed. No one can doubt the importance of security considerations. But alongside them, more and more constraints and conditions were piled onto the scales.

As the security demands of Barak's government were translated into practical terms—primarily, the fear of "invasion from the East," vital control over "key transportation roads," and the need for "comprehensive defense of settlement blocs" (i.e., most of the settlements) on the new border—the restrictions that Israel hoped to impose on a Palestinian state moved into sharper focus. Palestinian sovereignty and independence were meant to be not only partial but subject to long-term Israeli discretion; clear evidence of the asymmetry in the balance of power between the state of Israel and the PA as the governing body of the Palestinian people. Barak had from the start proclaimed "four *nos*" that were to shape a permanent settlement: "no" to returning to the 4 June 1967 borders, "no" to dismantling settlements, "no" to compromising over Jerusalem, and "no" to any right of return by Palestinian refugees to Israel's sovereign jurisdiction. It was the most straightforward and unequivocal statement on the topics to be negotiated and settled for permanent status. One might have assumed that, under these conditions, it would be impossible to reach an agreement. Yet his words did not trigger any meaningful or critical discussion in Israel. Various Arab spokespeople protested, but that did not spark pan-Arab discussion of the issue.

In the early months of his term, Barak worked hard to persuade the United States, Egypt, Jordan, and, of course, the Palestinian leadership to give his new political program a chance. Despite their esteem for him at this stage, almost all the leaders cautioned him about his new blueprint, pointing out that reneging on a signed agreement could have nasty consequences. The main impediment was having the Palestinians waive full Israeli implementation of existing agreements, notably the IDF's withdrawal from a good chunk of the West Bank. To them, Barak's readiness to forge ahead to final-status negotiations was a force of circumstance, not necessarily a gesture on Israel's part. In the first meeting between the two leaders (11 July 1999), Barak, without going into detail, informed Arafat of his intention: "progress on final-status negotiations would be integrated with the implementation of the Wye [Memorandum]."[8] In response, Chairman Arafat noted that for the political process to progress, the parties had to fulfill the commitments they had undertaken, especially the redeployment phases outlined in the Wye Memorandum. In conjunction, intensive talks would be conducted on a permanent settlement. Arafat had chalked up countless hours of discussion with Israeli leaders, and he soon realized that the new prime minister did not mean to implement the Wye Memorandum signed by Netanyahu. Apart from the questions and apprehensions this realization raised, the Palestinian leadership found it difficult to swallow the way in which Barak had laid down the plan before Arafat. Barak's associates, over the years, had grown accustomed to his manner and tactlessness. Not so his colleagues in the Labor Party, to say nothing of the Palestinian representatives.[9] They came away with a poor impression of the man and his plan, seeing it as an attempt to force impossible conditions on them.

Arafat and his close acquaintances mulled over the approach to adopt toward Barak: whether to take a firmer stance from the very beginning or to try to get him to change his ways through diplomatic channels.[10] This indecision was taken for lukewarm receptiveness. Palestinian leaders did not mask their disappointment with Barak in public declarations, of course, but they attributed his attitude to a lack of political experience. They expected the built-in dynamics of negotiations to undo his words. Meanwhile, Palestinian opponents of the Oslo process pronounced him no different from Netanyahu. Barak, in the next few months, was to restate his position at various opportunities. He had, in fact, broached his ideas about a new blueprint to Clinton on his first trip to Washington, D.C., in mid-July 1999. Months later, he was still in the preliminary stage of presenting his positions to seasoned decisionmakers both inside and outside the Middle East. Clinton and his advisers examined the new direction pursued by Barak and phrased their reservations in such a way that Barak and his associates could take it that the United States was not opposed, which was a serious mistake.[11] Clinton should have nipped the initiative in the bud. Instead, he undertook to promote a program of which he was not at all sure. His administration exerted all its influence to get Arafat to give Barak's new blueprint a chance. It also used its influence on governments in the Middle East (primarily Egypt) and in Europe to support the new diplomatic effort.

Barak's endeavors bore fruit. Although unconvinced of the need for the framework agreement that Barak saw as vital, US, Egyptian, and Palestinian administrations were all impressed by his determination to cut to the chase in the political process. They may have thought it preferable to endorse his blueprint rather than have an open confrontation, which would have further handicapped the foundering political process. The Palestinian leadership was compelled to negotiate with Israel on a framework agreement, and the negotiations ended on 4 September 1999 with the signing of the Sharm al-Sheikh Memorandum. Under the patronage of the Egyptian president, the Jordanian king, and the US Secretary of State, Israeli and PA leaders committed themselves "to full and mutual implementation of the Interim Agreement and all other agreements concluded between them since September 1993." In addition, provisions were made for two new agreements meant to embody the progress of the parties in resolving all disputed issues and arriving at a permanent-status settlement. The one—a framework agreement—was to be signed within five months, would define the commitments of the parties at this stage, and would spell out all the questions that were to make up the permanent-status settlement. The other—a comprehensive agreement—was to be concluded within a year and would finalize all the permanent-status issues. The latter agreement was to be regarded by the parties as "the implementation of Security Council Resolutions 242 and

338."[12] Armed with this memorandum and these understandings, the leaders began dispensing their own interpretations. The Palestinians highlighted the fact that by 13 September 2000, permanent-status negotiations would be concluded and Israel would implement its Interim Agreement commitments, including additional redeployment in the West Bank and the release of security prisoners. In Israel, there was a totally different interpretation as to the imminence of meeting prior commitments and the timetable.

The plans of Barak and his colleagues were disturbed by political developments that should have been foreseen. The signing of the Sharm al-Sheikh Memorandum ushered in the disintegration of Barak's coalition. It was a government in crisis that discussed and approved the memorandum. In the Knesset, all the Shas Party MKs voted with their feet, absenting themselves from the assembly. MKs of the National Religious Party (Mafdal) and the immigrant party (Yisrael Be'Aliya) voted against it. The Orthodox party of Yahadut HaTora had quit the coalition even prior to the Sharm al-Sheikh talks because of the government's decision to allow the Electricity Corporation to transport slow-moving heavy equipment on the country's roads on the Sabbath (13 August). At this stage, the evident differences between the component parties of Barak's government did not yet bring it down, though the widening gulf had been apparent within months of its establishment.[13] Israel's commitments as per the Sharm al-Sheikh Memorandum, especially the accelerated political schedule, were among the chief factors adding to the tensions around the cabinet table. Based on current information, there is no way of knowing how Barak assessed these developments or their implications for the political process with the Palestinians. He advocated coalition unity and spoke over and over again of the import of the moment and the responsibility toward future generations, but all these comments could be taken in more than one way.

The champions of the political process held up the Sharm al-Sheikh Memorandum as a positive sign for the future. In practical terms, the parties were now to tackle the nitty-gritty of permanent status, which entailed intensive groundwork. The Palestinians required only a few days to prepare, their negotiating teams and logistical base having worked in concert for some time. Israel, however, dragged its feet as to the makeup of the negotiating team. Barak clearly did not wish to leave matters to his Labor Party colleagues. Ministers Shimon Peres, Justice Minister Yossi Beilin, Haim Ramon, and many others were thus seen as the natural candidates only in their own eyes. But Barak found it equally difficult to hit on a suitable candidate outside the political realm. Weeks were wasted before he named the head of the Israeli team, Oded Eran of the Foreign Ministry, a professional diplomat. It only remained to be seen if he would be given sufficient authority.

The ineptness with which Israel's negotiating team was appointed was symptomatic of a far larger problem. According to a privileged few who occasionally enjoyed the prime minister's confidence, Barak, even at this stage, was still weighing alternatives to the course laid out by Oslo. On 2 October 1999, he invited Yossi Beilin to his home and, in a two-hour meeting, asked him what he thought about the possibility of progress in the Palestinian channel, in particular, about the agreements that Beilin had formulated four years earlier with Abu Mazen, the man considered to be number two in the Palestinian hierarchy, which had resulted in the Beilin–Abu Mazen Document (31 October 1995). After Beilin delivered a detailed report, Barak described his own perception of a settlement with the Palestinians. Above all, he showed a desire to deviate considerably from the Oslo path. According to Beilin's notes, Barak thought that

> the agreement should aim at separation between Israel and the Palestinians, meaning a 400-kilometer-long fence . . . with 7-8 border cross-points, easily negotiable on the basis of handprints. The Jerusalem area would stay open, but with an option to shut it off if need be. No settlements would be left on the Palestinian side of the fence, and there would be an overhead bridge between the Gaza Strip and the West Bank. He was also interested in economic separation.

As for the territory of the Palestinian state, Barak declared that, "even 50 percent of the West Bank looks like a state," and added, "several bridges and several tunnels, and you have full contiguity." In the Jordan Valley, Barak believed, the IDF camps and Israeli communities would remain. Beilin, one of the best-versed Israelis on the Palestinian position, summed up this "most candid political discussion" with Barak thus:

> I walked out into Kochav Ya'ir's chilly night feeling that here was a man who really wished to make peace, and fearing that the bid to expect Ben-Gurion-like traits from our interlocutor was overly optimistic, especially if our opening positions were so tight-fisted. Nor was I enthusiastic about barbed wire fences. But Barak's enthusiasm and confidence in his ability to bring it about in his own way lifted my hopes that this time we would make it to the finish line.[14]

It is hard to say how Barak envisioned the chances of realizing his idea of a Palestinian state. Three days after his talk with Beilin, he stuck to his commitment to open a safe passage in the southern route joining the Gaza Strip and the West Bank, a crucial component of the Interim Stage. The Palestinian leadership welcomed the move in view of the longtime claims by Palestinian oppositionists that Israel would never connect or allow free movement between the two areas. Its opening was vested with both practical and symbolic significance. The political channel, apart from coordination on security matters, had been at a virtual standstill.

Oodles of reckonings and forecasts saw out the year 1999. The twentieth-first century, the third millennium, was on the threshold. Data were published on the world population, and note was duly taken of the foci of wealth and poverty, religion and secularism. Prophecies of doom vied with predictions of untold delights for the dawning era. A drizzle began in the Israeli and Palestinian press, with the resurrection of an Israeli-Syrian channel of communications, with US mediation. The drizzle was soon a downpour. The initiative, as it transpired, had come from Israel's nimble prime minister but did not enjoy universal support. In early December 1999, the heads of Israel's Secret Services warned against making the Syrian channel a priority at this time: "This decision of yours could prove disastrous. You do not understand the Palestinian problem," the head of Shin Bet told the prime minister.[15]

One can only wonder at the odds Barak gave the Syria channel, at his choice of timing, and the information that prompted him to revive that of all options. Barak consistently pressed the US administration to launch peace negotiations between Israel and Syria. According to Clinton, toward the end of 1999, Barak told him "that he was prepared to give the Golan Heights back to Syria as long as Israel's concerns could be satisfied about its early warning station on the Golan and its dependence on Lake Tiberias."[16] In consequence, the Americans set to work persuading the Syrians. Political efforts in the Palestinian channel took a backseat. The Palestinian leadership subsided into apprehension and anxiety. Against their will, Barak had dragged them to Sharm al-Sheikh to sign the memorandum, and when he got what he wanted, he instructed his negotiators to focus on security issues. The complex topics of permanent status were hardly discussed and, even then, only in general terms. Instead of getting down to brass tacks, the prime minister's office was busy cultivating the Syrian channel. From Barak's public declarations and his tight rein on the negotiators, Arafat and his coterie concluded that Israel was turning its back on every opportunity to make significant progress with them. According to Palestinian spokespeople, Barak wished to use the Syrian channel as leverage against them. Months passed before there were any meaningful talks on permanent status.[17]

The Syrian channel dealt seriously with all the issues in dispute. The two sides came closer than ever to reaching an agreement. The many details published to date show the blueprint to have been based entirely on the principles of the Egyptian-Israeli peace treaty with regard to withdrawal, security arrangements, and normalization of relations. Pertinent messages were exchanged behind the scenes, and at the height of the talks, the Americans seemed to be leading the two sides to a historic peace treaty.[18] On 17 December 1999, the *Maariv* daily told readers that Clinton, Barak, and Syrian foreign minister Farouk al-Shar'a had "agreed that the year 2000 would be the year that Israel and Syria achieve a full and comprehensive peace." A thoroughly uncritical media again gave exposure to deliberate leaks. Only after the Syrian channel had failed was there a flurry of explanation in Israel's media for the fact that no treaty had been signed. Then, too, many reporters and commentators mostly echoed Barak's camp, which managed to plant the charge that there was no treaty because of Syria's unfathomable insistence on "sitting" on the Sea of Galilee. Still, from the heaps of articles published on the subject, it is worth noting the account by Barak's right-hand man at the time, Gilead Sher. He describes US shock on the eve of the Shepherdstown Summit (3 January 2000) at hearing Barak sing a new, unpleasant tune. After all their labor in working out the parameters of an Israeli-Syrian peace, the Americans learned on the eve of the summit itself, that Barak had changed his mind about going the full distance toward Assad for the sake of a peace treaty with the Syrians. According to the Americans, as soon as he landed in Washington, the prime minister had told them, "I'm sorry, but I can't budge. Politically, my hands are tied."[19] As it emerges from the testimonies of Clinton and Ross, from the start of the Shepherdstown talks it was clear to the American team that Barak had backtracked on the blueprint with Syria. It was the Syrians who were obviously flexible about the US draft of the peace agreement. In his memoirs, Clinton notes:

> The Syrians responded positively . . . and we began meetings on border and security issues. Again, the Syrians showed flexibility on both matters, saying they would accept an adjustment of the strip of land bordering Galilee to as much as 50 meters (164 feet), provided that Israel accepted the June 4 line as the basis for discussion. . . . I was encouraged, but it quickly became apparent that Barak still had not authorized anyone on his team to accept June 4, no matter what the Syrians offered. . . . Syria had shown flexibility on what Israel wanted, providing its needs were met; Israel had not responded in kind.[20]

High hopes for a breakthrough ended in disappointment, the responsibility for which fell upon the Israeli side, headed by Barak. Syrian disappointment could be heard in the summation by Foreign Minister Farouk al-Shar'a ("Barak was not sincere") and in President Assad's reaction at his meeting with Clinton in Geneva.[21]

Although Israeli and Palestinian negotiators had met in the seven months between the signing of the Sharm al-Sheikh Memorandum and the collapse of the Syrian channel, it was clear to all that Barak did not attribute much importance to the contacts. Convinced as ever that he had right on his side, he made a note that since no significant talks had begun on permanent status, Israel's position vis-à-vis the Palestinians had remained intact. Among other things, Barak was influenced by what he saw as the potential political consequences of pursuing negotiations on controversial issues with the Palestinians. His government, after all, represented also hawkish parties, which made compromise necessary. He preferred to leave decisive talks to summits, where the true positions of Israel and the Palestinians would be revealed and the painful compromises clarified if a peace treaty were to be reached and the heart of the Arab-Israeli conflict resolved. He did not regret the months of relative inaction. In this time, he and his coterie had begun to refer to the need for an "incubation" period—a time of vital "maturation" to prepare both peoples and especially their governments for the fateful summit.[22] The public and media discourse soon pounced on the new concept, oblivious to how it had come into the world or what it meant. It was spawned by legitimate considerations, chiefly Barak's evaluation of the disadvantages of protracted negotiations at the intermediate level and the inherent danger they posed to the political support for his government. He truly feared that months of palaver on sensitive topics would prematurely expose Israel's positions and the painful concessions it had to make. Throughout his term of office, he contended that the documentation of Israel's positions in negotiations, especially if leaked, could only narrow the maneuverability of its leadership at the crucial summit and shorten the life of his government.

Though the Israeli-Palestinian talks ran into a dead end in the first half of 2000, Barak looked like a skilled driver who knew the road well. The Palestinian leadership grew more and more disenchanted with his government and its refusal to fully meet its commitments, especially to make serious headway on permanent status. They were even more disappointed when Israel did not hand over control of a number of neighborhoods in Jerusalem, a measure it had approved. And their rage and frustration soared when they found that Israel was impeding and, in fact, disallowing the release of security prisoners—an issue that, over the years, had become the PA's greatest internal pressure point. Israel reacted by saying that the violence surrounding *al-Nakba* Day in mid-May had prevented Barak from approving the planned "gestures" toward the Palestinians. Increasingly, the Arab media argued that Barak was acting on the assumption that the Palestinians had no choice but to pursue his blueprint and that, given the current conditions, he exclusively could dictate the pace of progress.[23]

Barak's was not the only sorry conduct. One cannot ignore the US government's handling of the talks with the Palestinians at this stage. For months, the United States was content to dispatch envoys to futile negotiations. Even when it was clear as day that Barak was not sticking to the blueprint that he himself had forced on the Palestinians, the United States showed no real concern. Clinton and his aides knew that Barak wanted to reach an understanding with the Palestinians in direct negotiations. But they also knew—having learned from various Arab sources—that nothing was happening in the Palestinian channel and that Israel kept turning down suggestions to convene on permanent-status issues. Yet the Clinton administration seemed to have adopted an uncritical policy toward Barak's modus operandi. Any faith the Palestinians may have had in the sincerity of Barak's intentions was lost, and messages to this effect were conveyed to Israel. "The Palestinians felt cheated, humiliated, pushed into a corner," wrote Gilead Sher.[24] They found only one encouraging note: the key sponsors of the political process, topped by the United States, reiterated their commitment to the timetable for reaching an agreement on permanent status as set out in the Sharm al-Sheikh Memorandum. The Palestinian leadership now pinned their hopes on one date: 13 September 2000.

While communication slumped, there was no letup in mutual violence. Events hit a nadir in May 2000, when, according to the Sharm al-Sheikh Memorandum, the parties should have concluded the framework agreement and moved on to the highly charged issues of permanent status. The escalation had been noticeable from the start of May, harrowing the lives of Israelis and Palestinians. In mid-month, exactly when Israelis celebrated their Independence Day, Palestinians marked al-Nakba Day, their commemoration of the catastrophe that befell them in 1948. The demonstrations and clashes lasted three days and degenerated into the worst incidents since Barak's government had been sworn in. For the first time, gunmen of al-Tanzim took part. It was a wake-up call: members of a strong militia functioning under the auspices of the Palestinian leadership turned their weapons on Israel's armed forces. Worried about losing control and a full-scale flare-up that would make the chances of permanent-status talks even more remote, the PA leadership took steps to check the unrest. US and Egyptian envoys called on Israel to display similar self-restraint, and calm was restored.[25] At the same time, Israel announced that it did not intend to carry out the third redeployment phase. Barak asserted that the scope and character of IDF redeployment were subject to the discretion of the government of Israel, and it was thus within its rights to defer the third phase. His advisers were not all of one mind on this matter, and the Palestinians obviously rejected the analysis. Egyptian, Jordanian, and US spokespeople held that, in the absence of meaningful talks on permanent status, Israel should honor its commitments to redeploy.

Amid the escalation, Barak took a decision that was to be the major milestone of his term of office. To the chagrin of most IDF generals and the chief of general staff, he instructed the army to pull out of Lebanon. Only one stumbling block was left between Israel and Lebanon: control of a small portion of Mt. Dov (the Sheba'a Farm). Israel's sojourn in Lebanon had lasted almost eighteen years. Prime Minister Menachem Begin had launched Operation Peace for the Galilee on 4 June 1982, and the last of Israel's soldiers evacuated the "security belt" in southern Lebanon on 23 May 2000. Thousands of Israelis, Palestinians, and Lebanese had been killed in numerous battles. Enormous damage had been done. As the years passed, the IDF got more and more bogged down in Lebanon. The direct cause of the war ("the destruction of the PLO's terror infrastructure in Lebanon") had become irrelevant. Many PLO leaders and fighters had left Lebanon on the basis of a concluded agreement to become, within a few years, Israel's partners in the Oslo process. The war against Israel's presence in the land of the cedars had been taken over by Hizbollah, a Shiite group enjoying massive support from Iran and Syria. The longer Israel's occupation of southern Lebanon lasted, the more support the local organization garnered, its charismatic leaders succeeding in consolidating a political movement. The withdrawal of Israeli forces to the boundary line was covered (especially on television) as a flight of panic. Military posts and equipment were abandoned. Hizbollah's takeover was swift and had the air of a victory carnival. In the Arab media, the hasty retreat was depicted as the successful ouster of the IDF by the Shiite guerrilla movement.[26] The lesson did not go unnoticed in the Occupied Territories, particularly by Palestinian groups who advocate armed struggle and spurn political settlement. Hizbollah and Hamas share a common ideology of armed struggled against Israel based on an Islamic platform. Both "resistance" movements flourished in the hotbed of Lebanese and Palestinian failure to score any meaningful gains against Israel.

From early May 2000, there was an upsurge in the channels of confidential communication between Israeli and Palestinian officials. A format for secret talks was devised with the knowledge of US and Egyptian governments. It was the last significant attempt to conclude a framework agreement to define the principles and agenda of permanent-status negotiations. The contacts led to a number of rounds of secret talks under the patronage of the Swedish government. For the first time in months, there was meaningful discussion between Israeli (Minister Shlomo Ben-Ami and Gilead Sher, Barak's right-hand man) and Palestinian representatives (Abu 'Ala [Ahmed Qureia] and Hassan 'Asfur, among the senior negotiators from the start of the Oslo process). Nevertheless, though intensive and to the point, the talks in the "Stockholm channel" could not resolve the issues in the balance. Israel presented a redeployment map, and the Palestinians rejected it; they said they were not prepared to seriously consider Israel's annexation of the Occupied Territories, to the tune of more than 13 percent direct annexation of the West Bank and indirect annexation (through control of roads and military installations) of yet another 10 percent. Still, the talks gave the parties a chance to delineate positions more precisely and realistically, their own as well as the other side's, and to tag the key issues still outstanding: borders, settlements, security arrangements, Jerusalem, refugees, and the question of settling all claims and putting an end to the conflict.[27] There came a point when Barak and his advisers decided that the direct talks had run their course. They may have spelled progress and summed up certain issues, including Jerusalem, but from Israel's perspective the Stockholm channel was of dubious value. They were apprehensive about coming under pressure once a summit convened: "You are prepared to quash an entire agreement over a single point?" The Palestinians had similar qualms.

Media leaks about the existence of the Stockholm channel sealed its fate in early June. Israel's opposition, like the Palestinians', was furious at the far-reaching understandings ostensibly achieved in the Swedish capital. Barak welcomed the halt at this juncture. He could present himself as seriously pursuing every possible avenue toward a settlement with the Palestinians, especially to the US government, which was kept abreast of all the details. At home, the mere disclosure of the talks was an invitation to lambaste him. The domestic political pressures were real enough, but they also enhanced his image as a leader with the rare political courage to make mighty strides toward the Palestinians, a leader who could not relax his position any further, however, because he was under a barrage of criticism. Stopping the Stockholm talks obviously halted all further exploration of the positions held on crucial issues, chief among them Jerusalem and the refugees. The effects of aborting this vital preparatory stage were to be fully felt at the Camp David Summit to be convened in July 2000. Barak, meanwhile, turned his attention to the key component of his political program: getting the major partners to the peace process to back a summit in which the leaders would make the fateful decisions necessary for permanent status.

Based on the positions of the parties as stated in the various channels of communication between Israelis, Palestinians, and Americans, the chances of a breakthrough were rather slim. In fact, on a number of occasions US, Egyptian, and Jordanian envoys relayed information to the two sides that supported this assessment. On 15 June 2000, Arafat, meeting with Clinton at the White House, said that Barak was manipulating the political process as illustrated by his evasion of signed commitments (implementing the third phase of redeployment and releasing prisoners). He ran through his standpoints on each of the aspects of permanent status and voiced his doubts about convening a summit at this stage ("we need a lot of preparation"). He asked Clinton to shield him from what he feared were Barak's true intentions: "I think Barak has decided to put us in the position of the guilty party, and I need your promise that, wherever we go with the negotiations, you won't shift the blame for failure onto us and won't back us into a corner." Clinton rose to the challenge: "I promise you that under no circumstances will I place the blame for failure on you."[28]

After Arafat returned from the United States, the Palestinians worked feverishly to elucidate their stance and obtain the support of other major parties. They consulted with Egypt and gave Barak's delegates the same message they had given the Americans. At a meeting in Nablus on 25 June, Arafat told Shlomo Ben-Ami, Yossi Ginossar, and Gilead Sher: "We are not ready. We haven't even talked about Jerusalem or the refugee issue. . . . You're headed for failure. Go back with Abu 'Ala [Qureia], with Saeb [Erekat]; negotiate for one more month."[29] Three days later in Ramallah, Secretary of State Madeleine Albright heard the same message from the Palestinians. Albright reported to Clinton and Barak, telling both leaders what they were well aware of: Arafat's people had serious reservations about holding a summit in the present conditions.[30] Despite the odds, Barak, with characteristic tenacity, decided to press for the crucial summit. He obviously had his sights on two important dates. The first, stipulated in the Sharm al-Sheikh Memorandum, obliged the two sides to conclude permanent-status negotiations by September 2000. The second was the internal US political calendar. In early summer 2000, the United States was in the midst of presidential elections. There were also elections for some Senate seats, and Hillary Clinton was waging a tough, high-exposure campaign in New York State. There were only a few grains left in the diplomatic and political hourglass. The die was cast. Israel and the United States fixed it between them that a summit would convene at Camp David in mid-July.

Notes

1. Drucker, *Harakiri*, pp. 21–29.
2. Peri, *Between Battles and Ballots*; Ben-Eliezer, *The Making of Israeli Militarism*.
3. First session of the 15th Knesset, *Knesset Proceedings* 13, no. 26 (8 September 1999): 1305–1378.
4. First session of the 15th Knesset, *Knesset Proceedings* 8 (26 July 1999): 754–814. Barak's speech, pp. 762–768; the quote from p. 765.
5. "Joint statement by President Clinton and Prime Minister Ehud Barak, 19 July 1999," http://clinton6.nara.gov/1999/07/1999-07019-joint-statement-by-president-clinton-and-prime-minister-barak.html.
6. First session of the 15th Knesset, *Knesset Proceedings* 8 (26 July 1999): 763.
7. By August 1999, about a year before the collapse of the Camp David negotiations, the polls began to show a steady shift to the right by Israel's (Jewish) population. A solid majority were still in favor of "concessions," such as the establishment of a Palestinian state and the evacuation of the settlements from the Gaza Strip and most of the West Bank. A large majority opposed shared sovereignty over Jerusalem. And there was extremely broad consensus against recognizing a Palestinian right of return to the jurisdiction of the state of Israel. Drucker devoted an entire chapter to Barak's obsessive reliance on public opinion polls, see Drucker, *Harakiri*, pp. 75–86.
8. Gilead Sher, *Bemerhak neggi'ah*, 24.
9. The antagonism aroused by Barak's management of affairs was no secret in his close milieu. See Ben-Ami, *Chazit lelu oref*, 21, 64–66.
10. Evidence of this can be found in *Al-Ayam* (Ramallah), the editor of which, Akram Haniya, was closely associated with Arafat.
11. Clinton, in his memoirs, chose to ignore his first working session with Barak. Ross notes that Clinton was quite excited by Barak's ideas for the Palestinian channel but disappointed that Barak was not prepared to endorse Rabin's commitment to withdraw from the Golan Heights in exchange for a peace treaty that would meet Israel's security needs. Ross, *The Missing Peace*, pp. 497–501. For details of Rabin's commitment, see ibid., pp. 107–114.
12. US Department of State, "The Sharm el-Sheikh Memorandum on Implementation: Timeline of Outstanding Commitments of Agreements Signed and the Resumption of Permanent Status Negotiations," September 4, 1999. For the text, see http://www.state.gov/p/nea/rls/22696.htm.
13. For an elaborate treatment of Barak's poor management of the coalition "of all," including the Sabbath transport affair, see Drucker, *Harakiri*, pp. 167–178.
14. Beilin, *Madrikh le-yona petzu'a'*, p. 86.

15. Drucker, *Harakiri*, pp. 68–69.

16. Clinton, *My Life*, p. 883.

17. The Palestinian leadership confided their suspicions to the US administration. See Ross, *The Missing Peace*, pp. 501–508.

18. For a detailed account, see ibid., pp. 509–590.

19. Sher, *Bemerhak neggi'ah*, p. 65.

20. Clinton, *My Life*, pp. 886–887.

21. Ross, *The Missing Peace*, pp. 549–587.

22. Ben-Ami, *Chazit lelu oref*, pp. 21–36.

23. Graham Usher, "Accommodating Israel," *Al-Ahram Weekly*, 11–17 May 2000.

24. Sher, *Bemerhak neggi'ah*, p. 65.

25. On the attempts of the US government to stop the al-Nakba Day events via firm messages to the Palestinian leadership, see Ross, *The Missing Peace*, pp. 620–623.

26. A sure sign of this was the intensive coverage accorded the development by the al-Jazeera and Abu Dhabi Arab TV stations on 24–25 May 2000.

27. For a detailed account of the Stockholm channel, see Ben-Ami, *Chazit lelu oref*, pp. 41–55.

28. This exchange is quoted in Enderlin, *Shattered Dreams*, pp. 162–165. In their books, Clinton and Ross "skipped" this commitment to Arafat.

29. Ibid., p. 167. Ben-Ami described the meeting at length, although Arafat's words above do not appear in his account. See Ben-Ami, *Chazit lelu oref*, pp. 115–118.

30. For a brief account of the Secretary of State's visit to Ramallah, see Ross, *The Missing Peace*, pp. 643–644.

5

Camp David:
The Great Charade

By the eve of the decisive permanent-status negotiations, the advantages and disadvantages of the Oslo blueprint had been well delineated. Its greatest achievement remains the mutual recognition of the two peoples, attained by the leaders in signed agreements. The recognition was, of course, attended by myriad details of the painful compromise involved in partitioning the land and settling the decades-long bloody conflict between two national communities. One of the major flaws of the DOP was the decision of the two sides to avoid dealing with the end game between Israel and the Palestinian-entity-to-be. The DOP, like later agreements signed by the two sides, was open-ended. Many people took it for granted that the Oslo blueprint was based on a two-state solution. Yet the goal of establishing a Palestinian state does not appear at all in the DOP. The greatest defect was that the DOP and ensuing agreements did not provide for effective mechanisms to ensure that commitments were implemented. It was particularly conspicuous during the protracted interim stage, when the oppositionists went all-out to obstruct the political process. In addition, the leaders were little inclined to proffer goodwill gestures, and over the years, mutual trust dissolved. Distrust, in fact, was quite often fueled by the leaders themselves, who treated major violations too indulgently in the hope that the other side would do the same. For years, as Israelis and Palestinians mangled the accords in both letter and spirit, the United States simply stood by, delivering laconic statements that one move or another did not serve the cause of peace. This attitude from the main patron of the Middle East political process, which contented itself with mild rebukes while agreements were being trodden underfoot.

On the Palestinian side, evident violations included vastly enlarging its armed forces beyond what had been agreed, ignoring the strengthening of the armed militias, and turning a blind eye to rampant anti-Israel and anti-Jewish incitement (especially in the media and in textbooks).[1] Palestinian leaders, primarily Arafat, delivered coarse remarks that contradicted the spirit of Oslo. The Palestinian Authority was hard put to stop the terror perpetrated by various groups, and PA spokespeople distinguished between acts committed in Israel proper that hurt civilians and acts committed against settlers and soldiers in the Occupied Territories. The former were usually condemned. Not so the latter. Israelis and Israeli targets in the West Bank and the Gaza Strip were considered fair game.

On the Israeli side, violations took the form of disrupting timetables, implementing only partial redeployment (IDF withdrawal), and refusing to release Palestinian prisoners as intended by the letter and spirit of the agreements. But all of them were dwarfed by Israel's handling of the settlement issue. The crowning glory of the settlement endeavor has always been to create facts on the ground so as to prevent partition of the land and the establishment of a territorially contiguous, independent Palestinian state. The settler population and their numerous supporters have, over the years, become a political force to be reckoned with.[2] That not a single government has ever made it to full term attests to Israel's political instability. From time to time, the government table was shared by ministers opposed to Oslo and in favor of expanding settlements, resulting in demands to reopen topics that had already been finalized. It was obvious, too, that Israel did all it could to avert serious discussion on permanent status and to unilaterally establish facts liable to render negotiations meaningless.

All Israeli governments since 1993 lent a hand to steadily expanding settlements, expropriating land and generating friction with the Palestinians. In the first eight years of the "peace" "process," the settler population grew by almost 80 percent, an impressive figure in which natural increase accounted for only a small proportion.[3] The settlements have always attracted newcomers to the Occupied Territories, and the powers-that-be allowed them to follow their inclinations. In parallel, Israel initiated and permitted intensive construction around Jerusalem, including Jewish neighborhoods in densely populated Palestinian areas. The settler public is far from uniform with regard to religious conviction, ideology, or socioeconomic status; different groups are motivated by different reasons. Nevertheless, as large as the growth has been, it could not change the overall demographic balance in the Occupied Territories, and the settlers have remained a small-scale minority. They have nonetheless managed to fan out over the length and breadth of the West Bank and the Gaza Strip, to take over extensive lands, and to benefit from government water allocations for domestic and agricultural use. Their extension was matched by broader IDF deployment in an attempt to control major and minor traffic routes, which exacerbated the friction between the settlers and the IDF shield on the one hand and the Palestinians on the other. Reports of settler action against Palestinian life and property began to rise. Revenge for injury to

Jews became a common occurrence. The settlers became hateful to the Palestinians and a favorite target of the armed organizations.

In deciding to initiate a summit and conclude permanent-status negotiations, Barak was swayed also by information received from the United States, based on contacts between the Palestinians and the Americans. One such influential communication followed Clinton's White House meeting with Arafat on 15 June 2000, when Arafat sketched the guidelines for a permanent-status agreement on the most sensitive issues. He demanded the establishment of a Palestinian state along the 4 June 1967 borders but was prepared to make "minor changes" that would probably leave in place some of the settlements ("it [the settlements themselves] poisons the peace process"). Jerusalem would be a dual capital with the Palestinian capital in the eastern part of the city (al-Quds). Arafat was prepared "to take their [Israeli] needs into account" and weigh the idea of "an open city." As for the refugee question, "there's Resolution 194, but we have to find a happy medium between the Israelis' demographic worries and our own concerns." The Americans appended their own favorable impressions of Arafat's flexibility on the matter of borders, Jerusalem, and the refugees, and Barak could note that although there had been some movement in the explicit Palestinian position, the question remained whether it was enough to reach a permanent-status agreement.[4] Another reason for Barak's interest in a summit was the deadlocked political process at this stage. He had worked hard to persuade others of his program's potential, and he did not want to be identified with failure. Both in the Sharm al-Sheikh Memorandum (that he had also initiated) and in countless diplomatic contacts with colleagues inside and outside the region, he had committed himself to embarking on permanent-status negotiations by September 2000 and, in tandem, implementing the third phase of redeployment. The outbreak of violence on al-Nakba Day did not augur well. To prolong the status quo and fail to live up to signed agreements could have serious consequences.

One of Barak's tactical objectives was to obtain US support for the idea of a summit and maintain Clinton's continued personal trust in him. The Americans were well aware of what was happening in the talks, and they knew that Arafat and his people were not interested in a summit; there was a whole slew of outstanding issues (topped by Jerusalem) on which no understandings had been reached and that required a good deal of advance preparation. The Americans had been apprised of these reservations via a number of channels: from Clinton's talks with Arafat (at the White House), from Secretary of State Albright's talks (in Ramallah), and from messages relayed by Egypt and Jordan. The top US brass kicked around various options, and given the circumstances, some thought the chances of reaching a permanent-status agreement were slim.[5] Yet the United States did not caution any party whatsoever that to convene the planned summit might be a grave error. This reticence is baffling. Why did Clinton allow invitations to go out, if, according to his information, the odds were against a successful summit? How did the United States define the summit goals? What parameters would signal success in the prevailing conditions? Did his policymakers believe there was a reasonable chance of reaching agreement on permanent status? The answers to all these questions will have to wait for the opening of the Clinton administration archives in a generation's time.[6]

Meanwhile, as the summit drew near, the Americans succeeded in "persuading" the Palestinians to participate. Clinton's envoys, Palestinian sources insist, assured them that the president would not blame either side in the event of failure. The US message, understood by the Palestinian leadership as a promise and quasi-insurance policy, is one of many indications of the drama that went on behind the scenes between summit proponents and those who predicted that it would come to nothing. In the end, following frantic consultations, the Palestinians decided that not to participate might be worse for them than to participate and not reach an agreement.

Even prior to the Stockholm channel talks and the escalation on the ground, Barak had harbored serious doubts about the intentions of the Palestinian leadership. To close associates, he described the tactical advantages of "unmasking" them, especially Arafat, an attitude that since the spring of 2000 was reflected in his decisions and public statements. Gilead Sher, his trusted senior aide, documents its first manifestation. In a consultation on 5 May 2000, Barak instructed Sher on the line he was to take with the Palestinians: "The message to Arafat should be that this is a historic opportunity that won't be repeated. . . . The Palestinians must consent in principle to our jointly drafting a negotiated document, collating all our agreements and disagreements in advent of permanent settlement. Should they not consent, it will be proof that they have been conducting a ritual conducive to confrontation rather than true negotiations." Sher pointedly summed up what he had learned from the prime minister: "Here is the conception of 'unmasking' (the Palestinians), which came into usage at a later stage."[7]

The shaping of Barak's conception was also bolstered by internal political developments. All told, only a year had passed since he had been elected. On the one hand, he had kept his promise to pull the IDF out of Lebanon. On the other, his government was having a hard time, public and political support was dwindling, and he himself was being pummeled. By early June 2000, time was clearly running out for his government. To stem the swelling trend, his office hit on the idea that a successful permanent-status summit under US patronage might upend the hourglass. In the weeks preceding Camp David, the political arena in Israel seethed. Led by right-wing movements and associations such as Zu Artzeinu (This Is Our Land), Shenit Gamla Lo Tipol (Gamla Will Not Fall Again), Women in Green, the Judea and Samaria Council, and activists of the late Meir Kahana's Kach Party, mass demonstrations were organized against the measure Barak sought to promote. The "peace camp," including its most renowned spokesmen (among them, the writer Amos Oz), made feeble attempts to organize counterdemonstrations in support of Barak's government and issued calls "for the public of peace supporters" to take to the streets en masse. But apart from the youth guard at a number of major intersections, there was little response. Barak's premise was simple: if the negotiations succeeded, the agreement reached would be the focus of the impending election campaign and the "people would decide"; Camp David was thus a bid to save his bleak political career. If the negotiations failed, he in any case stood to lose little in the voters' eyes: he could always say that he had been tough and to the point, and if the negotiations had not yielded an agreement, it was because he had stood his ground on issues big and small regarding the vital interests of the state of Israel. The negotiations could thus be a lifesaver for a political career fast sinking in Israeli public opinion.

By early summer 2000, only a handful of supporters still rallied round "the government of all" that Barak had formed. About three weeks before the Israeli delegation departed for Camp David, the ministers and deputy ministers of three coalition parties—Shas, Yisrael Be'Aliya, and the National Religious (Mafdal)—announced their collective resignation. Barak stuck to his guns. "I will continue with the negotiations even if I am left with only nine ministers and a quarter of the MKs," he declared. As he put it, he was accountable only to the people who had elected him and the road he represented by a large majority, and he would therefore follow through with the negotiations even if he lost the support of the government and the Knesset. "It is the people who appointed me and gave me the mandate," he said, "and the people alone will decide."[8] Such open contempt on the part of a prime minister for the state's elected institutions and leaders had not been heard in Israel for a long time. It was a close-up of arrogance personified. His few supporters reiterated their intention to bring any agreement to a referendum, and by this procedure bypass the Knesset—where they already lost the support of majority. Meanwhile, Barak entertained the notion that he had a trump card up his sleeve to recoup public support: an end to the conflict. He was not gambling on merely one issue or another or one detail or another, but on the whole kit and caboodle. His policy, after only a year in office, had no parliamentary backing. Politically, the prime minister "of all" was washed up, having failed to assimilate Israel's civic dynamics and the workings of its house of representatives. The defects of Israel's new voting system for head of state were, once again, in plain view. Direct elections had awarded the top job first to Netanyahu and then to Barak. Neither man, at certain moments, enjoyed the confidence of a House majority. But so long as votes of no confidence fell short of sixty-one MKs, the prime minister was free to pursue his own course and cheerfully ignore the elected members of the Knesset.[9]

The Palestinian dilemma over the Camp David summit was twofold. Although they hoped for genuine negotiations under the US auspices, they feared that a fixed, weeklong framework in which to finalize permanent status would create a marketplace dynamic on the most acute issues. Some saw Clinton's acquiescence to the summit, in the face of Arafat's misgivings, as a sign of US-Israeli collusion, and they fretted this dynamic would only get worse during negotiations in an attempt to force their hand. With the US presidential campaign for the November elections in full swing, they were well aware that a summit had to be brief if Clinton were actively involved. Their apprehension aside, they nevertheless decided to participate.[10] They felt that to reject Clinton's invitation was to invite charges of having torpedoed any chance for significant progress. In public statements, they welcomed the positive role of the United States. At the same time, they gave the impression that they were being dragged to a summit for which conditions had not ripened. It was an expedient seed to plant. They could always turn around later and say, "we told you so." The Palestinians set out for Camp David having neglected to do their homework. They had erroneously envisioned a summit that, at most, would conclude with general agreements between the leaders, to be followed up by intensive negotiations in earnest.

Both sides, before leaving for the summit, spoke unstintingly about their expectations and bottom lines. They publicly shackled themselves in obligations toward both their peoples and their fellow bargainers. On the eve of fateful negotiations that would demand compromise, Israeli and Palestinian consensual opinions echoed the leaders who echoed the consensus. Barak, before flying out (on 10 July), reemphasized that Israel would not return to the 4 June 1967 borders and that Jerusalem would remain united under Israeli sovereignty, most of the settlers would remain in Judea and Samaria, in settlement blocs under Israeli sovereignty, and Israel would not acknowledge moral or legal responsibility for the refugee problem. Arafat reiterated his people's longed-for national goal: the establishment of a Palestinian state according to the 4 June 1967 borders, with its capital at al-Quds, and a solution to the refugee problem on the basis of Resolution 194. Journalists hardly probed the statements. They simply gave the leaders the floor and allowed them to capture headlines.

Instead of conditioning their peoples to the necessary compromises warranted by permanent settlement, both sides transmitted entirely different messages. Conducting quasi-public diplomacy, officials proclaimed that they would not relent on crucial issues, such as Jerusalem or the refugees, for the sake of a final settlement. To some extent, they were clarifying their positions. In retrospect, however, Barak's explicit and oblique public statements seem to have been preparing Israeli public opinion for a scenario of failure ("we will know shortly if we have a true partner for peace"). Moreover, according to anonymous intelligence leaks, Arafat had instructed the PA to get ready for a head-on collision with Israel if the summit failed. On 10 July, *Maariv* carried a story titled "Arafat to his People: Prepare for Confrontation with Israel."

This, on the eve of the decisive summit. The degree of mutual distrust between Israeli and Palestinian leaders, especially between Barak and Arafat, was out there for all to see.

Both sides, before leaving for Camp David, also sought the blessings of Egypt's President Mubarak. Egypt was pessimistic. Barak met with Mubarak for an hour in Cairo and tried to convey the sense that it was time for the leaders to take the hard decisions toward compromise and an end to the conflict. The press release drawn up by Barak's public relations adviser said that the Israeli prime minister had stressed to his host that his goal was to achieve "a settlement which will assure a secure future and a good life for our children in a framework which will be based on the principle of a stable and permanent separation between the two peoples."[11] It is doubtful that Mubarak absorbed the full gist of Barak's guiding principle. Ever since the Sadat-Begin-Carter negotiations at Camp David, Arab supporters of a political process had had only one guiding principle: "land for peace." To them, the Egyptian-Israeli peace treaty was the precedent and model for implementing the substance of Resolution 242. Available sources do not tell us what Mubarak said after Barak presented his new principle for settling the conflict ("stable and permanent separation between the two peoples"). What is known is that Barak pointed out to Mubarak the dangers of failed negotiations. The press release gave no details of Mubarak's response or position. Nor was it reported whether he had shared with Barak the impressions of his meeting with Arafat the previous day at his home in Burg al-'Arab. A statement by Egypt's foreign minister, 'Amr Mussa, furnished an inkling of what had happened at that meeting: Mussa said that Egypt and the Palestinians saw eye to eye on the need to discuss all the issues of permanent settlement, especially al-Quds. In any case, Mussa noted, there was no getting around the fact that the parties had to meet the commitments of the interim stages. The foreign minister also said that the five "nos" recently declared by Israel's prime minister clouded the prospects of arriving at a comprehensive agreement on permanent status. "Internal difficulties," he protested, "were not to be used as a pretext, by any of the parties. All governments have domestic difficulties, President Arafat himself is facing difficulties."[12] As in the past, Israeli spokespeople and commentators depicted Mussa as "the bad guy" of Cairo, instead of squarely facing the fact that this view had long been the starting point of Egyptian policy.

Camp David—The Second Time Around

The Camp David Summit opened at noon on 11 July 2000. From the very start, all eyes were glued on Israel's prime minister, the man who had worked so hard to convene the summit, envisioning the parties conducting fateful negotiations that compelled the leaders to relax their public positions and adopt painful decisions on behalf of their peoples. As the hours and days clocked up, it transpired that, for the first time in negotiations with the Palestinians, Israel was prepared to discuss all the long-postponed critical issues of permanent status. Barak impressed his counterparts as a leader conscious of the historic juncture and proceeding with exceptional courage in the face of the controversy aroused by his policies at home. But his negotiating tactics at Camp David elude assessment. He tried to stave off the moment that US mediators would press the parties to accept a middle-of-the-road proposal. He chose to pass on Israel's ideas on final status to the Americans, to convey the sense that Israel's stance was valiant and unprecedented, and to urge the United States to use all its influence to convince the Palestinians to accept the main points. Additionally, Barak was bothered by the prospect that the agreements and disagreements between the parties would be documented; at his request, the words of the negotiators were not recorded. He was uneasy about documentation being leaked and used against him by political rivals. His apprehensiveness had an impact on the rest of the Israeli team, as Gilead Sher observed: "The fear that our positions would be leaked to the outside, or documented, buttressed and fastened these positions beyond all recognition. At times it seemed as if, to play it safe, some of the members of the Israeli team were striving to obtain a seal of approval from the Judea and Samaria Council for any position that we might submit."[13]

At the start of negotiations, Barak appeared to endorse a new approach to several key issues formerly taboo on Israel's national agenda: primarily, the scope of withdrawal from the West Bank and the Gaza Strip and the arrangements for the division of Jerusalem and its holy sites. Toward the end of the summit (23 July), members of the Israeli team, meeting among themselves, were able to gauge the chief points of the permanent settlement for which Barak meant to seek support: the establishment of an independent sovereign Palestinian state "on 89 percent of the territory"; an overhead safe passage connecting the West Bank and the Gaza Strip; Israeli withdrawal from the Jordan Valley subject to security arrangements that left a limited military presence at agreed spots; a possible swap of land to satisfy the territorial demands, though not on a one-to-one basis; al-Quds as the capital of the Palestinian state, including villages around Jerusalem and neighborhoods in East Jerusalem (among them, the Muslim and Christian quarters of the Old City); Palestinian custodianship of, but Israeli sovereignty over, the Temple Mount; and a demilitarized Palestinian state with "a strong police force." As for the refugees, Israel remained adamantly opposed to a Palestinian right of return and rejected all responsibility for the problem. Palestinian refugees would be permitted to return only to their own state, although, as in the past, Israel would be prepared to allow in a limited number within the framework of family reunification or humanitarian gestures. In exchange for all these, the Palestinians were to agree to "a real end to the historical conflict," meaning settling all claims once and for all and strictly abiding by all the conditions of the agreement.[14] Barak's main goal, it was soon apparent, was an "end to the conflict." Historically, the demand had no precedent. In terms of international law, it had no footing. It is no accident that the peace treaties signed with Egypt and Jordan contained no clause on an "end to conflict."

The salient points of the Palestinian position at Camp David corresponded to the PA's longstanding explicit approach: the establishment of a sovereign Palestinian state according to the 4 June 1967 borders, with possible minor modifications on a one-to-one basis. Nothing less would do. Palestinian negotiators regarded Israel's security and settlement demands as a threat to their statehood, sovereignty, and territorial contiguity. East Jerusalem (al-Quds) and the mosques on the Temple Mount (al-Haram al-Sharif) were part of the occupied West Bank and, as such, had to fall within Palestinian sovereignty. The Palestinians argued that they could not waive sovereignty over al-Haram al-Sharif since the compound was holy to all Muslims, and no leader could relinquish it in the name of a billion and a quarter Muslim faithful. Jerusalem would thus serve as the capital for two states, though there would be free and open movement between the Israeli and Palestinian parts. Should the format be adopted, there would be two separate municipalities and one coordinating body to manage joint affairs such as transportation, sanitation, and the environment.[15] In exchange for recognizing Israeli sovereignty over city neighborhoods it had built in areas it had conquered in June 1967, such as the Jewish Quarter, the Western Wall, and the neighborhoods around Jerusalem, the Palestinians would receive comparable areas in quantity and quality. In Palestinian eyes, "ceding" the Jewish Quarter and the Western Wall—which by Islamic tradition was where the Prophet Muhammad had tethered his horse, al-Buraq, on his night journey to the al-Aqsa Mosque—was ultimate proof of their readiness to make painful concessions since in principle these sites were part of the Occupied Territories, and in the past, most of the assets concerned had been in Palestinian hands.

The Palestinians rejected Barak's "generous offer" because it lacked more than it contained. They were being asked to proclaim an end to conflict without receiving a satisfactory response to some of their major demands. Above all, the Israeli offer did not provide sufficiently for the sovereignty and independence of the state to rise. "Pockets" of Israeli settlements and military bases for the sake of Israel's vital interests would have segmented the Palestinian state into cantons that render its sovereignty hollow. They also found the offer inadequate with respect to the refugees and the holy sites, specifically al-Haram al-Sharif. On the refugee issue, they reiterated two principles: the recognition of their right of return and of Israel's responsibility for creating the problem. In exchange for such recognition, the Palestinians would accept Israel's claim that it would only allow in a number that did not harm its demographic or security interests, meaning, that it and it alone would decide if there were to be any serious discussion of the agreed number.[16] In Palestinian eyes, the Israeli offer was diametrically opposed to the premises of the Declaration of Principles (13 September 1993). Israel's "generous offer" did not translate into a sustainable Palestinian state and an agreed solution to permanent-status issues (among them, the refugees and al-Haram al-Sharif/Temple Mount). Barak's offer could not realize the longed-for objective of "a just, lasting and comprehensive peace."

Barak's offer was finally spelled out to the Palestinians as the summit drew to a close: Israel was prepared to withdraw from the Gaza Strip and most of the West Bank, but it wished to annex approximately 10 percent of the West Bank for "settlement blocs." Israel would totally control the borders of the Palestinian state: the IDF would hold an agreed number of posts along the Jordan Valley for a lengthy period of time, and the Palestinian state would be demilitarized and only partially control its airspace and territorial waters. It would also have restricted control of the aquifers. Roads would criss-cross the West Bank to enable Israeli access to the Jordan Valley posts. The Palestinian capital would be in al-Quds (including also the Muslim and Christian quarters of the Old City), and Palestinians would have custody of—but not recognized sovereignty over—al-Haram al-Sharif. The Palestinians could note with satisfaction that, as far as al-Quds and its Islamic holy sites were concerned, they had become the sole authority. In this connection, it is worth mentioning that Israel's peace treaty with Jordan stipulated the following: "When negotiations on the permanent status will take place, Israel will give high priority to the Jordanian historic role in these shrines," all this out of respect for the "special role of the Hashemite Kingdom of Jordan in Muslim Holy shrines in Jerusalem."[17] It seems that no one at Camp David—as far as is known—took account of this contractual obligation on Israel's part. As for the refugees, although many of them would finally be settled in either the Palestinian or other states, there was little chance that those who wished to return to Israel would be permitted to do so. Moreover, Israel refused to recognize its responsibility for the refugee problem or the right of the refugees to return to and settle within Israel proper. The Palestinians, for their part, emphasized the "concessions" expected of them: first and foremost, recognizing Israeli sovereignty over the Jewish neighborhoods of East Jerusalem, especially over the Western Wall and the Jewish Quarter; consenting to and, in fact, legitimating the continued presence of most of the settlers in the West Bank, attached to "settlement blocs"; agreeing to a limited Israeli military presence within Palestinian territory and access roads for Israeli forces to reach the posts, which could create a semblance of "cantonization"; and subordinating the resolution of the refugee problem to Israeli demographic and security concerns. Among themselves, the Palestinians could acknowledge that, compared to Israel's position in the not-so-distant past, there had been significant progress, but it was still a far cry from a just, satisfactory solution to all the problems. Under these conditions, to sign away all claims and seal the conflict meant to accept the unreasonable dictates of the United States and Israel.

Although the files of the expert staff at Camp David burst with essential information on the positions of the two sides as presented previously in various forums, the political echelons had not formulated lucid positions when the summit began. Nor was the daily agenda or its management any too clear. Thus opened one of the paramount negotiation chapters of the Israeli-Arab conflict. Even if members of the Israeli team were disturbed by this state of affairs, they did not raise the matter until the summit was in full swing and the crises already unmistakable. A case in point was the discussion on Jerusalem and the holy sites. In the middle of the talks on Saturday, 15 July, following a US "bridging proposal," the top Israeli bargainers retired to consult. The differences of opinion among them elicited a protest from then Minister of Tourism Amnon Lipkin-Shahak: "We're not even close to [defining] for ourselves how far we're prepared to go. . . . In what has been raised till now, there has been no solution for Jerusalem and therefore we have no agreement. We haven't clarified for ourselves what Jerusalem is. Kalandia, Shu'afat, the Temple Mount—are they all really one and the same? Would we fight to the end for them all?"[18] The deeper the talks delved into the question of Jerusalem, the clearer it became how many aspects were involved, all of which might have been foreseen. The sloppiness stuck out like a sore thumb. Israel wished to annex settlement blocs to its border, but they contained areas with tens of thousands of Palestinians. In Jerusalem, there was to be "territorial contiguity," but the attempt to translate this principle into practice ran into snag after snag. The Israelis found it hard to explain how contiguous sovereignty was to be ensured between their capital of Jerusalem and the suburb of Ma'aleh Adumim, when the two were separated by the Palestinian neighborhoods and communities of 'Isawiye, al-Z'aim, al-'Azariye, and Abu Dis, just as Jerusalem's northern neighborhoods (Mt. Scopus and Givat Shapira) were separated from Pisgat Ze'ev, Neveh Ya'akov, and the 'Atarot industrial zone by Shu'afat, the adjacent Shu'afat refugee camp, Beit Hanina, and al-Ram.

Equally obvious during the summit was just how far the Palestinians were from acknowledging Judaism's connection to the Temple Mount or the fact that all streams of Jewry identify it as the site of the First and Second Temples, on whose ruins the Dome of the Rock (Qubat al-Sahara) and the Mosque of 'Omar were built only centuries later. Whether this signified ignorance or posturing, it shows yet again how unprepared the parties were to tackle key issues. Historical, religious, and legal discussion of these questions had been going on for years in a variety of formats. The information was on tap, yet the leading negotiators were not acquainted with it. On the eve of a summit on these very issues, one might well have expected them to clarify in advance such matters as Judaism's bond to the Temple Mount or Islamic tradition on the Western Wall and the predictable implications of these issues for

talks on political agreements. They did not do so. And after years of deliberations with one and the same Palestinian leadership, it was striking that the Israelis had not managed to drive home to the Arabs, especially to the Palestinians, the fact of Judaism's bond to the Temple Mount. For years, Palestinian
spokespeople—including Arafat—maintained that the temple had not been in
Jerusalem at all, but in Shchem (Nablus). Such baseless statements had rarely
been dignified by an Israeli response.[19]

As the summit approached its end, the Israeli delegation consulted once
more on the question of Jerusalem. By now Barak estimated "that four rounds
of talks would be required for Jerusalem."[20] Apart from appreciating how
slapdash the preliminaries had been, most of the Israeli team were evidently
ready to relinquish sovereignty over Jerusalem's Arab neighborhoods without,
however, "ceding sovereignty over the Temple Mount." Barak shared this
view, with one major proviso: that Israel's assent be part of an agreement stip-
ulating an end to the Israeli-Palestinian conflict. A minority of the team considered the demand unrealistic. Most, moreover, were uncomfortable with
how Barak comported himself at the summit. Though he asked them for their
thoughts, they soon learned that he was not in the habit of sharing his own,
and in many instances, his decisions became comprehensible only in retrospect. Gilead Sher was aware of these sentiments. At the end of one consultation on Jerusalem, he had said to Barak: "We have to work these things out
among ourselves more thoroughly and much more openly, otherwise we
won't be able to proceed." Barak's response shed little light on the matter:
"We have inner red lines, real ones, sensed by everyone via basically describing the state's vital interests."[21]

Often, instead of searching for creative solutions, the negotiators simply
dug in their heels. The question of security is a good example. The Palestinian side gave Israel's demands far-reaching significance. Rather than discuss arrangements that would take into account the fears raised by the Israeli
side, the Palestinians simply rejected Israeli and US ideas and solutions,
though they were hard put throughout to come up with counterproposals.
Their polite but firm nay reinforced the impression that they had not come to
negotiate in goodwill unless their demands were met in full. The Israeli side,
however, seemed to view every issue through the prism of security and as a
"red line." Israel rightly regarded the question of security as a critical component of the entire permanent-status settlement. At the same time, the delegates
did overdo it on more than one occasion, for example, when they made the demand to deploy forces in Palestinian areas in times of emergency. Israeli attempts to justify the demand met with US, as well as Palestinian, objections.
Clinton exposed its weakness quite elegantly. After a long, drawn-out, and unconvincing talk by Major General Shlomo Yanai (arguing that in times of
emergency Israel can rely only on itself), Clinton simply wondered out loud:
"Who defines 'state of emergency'? After all, if I complain of headache, you

can't tell me that I don't have one."[22] Again, the preparations had been inadequate, this time with regard to security, an issue—it had been widely assumed—that would pose no special problem for reaching an agreement with the Palestinians. Certainly, no one in the Israeli delegation had expected any real differences with the United States on security matters. Had the negotiators done their homework properly, they would have carefully reviewed the US and Palestinian positions and might have devised a detailed list of situations that both sides could reasonably consider a state of emergency. As the summit proceeded, four team members who had been part of the limited forum convened by Barak on the eve of Camp David (7 July) realized that the formula they had worked out at the time for a possible deal fell short of the mark. Gilead Sher wrote of that meeting: "The discussion had given shape to a possible balance of 'give and take': territory versus elements of sovereignty; Jerusalem versus refugees. Refusing to yield on one side of the equation would entail greater flexibility on the other."[23] The parameters of flexibility for one formula or another to be translated into an agreement had not, however, been examined in detail. The negotiators had not broken the equation down into its components. Nor had they set out fallback positions or clear priorities and preferences to serve as guidelines.

The history of negotiations shows that lasting agreements have ensued from leadership decisions taken after painstaking preparation and repeated deliberations on divisive issues. The 1978 Camp David summit was preceded by a whole series of talks, negotiations, and elaborate groundwork. Moreover, after Israel and Egypt reached a framework agreement, negotiations continued for another half year, and even then, a peace treaty was attained only through President Carter's active intercession.[24] It follows that to attempt to wrap up a long, entangled dispute, such as the Israeli-Palestinian conflict, in a single summit is a dangerous gamble based on a naive perception of political negotiations, including the conflict at hand. The deliberations preceding the 2000 Camp David summit were fragmented. The chances of Barak's initiative succeeding were all too flimsy. Discussion of the complex issues involved—refugees, Jerusalem, the holy sites, an end to conflict, and all the subtopics that these issues entail—made precise preparation mandatory. Deliberations on Jerusalem required far more knowledge than the parties displayed, as well as creative thinking on territory, security, border crossings, sovereignty, and religious services for multiple groups. Jerusalem's division and some sort of decision about arrangements for the Temple Mount are not unfamiliar notions. Yet few people seemed to appreciate exactly what compromise meant. The nuts and bolts should have been worked out in advance. A summit is hardly the place and time to start grappling with them.

The course and outcome of negotiations are affected by style, too: not that a pleasant ambience guarantees a political settlement, but the personal conduct of the negotiators certainly helps set the tone of the talks. Many of

Camp David's participants, including no few Israelis, faulted Barak's negotiating manner. Most, by their own acknowledgment, had a hard time understanding it. In addition to Barak's personal traits, it is possible that his lack of experience with complex negotiations also came to the fore. His background was in security, but security was only one factor and not necessarily always the central one. He was not elastic enough when it came to defining either the goals of negotiation or the time frame required to translate them into agreements. He kept fending off suggestions that the delegation leaders get together for working sessions and, apart from one chance meeting, never sat down to direct talks with Arafat. He evaded direct discussion with Arafat from the very beginning, participating only in meetings with Israeli delegates and the heads of the US team. Later, when it became apparent that the Palestinians objected to most of the Israeli proposals and were not receptive to US brokering endeavors, he obstinately adopted a "reclusive" tactic, holing up in his cabin for days on end.[25] He rejected suggestions to meet with Arafat to discuss the issues in dispute and the US "bridging paper." He announced that there would be no negotiations so long as the Palestinians did not respond in the affirmative. More and more summit participants began to think that Barak's tactic was "take it or leave it"; this was only partially true, for there had been no few changes in the Israeli position during the summit. Yet, there was some truth to it since there were hardly any direct negotiations between the two sides, notably between the leaders. In referring to Israel's tactical mishandling at the summit, Shlomo Ben-Ami subsequently noted: "Barak's stubborn refusal to meet with Arafat was a big obstacle."[26]

The conduct of the US participants and the role of the president also deserve a word. Clinton devoted all his time and energy trying to get down to brass tacks. He was apt to initiate discussion of minute details, occasionally before the working teams themselves. The American delegation took the traditional US stand that the parties themselves had to be interested in a settlement and that no settlement was to be imposed. They shuttled between the two sides around the clock, acting as "postman." Since most of the proposals emanated from the Israelis, however, the said "postal service" gave the appearance of US support for the Israeli position. President Clinton and Secretary Albright gave the impression that they were enormously appreciative of Barak's sacrifice given the latter's domestic tribulations, whereas Palestinian constraints did not elicit similar empathy.[27] The Americans made the common US and Israeli mistake of regarding the Palestinian political arena as virtually irrelevant. More than once, they made a point of listing Barak's problems before the Palestinians, whereas in talks with the Israelis, the Palestinian arena rarely came up.

The summit was disorganized, and administrative slipups were frequent. Because the US hosts acquiesced to Barak's demand not to document the positions of the parties, there were no written responses to the proposals put forth, even though oral statements proved to be a sure recipe for divergence and distrust. There were no orderly follow-up sessions to monitor progress on any one topic. Frequently, the set agenda was simply ignored. At times, the American delegation did not have an adequate grasp of the understandings reached by the parties in presummit talks. Clinton tended to give way during the summit whenever Barak was averse to or rejected one or another suggestion by the US team. Even more serious, when Barak submitted his final positions to Clinton on the eighth day of the summit, Clinton not only endorsed them but presented them to the Palestinians as US positions.[28] All this compounded the mistaken decision of his administration to convene a summit when it was eminently clear that the sides were widely divided on critical issues. By the same token, the Americans were wrong to persistently press the Palestinians to consent to an "end to conflict" before having received their agreement to final-status issues. The attempt to win the support of Arab heads of state was made only once it became universally clear that the negotiations had broken down. The summit thus proceeded amid US attempts to conduct negotiations on one topic or another, Israelis pushing for a historic decision ("end to conflict"), and Palestinians courteously fending off Israeli or US suggestions and emphasizing that the gulf between the sides made agreement impossible.

The public diplomacy waged by the Americans at the summit's closing and in the weeks to come was also crucially misguided. The Americans grew increasingly frustrated at the lack of progress. Clinton voiced his anger to the negotiators, particularly to the Palestinians and Arafat, who, he felt, had not shown the necessary flexibility for the critical stage of negotiations. "I'm very disappointed," he told Arafat (19 July). "You're going to lose my friendship. You're going to ruin the opportunity to conclude an agreement for [the next] twenty years."[29] Nonetheless, much was made of the impending closing statements and what the president was going to say. Clinton, as behooved the occasion, chose his words with care, delivering a relatively balanced summation. He noted the great progress that had been made and showered Barak with praise for having gone a long way and displayed vision and courage. When it came to Arafat, his words were sparing and lukewarm. In his memoirs, Clinton confessed that his intention at that stage was "to give Barak some cover back home and indicate what had occurred."[30] Ostensibly, he kept his promise not to blame either side for the failure of negotiations. But his closing and subsequent statements placed the blame squarely on the Palestinians and Arafat, which had far-reaching consequences for the construction of the media and political discourse on the Camp David summit. In many places in the West, as in Israel and the United States, of course, Clinton's words were taken at face value: Arafat's tendency to reject Israeli overtures caused Camp David to fail and stymied all possibility of concluding an Israeli-Palestinian peace treaty.

This simplistic diagnosis was voiced on various occasions by the heads of the Clinton administration and soon became the prevalent evaluation. The memoirs of Clinton, Albright, and Ross documented the exclusive responsibility of Arafat for the failure to reach a peace agreement. These claims were consistent with the declarations Barak made at and, in particular, following Camp David. Upon his return from the failed summit, he stated: "We did not succeed for we did not find a partner prepared to make decisions. . . . we did what we could, we left no stone unturned, we exhausted every possibility to bring about an end to conflict and a secure future for Israel." Few were aware that the blame for the failure and even the formulation of the accusations had already been composed by Barak's advisers during the early days of the summit, long before serious negotiations had begun.[31]

Kissing the Political Process Good-Bye

The first months of the al-Aqsa intifada overlapped with the end of the Clinton administration. For their two terms in office, the US president and his senior staff had been up to their necks in the Israeli-Palestinian conflict. The first thing Clinton wanted when the intifada erupted was to stem the violence and speedily return the two sides to the negotiating table. Many in Israel claimed that Arafat had planned the intifada in advance or controlled "the size of its flames," but the administration did not believe that there was sufficient evidence to support the contention. Nevertheless, the Clinton administration fully expected Arafat to make a real effort to stop the violence and certainly to condemn it.[32] Washington was also concerned by Barak's shrinking domestic support from day to day. US diplomats posted in Israel reported on the intensive campaign waged by rightist parties and groups against the political process with the Palestinians and Barak's government. Press advertisements, posters, graffiti, and car stickers carried the terrible slogan, "Oslo criminals should be prosecuted." On 22 November 2000, the thirty-third anniversary of Resolution 242, there was a demonstration at Jerusalem's Zion Square under the banner, "Let the IDF Triumph." Elections were around the corner, but that was no election slogan. For months, the right had been spreading the baseless charge that the government was preventing the IDF from quelling Palestinian violence. Countless Israelis had simply turned a blind eye to the IDF's daily combat in the Occupied Territories since the outbreak of the intifada. Warplanes, helicopters, tanks, and special forces were put into operation every day against armed Palestinians and civilians alike. The number of casualties among the Palestinians was much higher than among Israelis. Palestinian groups sought to embroil Israel in guerrilla warfare to counter the IDF's vast military superiority and raise its casualty toll. Acts of terror were aimed at sowing grief in Israeli society. Tens of thousands of demonstrators at Zion

Square heard the Likud candidate for prime minister, Ariel Sharon, deliver his curt political platform: "Arafat is not a partner. He is a brutal enemy! . . . The witless Oslo agreement no longer exists!"[33]

The violence and terror, the constant rise in dead and wounded Israelis and Palestinians, the strident public discourse in both societies, and the atmosphere of hostility and distrust threatened to topple the entire Oslo process and had a serious effect on key Arab states, primarily Egypt and Jordan. The State Department and White House explored a variety of options to restore calm and resume the political process, reassured that alongside the drastic deterioration, dozens of meetings were being held by Israelis, Palestinians, and Americans, mostly "graduates" of the failed Camp David negotiations. On 23 December 2000, President Clinton decided on a new political initiative and presented the parties with his ideas on permanent status. In terms of substance, timing, and the reactions of the parties, it was an unusual step. For the first time, a US president put forward his own program on permanent status, explicitly indicating a direction for most of the divisive issues.

The Clinton initiative synthesized the proposals in five chapters. He dictated his formula to the parties but did not leave them a written document.[34] On the question of territory, he said he believed that "a fair and lasting agreement" would lead to the establishment of a Palestinian state consisting of 94–96 percent of the West Bank with the Palestinians being compensated in the amount of 1–3 percent for areas Israel annexed. Most of the settlers would concentrate in settlement blocs. Security arrangements would include, among other things, an international presence to replace the Israeli presence and help implement the agreements. Israel's withdrawal should be phased in over thirty-six months, with the last of its forces quitting the military posts in the Jordan Valley by the end of another thirty-six months. Israel would have three early-warning stations, their status to be reviewed at the end of ten years. The parties would reach an agreement on the deployment of forces for situations of "imminent and demonstrable threat to Israel's national security of a military nature that requires the activation of a national state emergency." The Palestinian state would have sovereignty over its airspace, though there would be special arrangements for overhead flights by Israel's air force. The Palestinian state would be declared "non-militarized," with "strong Palestinian security forces" and an international force "for border security and deterrent purposes." On the question of Jerusalem and the Old City, Clinton proposed formalizing the existing ethnic-religious status quo according to the principle that what is Arab would be Palestinian and what is Jewish would be Israeli. The Palestinian section would constitute al-Quds and be proclaimed the capital of the Palestinian state. There would be special arrangements for the sovereignty and administrative responsibility of al-Haram al-Sharif/Temple Mount and the Western Wall. The basis would be divided sovereignty: al-Haram al-Sharif under Palestinian control and the Western Wall under Israeli control. In addition, there would be agreed special arrangements, international monitoring, and an understanding that excavations beneath "the Haram and behind the wall" would be conducted only with the consent of the two sides.

As for the highly charged refugee issue—Clinton hoped that it would be solved by partitioning the country into two states. In principle, for Palestinian refugees wishing to return to their homeland, the Palestinian state would be "the focal point," without precluding the possibility "that Israel will accept some of these refugees." He noted that the formulations fixed by the two sides would make it clear that "there is no specific right of return to Israel itself, but that does not negate the aspiration of the Palestinian people to return to the area." The refugees were to be offered five options, with priority going to the populace in Lebanon: returning to the Palestinian state, returning to areas Israel would transfer to the Palestinians in an exchange of territory, being settled in the states in which they live, being resettled in other states, or applying to return to Israel proper (contingent on Israel's sovereign policies and decisions). In parallel, Israel would be asked to recognize the suffering caused the Palestinian people as a result of the 1948 war and would participate in the (US-led) efforts of the international community to resolve the problem. The parties would declare this to be the implementation of Resolution 194 on the matter of the refugees. In the final part, Clinton proposed that a "fair and lasting" permanent-status accord based on the parameters proposed explicitly stipulate "the end of the conflict" and its implementation "put an end to all claims."

Clinton's ideas had drawn significantly nearer the Palestinian demands made at Camp David. Why? After months in which he and his administration had accused Arafat and his aides of adopting positions that torpedoed a permanent-status agreement, how is it that his own ideas were now closer to those of the Palestinians? Had he and his aides been persuaded that the Palestinian demands were not so far-fetched and extraordinary? In addition, why had he dragged his feet for months, only to put forth his ideas on the eve of George W. Bush taking office and of Israel's general elections? Why had he not presented these ideas at Camp David, where they might have served as a promising basis for a settlement? Their drawback, when they were presented, was the timing. At the start of 2001, the political hourglass in both the United States and Israel was a great impediment to any chance of a breakthrough. Clinton presented his ideas about a month and a half after the US elections, only three weeks before George W. Bush was to be sworn in (20 January 2001) and five weeks before Israel's general elections (6 February 2001). The information currently available provides no clue as to his choice of timing, especially because he had formulated the ideas months earlier.

Israel and the Palestinians were asked to respond if they were prepared to resume discussions based on Clinton's ideas. They were told that if the ideas were not acceptable, they would be removed from the agenda at once and certainly have no validity after this president left the White House. Barak's gov-

ernment decided to accept the invitation, but expressed a number of reservations, mainly as to the scale of withdrawal, Jerusalem and sovereignty over
the holy sites, security arrangements, and the refugee problem. With their affirmative response, Barak and his government went further than they had
done at Camp David, and they were sharply criticized at home.[35] Once again,
an Israeli prime minister was the object of unveiled threats. MK Rehavam
Ze'evi was quoted as wishing to remind Barak that "there is a law in Israel
which rules that anyone acting to transfer territory from the state to the enemy
is to be deemed a traitor, which is punishable by death."[36] Elections were at
hand, and the polls predicted a sweeping victory for the head of the Likud and
the establishment of a new government. How appropriate, under these circumstances, was it to even approve negotiating principles that could shackle
the next government? And yet, could the Israeli government ignore a political
initiative emanating from a US president?

The IDF senior command was perturbed by Clinton's initiative and made
sure to leak its opposition to the media. On the final morning of the year 2000,
readers of *Haaretz* had this piece of news from senior military columnist
Ze'ev Schiff: "various publications stated that the Chief of General Staff had
said that the US proposals posed a threat to the state." Chief of General Staff
Shaul Mofaz—according to Schiff—had "said, among other things, that his
professional opinion was based on an evaluation of the situation at headquarters and his opinion is not aimed at hurting the negotiating process, in which
the IDF believes." Clinton's initiative presented also the Palestinian leadership with a dilemma. Ten nerve-wracking days passed before they sent in a
positive response, and, even then, their reply was so couched in conditions
that the Americans and Israelis felt that their reservations outweighed their
acceptance. Publicly, the Palestinian leadership was reticent about Clinton's
initiative. The Arab media, however, made no bones about its shortcomings.
It was depicted as a not especially successful attempt to stop the intifada and
force the Palestinians to accept an end to conflict without final-status issues
having been resolved. Many spokespeople described the parameters of Clinton's initiative, which were to replace negotiations, in a false light. This description may have been rooted in US pressure on the sides to respond instantly, whether with a "yes" or "no," to the most intricate questions of the
Arab-Israeli conflict, primarily the refugee issue and Jerusalem. On both these
issues, Clinton's initiative was described as closer in principle to Barak's position than to the Palestinians'. The territorial and security restrictions aimed
at curtailing the sovereignty of the proposed Palestinian state also drew sharp
criticism. Commentators portrayed the urgency of the answers demanded as a
last-ditch attempt to help Barak in Israel's upcoming elections and Clinton's
shot at finishing his own term in office with a significant political achievement. Oslo opponents wrapped up their criticism of the parameters by taking
to task the PA's consent to discuss the suggestions in principle.[37]

The qualms, problematic timing, and doubts did not prevent Barak and Arafat from dispatching delegates to talks represented as definitely the last opportunity to reach an understanding on permanent status. The stopwatch of Barak's government could be heard ticking in the background. When the parley opened in Taba, Egypt, on 21 January 2001, the two leaders did not take direct part in the discussions, nor did US representatives attend them. It was a last-ditch effort to conclude permanent status, and Barak may have hoped that a breakthrough would save his political career in the elections two weeks down the road. The decision to hold serious talks at this juncture was, however, thoroughly misguided, a sorry reminder of the political obtuseness of Israel's prime minister who, in his last months in office, seemed to have lost his way completely.[38] The Palestinians feared that understandings reached at Taba would not be recognized by a new Israeli government, that once more, Israel's new leaders would ask them to reopen hard-won agreements and submit new concessions. They accepted the invitation mainly in the hope that it would repair their image as peace "rejectionists."

According to the summation and testimony of some of the participants, the Taba talks were profound and practical, and "substantial progress" was made. The seven-day conclave ended with a statement that the sides had "never been closer to reaching an agreement." And, indeed, understandings were reached and gaps narrowed on a number of key issues, including the scale of withdrawal, the settlements, and security arrangements. This time, the Palestinians did not stop at saying they would weigh Israeli proposals but offered detailed ideas of their own. For the first time, they presented a map showing their acceptance of Israel's annexation of Jewish neighborhoods in East Jerusalem.[39] In contrast, Minister Yossi Beilin's proposal on the refugee question, obliging Israel to take in a certain quota over a number of years, was not supported by most of the Israeli representatives. Delegation members relayed messages to this effect to the Palestinian team. Meanwhile, in Israel, public pressure mounted on Barak's government to bring the Taba team home and refrain from making commitments in light of the imminent elections. The delegation was instructed to come home after six days of talks. The joint closing statement was optimistic, but it did not inhibit the Taba parley from joining a long list of successful Israeli-Palestinian meetings that ended in pretty words and had little practical value.

One illuminating conclusion can be drawn from the Taba talks. Five months after the Camp David summit, Barak's "generous offer" was shown up as somewhat less than generous. Barak, it will be recalled, declared at the end of the summit that no Israeli leader could make the Palestinians a more far-reaching offer than he had. Come Taba, and suddenly Barak's representatives could make the same Palestinians an inestimably better offer. On the question of territory, Israel now spoke of annexing some 6 percent, not the 10 percent–plus it had demanded at Camp David. With regard to territorial exchange, Israel suggested raising the figure from 1 to 3 percent. All told, Israel offered to withdraw from some 97 percent of the total area of the West Bank and Gaza Strip. The Palestinians were ready for Israel to annex more than 3 percent of the West Bank but demanded compensation on a one-to-one basis, meaning that Israel would transfer to the Palestinian state areas identical in size to the annexed settlement blocs.

But what does it tell us, if even these terms did not lead to the hoped-for breakthrough? Some in Israel saw it as proof of the bottomless Palestinian demands, that deep inside they were not really interested in a comprehensive agreement that spelled an end to all claims. Others believed it was yet another missed opportunity on the part of the Palestinian leadership, who had blundered at every stage of the negotiations. To these, a third version may be added: from the start of the Oslo process, many in Israel assumed that at the decisive stage of permanent-status negotiations, the Palestinians would be forced to accept a compromise and face reality, namely that they would not receive the whole of the West Bank and Gaza Strip. This widespread assumption on the ultimate positions of the Palestinians and Arafat was obviously wrong. The common explanations in Israel's public discourse ignored the fact that the Taba parley died a natural death in view of Israeli and US political circumstances. There is no truth to the allegation that the Palestinians again rejected a generous peace offer since the summations as a whole were not put to the leaders for approval. What was placed before the Palestinians at Taba was the closest offer yet to their minimal positions on permanent status, though not all the differences had been ironed out. Be that as it may, it was mainly the impossible timing that left the negotiations hanging. Moreover, in the absence of the leaders, there could be no finalization of a settlement or a trade-off on the critical questions of permanent status. Senior Palestinian negotiator Nabil Sha'ath summed up the Taba talks in a nutshell: If what was proposed at Camp David "was too little, Taba, was too late."[40]

Notes

1. The question of textbooks was widely treated, and a number of studies on the subject were published. See Israel/Palestine Center for Research and Information (IPCRI), "Analysis and Evaluation of the New Palestinian Curriculum: Reviewing Palestinian Textbooks and Tolerance Education Program," Jerusalem, Report 1, March 2003; Report 2, June 2004; "Examination of Israeli Textbooks in Elementary Schools of the State Educational System," Jerusalem, April 2004.

2. Eldar and Zertal, *Adunei Ha'aretz* [Lords of the Land]; Newman, *Population, Settlements, and Conflict;* Aronson, *Settlements and the Israel-Palestinian Negotiations.*

3. According to the Central Bureau of Statistics, in 1993 there were 110,900 settlers, and in 2001, the number was estimated at 198,000. Official figures broadcast by Israel Radio on 24 July 2003 gave the number as 231,443, of whom 7,700 lived in the

Gaza Strip. In September 2004, the number of settlers was estimated at 239,800, of whom nearly 8,000 were in the Gaza Strip.

4. Enderlin, *Shattered Dreams,* pp. 163–164.

5. On the administration's doubts on the eve of the decision, see Ross, *The Missing Peace,* pp. 628–631, 645–649.

6. In his memoirs, Clinton supplied a rather weak excuse for the decision: "There was not a high probability of success for the summit. I called it because I believed that the collapse of the peace process would be a near certainty if I didn't." Clinton, *My Life,* p. 912.

7. Sher, *Bemerhak neggi'ah,* pp. 80–81. Barak also demanded that the US government relay a similar message to Arafat. See Ross, *The Missing Peace,* pp. 628–629.

8. *Maariv,* 6 July 2000.

9. On the eve of the 1996 elections, new legislation—the Law for the Direct Elections of the Prime Minister—severed the vote for party from the vote for prime minister. Until that time, the power to impose the formation of a government on a candidate likely to be able to do so was vested in the state president. The new law was in effect for the 1996, 1999, and 2001 elections. But in view of its many drawbacks, the law was again amended to revert to the previous one-ballot system. That was the format of the 2003 elections.

10. Hanieh, "The Camp David Papers," pp. 75–97.

11. "PM Barak Meets Egyptian President Mubarak," communication issued by Prime Minister Media Advisor, Jerusalem, 11 July 2000.

12. "President Mubarak Hopeful on Camp David Negotiations to Come up with Serious Work," statement issued by Egyptian Ministry of Foreign Affairs, 9 July 2000.

13. Sher, *Bemerhak neggi'ah,* p. 185; Ben-Ami, *Chazit lelu oref,* p. 88.

14. Sher, *Bemerhak neggi'ah,* pp. 218–219.

15. Saeb Erekat, *al-Hayat al-Jadida,* 2 August 2000; *al-Ayam,* 26 July 2000.

16. Malley and Agha, "A Reply to Ehud Barak."

17. "Treaty of Peace Between the State of Israel and the Hashemite Kingdom of Jordan," 26 October 1994, Article 9/2. The treaty is available at http://www.mfa.gov.il/ MFA/Peace+Process/Guide+to+the+Peace+Process/Israel-Jordan+Peace+Treaty.htm.

18. Sher, *Bemerhak neggi'ah,* p. 165. The question of Israel's positions on Jerusalem was far from being resolved, as is evident from the further penetrating discussion held by delegation members two days later (17 July). See Ben-Ami, *Chazit lelu oref,* pp. 173–178.

19. In Israel, too, one view—held especially by messianic right-wingers (e.g., the Movement to Establish the Third Temple and the Temple Mount Faithful)—has it that Muslims have no connection to the Temple Mount. The attempts of these groups to "remove the abomination" (i.e., the Muslim mosques and presence) should not be taken lightly.

20. Sher, *Bemerhak neggi'ah,* p. 228.

21. Ibid., p. 165.

22. Ibid., p. 221.

23. Ibid., p. 145. Ben-Ami also noted that one of the chief bones of contention, Jerusalem, had not been sufficiently examined prior to the summit. See the interview with him (15 July 2002) at www.bitterlemons.org/previous/bl150702ed26.html.

24. Quandt, *Camp David.*

25. For the US team's ideas on breaking the deadlock, see Ross, *The Missing Peace,* pp. 657–666. Ross, like most of the writers on the Camp David summit, does not mention that in fact the Americans did not present a written suggestion; instead, they voiced a whole series of ideas and suggestions before the teams.

26. Interview with Ben-Ami, www.bitterlemons.org/previous/bl150702ed26.html.

27. This empathy was fully expressed in Clinton, *My Life,* pp. 678–680; Albright, *Madam Secretary.*

28. On Barak's positions and their presentation by Clinton to the Palestinians, see Ross, *The Missing Peace,* pp. 688–689, and more on Clinton's "buckling under" before Barak, ibid., pp. 663–666.

29. Enderlin, *Shattered Dreams,* p. 234.

30. Clinton, *My Life,* p. 916.

31. Drucker presented the original document ("Mis'hak milhama: Halufot efshariot le-astrateggia tikshortit be-ikvot totzaot ha-pisga" [War game: Alternative possibilities to communication strategies in wake of the summit results]), showing how devoutly "Barak had embraced the recommendation to throw all [blame] on the Palestinians." Drucker, *Harakiri,* pp. 284–286.

32. Referring to the al-Aqsa intifada, Dennis Ross, the Clinton administration's special envoy to the Middle East, noted in December 2002: "I am not one of those who believe that Arafat planned the whole thing. Arafat does not plan anything. He reacts. What happened was that violence took on a life of its own. The Israelis cracked down very hard to begin with and caused a lot of deaths. That triggered more Palestinian violence, and then the Israelis did more. Arafat, again, acted like a surfer. He rides the wave—he doesn't try to stop it." *Al-Ahram Weekly,* 5 December 2002. Subsequently, Ross revealed that after Sharon had gone up to the Temple Mount, the Clinton administration had contacted Arafat and asked him to take steps to calm things down, but Arafat had refused, saying, "that he would not lift even a finger." According to Ross, the United States had intelligence information that Arafat encouraged the demonstrations and clashes with Israeli forces instead of trying to stop them.

33. *Haaretz,* 23 November 2000; *Makor Rishon,* 24 November 2000.

34. The origin of the different versions of Clinton's parameters is the fact that the president did not deposit any written document with the sides. Ross was asked to dictate the president's words to Israeli and Palestinian representatives. His recently published book gives a text that is apparently the most precise version that we have. See Ross, *The Missing Peace,* pp. 801–805.

35. See Israel's response to Clinton's ideas in Sher, *Bemerhak neggi'ah,* pp. 372–374. Menachem Klein, then a member of the political staff at the prime minister's office, confirmed Israel's reservations on Jerusalem and the holy sites: "The Israeli side was not prepared to relinquish sovereignty over the Temple Mount and demanded that sovereign territorial contiguity be assured between Mt. of Olives, Mt. Scopus, the City of David, and the Old City's Jewish Quarter, as well as between the settlements to be annexed (Ma'aleh Adumim, Givat Ze'ev, and the 'Etzion Bloc) and West Jerusalem." Klein, *Shovrim taboo,* p. 74. Klein had his own evaluation: "One cannot ignore the impact of election considerations on Barak's lack of consent to Palestinian sovereignty over Judaism's Holy Sites in Jerusalem, especially the Temple Mount." Ibid.

36. *Makor Rishon,* 29 December 2000.

37. "Qadaya wa-a'ra" [Problems and Opinions], *al-Ahram,* 3 January 2001; for criticism of the Palestinian leadership, see "Clinton's Suggestions: An American-Zionist Plot Doomed to Failure," at the Palestinian Information Center: www.palestine-info .com/arabic/analysis.

38. Drucker, *Harakiri,* pp. 307–323, 347–359.

39. Klein, *Shovrim taboo,* p. 75.

40. *New York Times,* 26 July 2001. Shaat's words were quoted on many occasions, see www.gush-shalom.org/archives/campdavid2.html.

Part 2

The Outcome: Peace in Tatters

6

The al-Aqsa Intifada

The utter failure of the negotiations on permanent status brought the menace of violence closer. The seven years that had elapsed since the start of the "peace process" were marked by countless hostilities, defiant declarations, and measures that undermined trust. Clashes in the weeks preceding the Camp David summit were an omen of things to come, should yet another attempt at a permanent settlement go awry. Anonymous sources on both sides exploited the media to feed the public information that preparations were under way for a full-blown confrontation. The fear was of an armed uprising more bitter than the (first) intifada, which had furnished the background for the Oslo process. The failure of Camp David provided both sides with an opportunity to blame the other and hold it responsible for the anticipated consequences. The storm was about to break. Yet when the violence actually broke out, everyone was taken aback by its force and scale. Suddenly, the whole disputed land was awash in a flood that knew no boundaries, fanned by gusts of deeds and declarations while the Emergency Services busied themselves with SOS calls elsewhere. The eruption at the end of September 2000 was the worst crisis yet since Israelis and Palestinians had begun to steer a common course through Oslo's stormy waters. It was a new situation, and it earned a new name: the al-Aqsa intifada.

Its outbreak is mostly associated with the "visit" by Ariel Sharon to the Temple Mount on 28 September 2000 and the ensuing clashes. The timing and context of the affair belong to the sphere of internal Israeli politics. Most of the coalition parties had resigned from the Labor Party government and left Prime Minister Barak in an intolerable predicament. His domestic problems were aggravated by the failure of Camp David. Meanwhile, Sharon's position as head of the Likud was being challenged by Benjamin Netanyahu, who hoped to seize the party reins a second time. Sharon used every available platform to portray his party as a true alternative to Labor and his personal endowments for head of state as superior to any other candidate's. His visit to the Temple Mount was a stab at walking on the thinnest ice of the Arab-Israeli conflict. It was not an original attempt; every now and then, various groups in Israeli society would try to do the same to demonstrate not only Israel's control of the Temple Mount but, above all, the Jewish people's bond to the sanctified site. Control of the Temple Mount and Jewish visits there have been a controversial political and national issue since the site's conquest in the Six Day War. On the whole, whenever a flare-up threatened, the authorities barred the site to Jewish groups and individuals. Sharon's announced intention to go up to the Temple Mount was prompted by the Camp David failure, which, among other things, had illustrated just how difficult it would be to reach an agreement about the status of the site in a permanent settlement. Against the backdrop of Israeli elections, Sharon strove to underscore by his visit how Likud's position differed from Labor's on the question of Jerusalem and the Temple Mount. Barak's decision to approve the visit is certainly a cause for wonder. He was well aware that it was a provocative move liable to enflame passions.

Nevertheless, Sharon's visit was neither the exclusive nor even the chief factor in the intifada's explosion or continuation. Even if Barak had vetoed the visit, Israeli-Palestinian violence was in the air. Like its forerunner, the al-Aqsa intifada was not planned or shaped as part of the policy of one side or another, and most probably, no party could really have kept it in check. Like the first, it too erupted from the "bottom," and the efforts of the Palestinian leadership to control it were doomed. The collisions following Sharon's visit and the large number of casualties, especially among Palestinians, sounded the intifada's opening chord and, with it, the loss of hope among most of the public in both societies for a peaceful resolution. The brunt of the blame for the escalation cannot be attributed to either side and certainly not to any one leader. It was variously fanned by the acts of armed Palestinian groups (primarily Hamas, Islamic Jihad, and al-Tanzim) and the PA's regular forces, as well as by the Israeli government via the IDF. Violence, suppressive measures, and acts of terror only bared more teeth as the intifada continued. Palestinian terror invited Israeli reprisal. IDF action aroused Palestinian reaction. And so on. The vicious cycle of brutality and rabid hatred was both self-sustaining and spiraling. The toll of dead and injured rose daily: 3,124 Palestinians had been killed by 30 November 2004, and 1,030 Israelis by 3 January 2005; tens of thousands had been wounded; and property incurred heavy damage.[1] Several of the incidents became etched in the minds of Israelis and Palestinians: the killing of twelve-year-old Muhammad al-Dureh by IDF gunfire at Netzarim Junction (30 September 2000); furious demonstrations in several Arab towns within Israel on 1–9 October 2000, which the police tried to quell with, among other things, live fire, killing thirteen demonstrators—all Israeli-Arab citizens; and the Palestinian lynching of Israeli reserve soldiers

Yosef Avrahami and Vadim Novesche (12 October 2000), who had lost their way and then their lives at the Ramallah police station.

When the intifada started, it was Hamas, Islamic Jihad, and the PFLP that committed almost all the deadly acts by Palestinians. Gradually, these groups were joined by the PA security forces. Throughout Israel, rightist demonstrators clamored "to allow the IDF to triumph," and in some places, took to blocking roads and burning tires. Increasingly, official spokespeople pointed an accusing finger at Arafat, holding him chiefly responsible for the violence and terror. On the morning of 20 November 2000, an explosive device was set off next to a bus carrying Israeli schoolchildren from the settlement of Kfar Darom in the Gaza Strip. This act—even though Hamas claimed responsibility for it—triggered the turning point in Israeli policy toward the PA. The prime minister told the IDF to counter with a show of power, and warplanes promptly attacked Gaza targets; from this stage on, the PA, its facilities, and its forces became fair game. Israel declared all-out war on the PA leadership, primarily on Yasser Arafat and his associates. More and more, Israel approved IDF actions against Palestinian leaders in the field and groups identified with the PA. Al-Tanzim, as it transpired early on in the armed confrontation, stepped up its role in the anti-Israel struggle, and the IDF sought to deal its leadership a mortal blow. On 14 January 2000, al-Tanzim commander Raed al-Carmi was struck down in his hometown of Tulkarm. In Israel, his assassination stirred up some public controversy, the very deed eliciting objection. Among the Tanzim, the slaying of their respected leader convinced many of them that there was no longer any doubt about Israel's intentions or the value of conducting talks. Carmi's assassination was followed by surging violence, and PA forces, who until then had hardly participated in the armed struggle, began to play a more active part. The IDF inflicted severe damage on Palestinian governmental and civilian infrastructure. But far worse was the damage done to the idea of a "partner." Israel's delegitimization of Arafat and his rule were the basis for ensuing actions aimed at toppling the PA.

The Construction of the Public Discourse

Soon after the failure of the Camp David summit and the outbreak of the intifada, claims began to surface that were to make up the dominant narratives in both societies over the coming years. Each regime went to a great deal of trouble to establish its version of both the flop and the violence. These narratives, in turn, provided fertile ground for mischief making. In both societies, mutual aggression nourished the public discourse and vice versa. Israelis and Palestinians were sucked into a vicious cycle of violence, terror, incitement, and hatred, a nightmare in which terror and brute force vied with innumerable discussions, declarations, and programs on both sides. In both societies, violence and terror sprouted in furrows cultivated by exponents of simplistic narratives that linked what had ostensibly emerged at Camp David with the ensuing rash of violence. The approach to "Arab" topics in Israel's establishment and media discourse started to resemble the discourse on "Israeli" topics in Arab—especially state—media. Both suffered from a hyperfocus on the personality and alleged malevolence of the opposing leader. Most spokespeople ignored the constraints and considerations that trammel decisionmaking and omit the context of key events. They shared also another weakness: they were oblivious to the repercussions of the deeds and statements of their own camp on the positions and policy of the rival camp.

The positions of different groups on the Israeli-Palestinian conflict were neither preordained nor born out of thin air. They were formed by diverse processes and disseminated by varied means. As a chief source of public information and analysis, the media discourse plays a major role in these processes. To a certain extent, it "reflects" prevalent positions and moods, but mostly it helps to construct them. Journalism products are not a "mirror" reflecting reality, producing its details according to professional criteria alone and then presenting them to media consumers for their judgment. The tools of the trade (including words, phrases, photography, and even camera placement) are part of an inevitable process of subjective choice that governs the encoding and molding of various details into a journalistic product. Nor are media consumers all of a piece; a whole range of variables affect the way that readers and viewers decode a media product and respond to a message, as has been adeptly shown by Stuart Hall, one of the groundbreaking researchers in the field of cultural studies.[2] Different groups of viewers understand broadcast messages in different ways. Moreover, the media discourse in general and the products of journalism in particular are still the chief source of information and commentary for most of the public. One cannot ignore the possibility that protracted exposure to simplistic presentations of key issues in the media discourse has repercussions for the positions held by broad sectors of the public.

The unstable (security, economic, and political) environment that has long framed the lives of Israelis and Palestinians has turned them into media addicts, especially when it comes to news: they listen daily to radio broadcasts, scan press headlines, and watch TV evening news with a finger on the remote to take them from one talk show to another. At the same time, relatively few Israelis are exposed to the non-Israeli media discourse, and relatively few Palestinians are exposed to the non-Arab media discourse. Yet, there is no exaggerating the importance of reliable information and analysis on the Arab-Israeli conflict for both societies. The conflict has ruled the public and national agendas and has been the object of intensive media coverage for decades. Most Israeli and Arab media resources employ correspondents specializing in "Arab" or "Israeli" affairs. In addition, diplomatic, security, and political affairs correspondents also contribute to the discourse on the Israeli-Palestinian conflict.

As the al-Aqsa intifada grew more ferocious, both sides closed ranks and withdrew into themselves. A spreading sense of emergency caused domestic parties and factions to place their differences on the back burner. The media discourse now appeared more homogeneous than ever. Mass media, particularly independent television stations, became the main podium for public discussion, efficiently disseminating the foremost arguments put before the Israeli and Palestinian publics. The sights and sounds of news editions and host shows brought gruesome pictures into the private domain, along with analyses that underpinned the dominant narrative, describing the parties responsible for the hostilities and speculating on the possibility of bringing them to an end. The media discourse became standardized, availing itself of a new terminology. "Settlements" (*hitnahluyot*) and "settlers" (*mitnahlim*) almost overnight became *yishuvim* and *mityashvim*.[3] Military terms (*hissul memukad* [targeted killing], *segger* [closure], *keter* [blockade], and *pe'ulat khissuf* [exposure]) entered the public discourse. Concepts embodying the colonial praxis of conquest-sanctioned settlement were thus disguised by the media, clouding the distinction between the main and the minor issues. Rarely does Israel's media discourse mention the term "Occupied Territories," which is the chief context of the Israeli-Palestinian conflict; instead, one hears the designation "Judea and Samaria." Similar processes affect the Arab and Palestinian media discourse. Such terms as "the enemy" and "the Zionist entity" were restored to star billing. Palestinians who committed clear-cut acts of terror were called *shuhada* (plural of *shahid*, or "martyr"), towns and villages within Israel were sometimes dubbed *mustawtanat* (like settlements in the Occupied Territories), and the Israeli government was referred to as "Tel Aviv's government." No briefing "from above" was needed for all this. "National responsibility" proved to be a highly effective recruiting agent for many Israeli and Palestinian correspondents, interviewers, and analysts. Fine journalists readily enlisted in the media campaign, which quickly became a central battle arena for the Israeli-Palestinian confrontation.

Against this background, the Israeli right-wing camp dusted off the slogan that "Jordan is Palestine." The cry nicely dovetailed with the view that Oslo had been a historic blunder and the situation had to be rectified at all costs. From this standpoint, so long as a permanent-status settlement was not signed and the establishment of a Palestinian state not finalized, the vision remained intact that Israel would rule "Judea, Samaria, and Gaza" eternally; Jordan would be proclaimed the Palestinian state. The spokespeople of this camp have, for decades, contended that the Palestinian problem could be resolved beyond the historical boundaries of the land of Israel. They point out that the Palestinians in any case comprise the majority of Jordan's population and that Jordanian national identity is artificial, lacking any historical basis. They scoff at the peace treaty Israel signed with Jordan and the relations built up by the two states over the years. As they see it, the Arabs' sweeping rejection of this

solution is primarily symptomatic of their built-in objection to the very existence of the state of Israel as the homeland of the Jewish people. As for the slogan's practical implementation, opinion has been divided between the majority who backed the immoral idea of population transfer in one form or another
and the minority who assumed that the same results could be achieved as part
of a political process leading to real peace.

Concord in the Shadow of Domestic Controversy

The Arab media covered the al-Aqsa intifada nonstop, at times depicting Israel's strong-arm tactics and collective punishment as war crimes. Various programs, on a daily basis, broadcast and dwelled on the pounding by Israeli
forces of the innocent Palestinian population and on the rising toll of the dead
and wounded. On more than one occasion, ongoing reportage of events in the
occupied Palestinian territories and in Israel was accompanied by simplistic
commentary about the character of the Jewish state and the inhuman traits of
Israelis. At the start of the intifada, Palestinian demonstrations against Sharon's
visit to the al-Aqsa compound and Israel's immoderate use of live fire, which
resulted in numerous casualties, were covered intensively. Muslims all over the
world were offended by the film footage of Israeli soldiers and police officers
shooting in the compound of al-Haram al-Sharif. Other footage that had a similar effect was the ghastly killing of twelve-year-old Muhammad al-Dureh at
Netzarim Junction and the IDF's unconvincing attempts to shake off responsibility for it and Israeli gunships firing missiles at buildings in residential neighborhoods in the West Bank and Gaza.

The large number of Palestinian casualties and Israel's undue use of force
in the first month of the al-Aqsa intifada affected Arabs everywhere. The
protest was evident in demonstrations organized by various bodies and in
items published in the press—including numerous manifestos and advertisements. The lion's share of the remonstration, however, found expression in
satellite television stations. Sparing no censure for Israel, they criticized also
the impotence of Arab regimes, especially Egypt and Jordan, that had signed
peace treaties with Israel. In these two states, opposition parties, trade unions,
trendsetters, and most of the intellectuals and academics showed, in different
ways, that they objected to Israeli policy, to the peace treaties with Israel, and
above all, to any signs of normalization in the given conditions. The call of
various opposition groups to break off diplomatic relations with Israel in view
of the harsh measures it continued to adopt against the Palestinians won widespread support. Egypt's and Jordan's peace advocates were well-nigh silenced. Many Israelis, some of the Jordanian elite, and very few Egyptians
had nursed the hope that "warm" peace was imminent; that hope now evaporated. It turned out to be misguided because it rested on the false premise that

there was no direct link between the peace treaties and persistent hostility and combat on other fronts of the Arab-Israeli conflict, primarily the confrontation with the Palestinians.

Israeli-Palestinian escalation made short shrift of certain assumptions taken for granted in Israel. Israelis believed that the "warm" peace with Jordan would not be dented since "everything depends on the king." One should not, of course, underrate the abiding commitment of Jordan's royal house to peace with Israel or the close relations between Israeli and Jordanian decisionmakers, which have endured. Commitment to the peace treaty and the political process, along with cooperation on security matters, has remained intact even in times of crisis. But they are only part of a whole slew of factors that affect relations between the two states. More so than any other Arab society, Jordanian society, including its ruling elite, is tightly interwoven with Palestinian society. Any political process aimed at a permanent settlement between Israel and the Palestinians is of crucial importance to Jordan's government and society. The kingdom's public and political agenda is decisively influenced by internal political and social processes.[4]

Some three weeks after the intifada started, an Arab summit convened in Cairo (21–22 October 2000), where the buildup of tension in the Arab world came to a head. The summit was rent by leaders who clamored for a strong Arab response to Israeli actions and others who felt that adding to the tension would not serve Arab and Palestinian interests. The hard-liners wished to take up the armed struggle shoulder to shoulder with the Palestinians and have all ties with Israel broken off; they were checked by Egypt and Jordan, working in concert.[5] Nonetheless, as the violence persisted, Arab public opinion became tempestuous. And Egypt and Jordan resolved to act. Ambassador Muhammad Bassiouni was recalled from Israel (21 November 2000), and the Egyptian representation in Tel Aviv was downgraded. Jordan decided not to dispatch a new ambassador to Israel in place of Marwan Muasher, who had completed his term some months previously. Arab states that had established special relations with Israel since Oslo followed suit. Morocco recalled its diplomats and evacuated its premises next to Tel Aviv's Kikar Ha-Medina Square. Tunisia severed ties, and Oman shut down the offices of the Israeli legation in its capital. Once again, Arab polemics questioned whether Israel was a partner for peace. On Palestine Day (29 November 2000—the anniversary of the 1947 UN vote on partition), al-Jazeera TV broadcast the program "Bela' Hudud" [Without Borders], in which the interviewer, Ahmed Mansur, wondered if Israel were a legitimate negotiating party, seeing that its establishment had been unjust and the Oslo agreements fell far short of the minimal moral and political requirements to resolve the conflict. His guest in the studio was Edward Said. Said's words took the interviewer by surprise and reverberated far and wide. The prominent Palestinian intellectual noted that the Palestinian nation did not need to rise on the ruins of another people (the

Jews). He himself, so he declared, had many Jewish friends in the United States and even in Israel who did not support the policies of the government of Israel and were aware that the Oslo process had aggravated the occupation.

Arab spokespeople, especially Palestinian, generally explained the al-Aqsa intifada as a reaction to the sterile Israeli and US attempt to foist unacceptable permanent-status conditions on the Palestinians and force them to concede on two major issues: Jerusalem (including control of al-Haram al-Sharif) and the refugee problem. A common motif was the "imposed settlement" sought by Israel and the United States and an agreement that was tailor-made for Israel. Barak claimed that he had succeeded in unmasking the Palestinians and exposing their malice for Israel; actually, the mask had been ripped from Israel's leadership, left as well as right. They, it transpired, desired a peace that meant forcing Israeli positions and interests on the Palestinians. Far better, under these conditions, not to seal an agreement. Sharon's walk on al-Haram al-Sharif and the killing of Palestinians who demonstrated in protest in the next few days were the match that lit the fire. But some of the Palestinian leaders welcomed the escalation as an opportunity to break the stalemate and involve external powers that would coerce Israel into far greater flexibility. The longer the intifada lasted, the more the measures employed came to represent a legitimate struggle borne by all factions and sectors of Palestinian society and aimed at national liberation from the yoke of prolonged occupation.

For decades, the Palestinian public had vested al-Haram al-Sharif and al-Aqsa Mosque with the cardinal symbolism of the national, religious, and historical struggle between Arabs and Zionism. Innumerable publications, literary works, and artworks were devoted to this site, which became a religious, national, and cultural icon widely familiar to the Muslim and Arab public, both within the region and beyond. Upon the eruption of the al-Aqsa intifada, the audiovisual exposure of al-Haram al-Sharif and al-Aqsa Mosque reached new heights. In the mounting turbulence the intifada became *the* Palestinian national-religious symbol of the times. Its design as such was enhanced by both official and unofficial parties, its dissemination was assured by diverse means, and its interpretation was left to different groups as they saw fit. The second intifada was thus presented as a holy war, and its casualties were *shuhada* (martyrs of the holy campaign).

Satellite television provided thorough coverage of the intifada. The realities of life under occupation were regularly beamed into the homes of millions of Palestinians and Arabs by a plethora of media channels. Steady daily fare included clashes and Palestinian suffering. Arab solidarity with the Palestinian struggle was greatly boosted, in particular by al-Jazeera and Abu Dhabi TV. The well-known veteran Arab singer, Feiruz, who continues to make appearances, delivered a new rendition of her song "Zahrat al-Mada'in" (Splendor of the Cities)—a paean to al-Quds (Jerusalem) as the most coveted of cities and the object of the Palestinian liberation struggle. The song was played over and over again in the media and enjoyed several new arrangements. In November 2000, readers of Egypt's *al-Ahram* were treated to an unexpected gift when one of the weekend editions was accompanied by a tape of Feiruz's song. The top part of the tape cover said, "Feiruz—al-Quds fi al-bal" (Feiruz—al-Quds in the mind); the bottom said, "Lan nansa'ki" (We will not forget you). In the center, there was a photo montage of the al-Aqsa Mosque and beneath it, twelve-year-old Muhammad al-Dureh lying dead across the lap of his wounded father. The cover was directed against what most Arabs saw as Israel's unwavering goal: to change the Arab and Islamic character of al-Quds and the Temple Mount. Broadcast all over the world, the footage on the shooting of Muhammad al-Dureh as his father tried to shield him at the junction they had strayed across had appalled viewers. The boy's tragic death was used on the tape cover and at other opportunities to put across a message that caught on quickly and was embraced by various public sectors, especially in Arab society: the Palestinians as victims rising up against a cruel, oppressive occupation.

The al-Aqsa intifada won the support of Palestinian factions, the broad Arab public, Arab governments, and sundry nongovernmental organizations (NGOs) throughout the world. Many Palestinians applauded the acts of terror against Israelis in the Occupied Territories and even within Israel proper, popularly referring to them as self-sacrifice (*'amaliyyat istishadiyya*). Even wider legitimacy was accorded the uprising against the occupying forces and the settlers. Numerous petitions were signed and published in favor of continuing the intifada.[6] The public discourse dwelt on the importance of "resistance," "standing firm," and "the struggle." Old concepts long rooted in the Palestinian national ethos, they were now dressed up to fit the unique circumstances of the al-Aqsa intifada. Despite its sectarianism, the concepts spoke to all streams and groups of Palestinian society and underlay the public sympathy for both stone throwers, who clashed with Israeli troops, and to a large extent for suicide bombers within Israel. IDF actions, the disruption of daily routine due to restricted movement, and repeated incidents with settlers greatly swelled support for the armed struggle. Decades of confrontation with Israel had made struggle and resistance central components of the Palestinian national identity. The intifada, as an expression of the legitimate struggle of the Palestinian people, was upheld by the broader Arab public and lauded by writers, poets, artists, and intellectuals. Television and radio, the Internet, newspapers, and magazines all revolved around it. Literature, poetry, theater, documentaries, and feature films served as rich, unique sources, conveying how different Arab publics perceived, embedded, and accepted the intifada from September 2000 on. The humiliation and despair of life under occupation were recurrent themes, coupled with the fact that for most Palestinians the words *peace process* had become an empty phrase. Above all, these sources and cultural products were an indication of the divergent Palestinian and Israeli perspectives on the Oslo process with regard to expectations and the responsibility for its failure. Yet the sources were not a mirror image of the realities. The texts are complex and should be read critically while bearing the realities in mind. They provide a wealth of detail relevant to an understanding of the construction of symbols in the Palestinian national struggle and of their significance for different publics.

Al-Karmel, a journal published in Ramallah and edited by Mahmoud Darwish, who occupies a place of honor in modern Arabic poetry, served as an esteemed podium for Arab writers and poets. Arab thinkers during the intifada grappled on its pages with the question of whether it was possible at all to compose poetry when so much blood was being spilled. The question sparked numerous articles, essays, and poems, an additional indication that the al-Aqsa intifada was constructed as both a Palestinian and a pan-Arab phenomenon. How different was *al-Karmel*'s content from what appeared in the mass media? The themes and motifs were highly similar. The difference lay in the language, metaphors, and symbols chosen. The political rhetoric of Palestinian spokespeople from different currents (notably the nationalist one) was given ample voice in the press, on Palestinian radio, and even in periodicals such as the *Journal of Palestine Studies*. *Al-Karmel*, like Arab satellite TV, created a different sort of shell for the discussion of national issues, chiefly because it was a platform for voices seldom heard elsewhere. The fact that many of its authors were writers and poets lent weight to their choice of language, especially concerning the construction of symbolic meanings and the depiction of the intifada as a potential framework for reviewing basic questions troubling Palestinians as well as the larger Arab public. The intifada was described as the most important campaign for Palestinian interests to emerge in a long time, a "revolution" of both consciousness and action.[7]

Most of *al-Karmel*'s authors dealt with the context of the intifada's eruption. Their arguments were summarized in an article by prominent writer Abd al-Rahman Munif. At the heart of the Palestinian uprising, according to Munif, lay a successful attempt to undo the Oslo equation that had provided Israel with a framework to dictate conditions and, in effect, to perpetuate the oppression, occupation, and settlement of the Occupied Territories. The intifada also restored the refugee question to the top of the Arab public agenda. Though the intifada itself would not lead to a resolution of the conflict, it had scored a major achievement, smashing "the cage in which some sought to lock up the Palestinian problem in keeping with the will of Israel and the pressure of the US and the impotence of the Arab regimes."[8]

With regard to the construction of symbols of the al-Aqsa intifada, it is interesting to note *al-Karmel*'s inclusions and omissions. The symbols, messages, and rhetoric of the Islamist current found no voice here. The terms *shahid, jihad,* and *al-Aqsa* were commonly mentioned, but nearly always in the context of the just Palestinian national struggle. The phenomenon of suicide bombers was largely ignored. In contrast, child and stone were presented as the real heroes of the intifada. The circumstances surrounding the death of the boy, Muhammad al-Dureh, at the start of the intifada, along with the large number of children hurt by Israeli security forces, endowed the image of the Palestinian child with the power of a modern-day David with a mere slingshot standing up to a terrible, armed Goliath. In *al-Karmel*'s pages, Egyptian writer and critic Yusuf al-Qaid lauded the brave young Palestinians fearlessly confronting Israeli soldiers who commanded the most sophisticated weaponry. In al-Qaid's eyes, the stone in the hands of the young was the intifada's most significant symbol ("*the* great surprise").[9]

The rage of the broader Arab public at the continued blows suffered by Palestinians turned, at times, on Arab leaders and the press. After decades of struggle for freedom of expression in Arab societies, the intifada—overnight—made the "street" a factor to be reckoned with in the public discourse. For writer Abd al-Rahman Munif, it was one of the intifada's more welcome developments. Arab leaders came to realize that they could no longer ignore public opinion. More importantly, the phenomenon is not confined to any specific local-national interest. Beyond the rage at Palestinian suffering, there is wide public protest over the impotence of Arab leaders in various spheres. Yes, the Arab "street" is demanding assistance for Palestinians, but it is also calling for greater reform and domestic change.[10] Egyptian writer Jamal al-Ghitani noted that the impact of the intifada on the young in Arab states is evident in the participation of pupils, students, and unionists in rallies of solidarity with Palestinians and protest against Israel and the United States. In his words, the demonstrators belong to a generation whose "consciousness was molded under what the Arab press calls the 'culture of peace,'" and suddenly along comes the intifada and lays bare for all to see the falsehood of a peace aimed at obliterating reality, counterfeiting the present, and accepting a situation based on myths. The demonstrations exposed the fact that a large Arab public holds views at variance with their leaders. This public can now publicize their critical opinions in the media and on the Internet.[11]

Another accomplishment of the uprising, as Darwish put it, was the "return to square one." On the second anniversary of the intifada, *al-Karmel*'s editor welcomed the fact that the basic questions of the conflict were being reviewed again, a development he considered far preferable to the thoroughly misguided Oslo route. It was the intifada that had created the conditions for this review. Israel's ongoing occupation and present attempt to suppress the intifada with an iron fist, he said, attested to Israel's inability to define itself unless it erased the characteristics of Palestinian national existence. His conclusion was gloomy: Israeli society is unable to live in peace with itself outside of a state of war with "the other"—Palestinian and Arab. In truth, the Israeli's endless war is "a war with our very existence." The aim of Israel's current war against Palestinians "is not to put an end to violence, but to put an end to the dream. Forever." "Have we grown weary?" Darwish asks, and then answers: "Yes. We have grown weary of prison, of siege and occupation. We shall not grow tired of hope."[12]

The intifada also saw growing rapprochement between the assorted Palestinian organizations as Fatah activists found themselves fighting shoulder to shoulder with their domestic rivals, Hamas, the Islamic Jihad, and the PFLP and PDFLP. Still, the closing of the ranks could not scrap or obscure the basic rifts that had deepened since the start of Oslo. Palestinian opposition ranks regarded the intifada as an uprising aimed primarily at the Israeli enemy, but it was also a counter to the political course of Arafat's leadership and the spreading corruption of the regime under the mantle of Oslo. To a certain degree, the intifada was set forth as an alternative to the political process, the signed agreements with Israel that had not really changed the lives of Palestinians but had left the occupation and settlements in place. Upon the return of the Palestinian delegation from Camp David, the opposition awarded the leadership an enthusiastic welcome and showered them with praise for holding out under heavy US and Israeli pressure. Alongside the public embrace, the opposition upheld the summit's failure as proof that there was no true chance of peace with Israel, that summits under US patronage tend to side with the Jews, distancing the Palestinians from their goals. Only continued armed struggle would force Israel to change its position.

Hamas extolled the self-sacrifice of suicide bombers against Israelis everywhere, presenting their actions as a concrete alternative to the PA course: suicide bombers were the harbingers of a new phase tenfold more effective than popular struggle, which, in the al-Aqsa intifada, had not produced the desired result. The occupation continued as harsh as ever, and Palestinian life had become insupportable precisely because of the agreements with Israel and the shadow they cast. There was sympathy for stone throwers, but it was the suicide bombers who came mostly from Hamas and Jihad that attracted the limelight and much of the support. It was they who embodied the new promising phase, exposing the Israeli enemy's soft belly. Against stones and gunfire, Israeli forces had developed effective defenses. But, Hamas and Jihad spokespeople pointed out, Israel had not come up with a solution for the suicide bombers who were motivated to sacrifice their lives for a noble cause. Indirectly, the suicide bombers, their commanders, and their sympathizers reflected the notion that Israel understood only the language of force, meaning that only severe violence would achieve results. In this context, Palestinian spokespeople cited the struggle of Lebanon's Hizbollah. Israel's retreat from southern Lebanon in May 2000 was depicted as buckling under the heavy fire to which Hizbollah had subjected the IDF and the residents along Israel's northern border. Nevertheless, there emerged a group among the Palestinian leadership, headed by Abu Mazen, who maintained that suicide bombers did more harm than good. Moreover, other interpretations were heard in the national current, different from that of Hamas and the claim that suicide bombers were motivated by fervent religious devotion whose reward was assured (a pleasant existence in the Garden of Eden). Relating to the *shuhada* in his book *A State of Siege* (*Halat hisar*), Mahmoud Darwish writes:[13]

> The *shahid* makes it clear to me:
> I did not seek beyond the horizon
> Virgins of eternity, for I loved my life
> On earth, amid pine and fig, but
> The path to my life was blocked,
> And I searched for it in the only thing that I had—
> Blood in azurite stone
>
> ⋆ ⋆ ⋆
>
> The *shahid* teaches me:
> There is no beauty outside of my freedom

With these words, the Palestinian poet gave voice to the national camp that viewed the actions of the *shuhada* as a consequence of the situation created by occupation and aimed at national liberation. His words uncover the basic dispute between the two key Palestinian camps: the national and the religious. The struggle against Israeli occupation is common to both, but that fact does not cancel the different agendas of each camp.

The discord between the PA and the oppositionist forces, especially Hamas, became more shrill whenever there was talk of cease-fire or resuming the political process. The PA was supposed to take responsibility for meticulously implementing the terms of cease-fire, which meant instituting tough measures against armed groups, especially Hamas, Islamic Jihad, and al-Tanzim. This prospect unleashed impassioned public debate for fear that the Palestinian internal struggle would degenerate into bloody civil war. In Hamas eyes, the intifada was *al-muqawama* (resistance); after all, it calls itself the Islamic Resistance Movement. Since its inception, its actions have always been depicted by spokespeople and sympathizers as synonymous with "resistance."[14] The continuation of the intifada was often glorified and the "resistance" portrayed as an authentic expression of the people's will, as a force that no one had the right to stanch. In so doing, members of Hamas, the largest Palestinian oppositionist movement, sought to delegitimize PA consideration of any sort of cease-fire that spelled a return to the Oslo blueprint. For the same reason, Hamas, Islamic Jihad, and the PFLP and PDFLP also objected to a number of cease-fire proposals broached during the intifada. They showcased the chain of terror acts committed by their people against Israelis as an unprecedented accomplishment that wreaked havoc on Israel. Highlighting the chasm between themselves and the PA, they noted that cease-fire was in Israeli interests. An editorial published at the height of the uprising in the organ of Islamic Jihad outlined the organization's opposition to cease-fire and called for continued action against Israel.

"Common sense has it that a victim would spurn all appeasement and ceasefire with his murderer. . . . Free, self-respecting Palestinians are not prepared to throw their murderers and the robbers of their lands and shrines a lifesaver. . . . We reject this ceasefire with the robbers . . . and demand more courageous acts of self-sacrifice against them."[15]

Notes

1. The figures do not distinguish between civilians and noncivilians. Israeli casualties are based on IDF official websites (updated 12 January 2004), www.idf.il/SIP_STORAGE/DOVER/files/4/21834.doc. Palestinian casualties come from B'Tselem, the Israeli Information Center for Human Rights in the Occupied Territories, www.btselem.org.

2. In an innovative article, Stuart Hall examines the processes of constructing television information and its decoding by groups of viewers. He convincingly shows that there are no grounds to assume that "the public" is an indiscriminate consumer of media messages. Hall, "Encoding and Decoding," pp. 90–103. For studies showing that publics interpret identical images differently, see Katz and Liebes, "Mutual Aid in the Decoding of Dallas," pp. 187–198; Abu Lughod, *Dramas of Nationhood*, pp. 29–53.

3. Both terms—*hitnahlut* and *yishuv*—are usually rendered as "settlement" in English. *Hitnahlut* comes from the biblical *nahala* (Numbers 26:54), which means "inheritance," "share," "estate," and so on. *Yishuv* denotes a place that is settled or inhabited. The prestate Jewish community in Palestine, for example, was known as the *Yishuv*; the Zionist movement established settlements, or *yishuvim*. Since the Six Day War, the term *hitnahlut* has come to mean settlements in the Occupied Territories.

4. Nevo, "Jordan, the Palestinians and the al-Aqsa Intifada," pp. 70–85.

5. For the resolutions of the Cairo Summit, see www.sis.gov.eg/online/html3/o221020f.htm.

6. For a petition signed by thousands of Palestinians, including prominent intellectuals from the entire political spectrum, see *al-Hayat al-Jadida*, 10 October 2000.

7. A summary of this motif can be found in an article by Elias Houri, "Surafat al-Intifada" [The eminent Intifada], *al-Karmel* 66 (2001): 28.

8. Abd al-Rahman Munif, "Al-Ma'na wal-Mabna" [Meanings and Form], *al-Karmel* 66 (2001): 12. According to Darwish, from the early stages of the Oslo process, "it was clear that the Israeli side was not interested in the peace process but only in the security aspect, which would assure continued occupation." Mahmoud Darwish, "Preface," *al-Karmel* 67 (2001): 1.

9. Yusuf al-Qaid, "Intifadat Awlad Misr" [Egypt's Sons Intifada], *al-Karmel* 66 (2001): 23–25. The motif of the stone as the chief symbol of the intifada can be gleaned also from cartoons in the Arab press. Cartoonists found the stone an excellent metaphor for a whole slew of messages. In many drawings, it was a catalyst for the building of a Palestinian state, as in the depiction of young Palestinians throwing hundreds of stones that land to erect a building flying the Palestinian flag. A similar motif by the same cartoonist shows the stones flung to be a barrier against tanks, helicopters, and warplanes, while the barrier itself forms the word "Palestine." See *Al-Ahram Weekly*, 3 October 2002, 20 September 2004.

10. Munif, "Al-Ma'na wal-Mabna" [Meanings and Form], *al-Karmel* 66 (2001): 12.

11. al-Ghitani, Jamal, "Al-'Awda ila al-Asl" [The Return to Square One], *al-Karmel* 66 (2001): 20.

12. Darwish, *al-Karmel* 72–73 (Summer–Winter 2002): 4. Yusuf al-Qaid, too, claimed that the intifada had returned the conflict to the starting position: a conflict over existence rather than over specific territory. "Anyone who thought otherwise is wrong." Al-Qaid, "Intifadat Awlad Misr" [Egypt's Sons Intifada], *al-Karmel* 66 (2001): 23–25.

13. Darwish, *Halat hisar* [A State of Siege], pp. 76–77. My translation.

14. See the London-based *Filistin Al-Muslima*. Other websites expressing Hamas voice include the renowned Islam Online at http://www.islamonline.net/English/index.shtml.

15. *al-Istiqlal*, 7 June 2001.

7

The "No Partner" Approach

In Israel and to a large extent in the United States, the public discourse presented the al-Aqsa intifada as the attempt of the PA leadership to obtain by violence what they had failed to obtain at the Camp David negotiating table. According to this reasoning, the Palestinians were never interested in real peace with Israel but merely in obtaining territories that would enable them to continue the struggle under more convenient conditions. Their leadership did not whole-heartedly embrace the Oslo process as a basis for establishing two states. Even though most of the Israeli public had come to accept the existence of a Palestinian people and supported partitioning the land into two states, the Palestinian side had not seen a parallel development.

The demonization of the Palestinian side thus took increasing shape in the Israeli media. Against the swelling violence and loss of hope, more and more voices depicted the Palestinians as holding life cheap, as animals do.[1] Pictures of Palestinian youngsters throwing stones at IDF soldiers had become, as I pointed out in Chapter 6, the symbol of resistance in Arab society. They were often shown in Israel's media as an example of the cynical use Palestinian society made of children and even as an expression of the little value Arab culture placed on human life. The context of the national struggle was muted and replaced by reams of cultural and social commentary on the "nature" of Palestinians, Arabs, and Muslims. A knee-jerk reaction to the negative, disdainful attitude toward these groups could be found in satires on Israeli TV. The Eli Yatzpan show, which enjoys one of the highest ratings, frequently dealt with "the Arabs" by mocking and patronizing their leaders. In early June 2001, Yatzpan mimicked Mubarak by depicting him as an ape-man with slurred speech. Egypt protested through diplomatic channels and the press. Yatzpan's portrayal became the talk of the day in Israel, inviting a host of media reactions. On one occasion, Yatzpan appeared on Channel Two's entertaining talk show hosted by Ya'ir Lapid and again mimicked Mubarak. The next day *Haaretz* reported what went on in the studio. "The audience and Lapid were beside themselves with laughter as Yatzpan delivered his piece, sounding like a baboon and making rude gestures." The TV critic astutely reflected the public's identification with the delivery: "Yatzpan was borne high because he made a fool of the leader of the Arab world, both angering and humiliating him, and in the current public climate, this is enough to make [Israelis] stand up straight and raise morale. . . . it sheds light on the image of the Arab in the eyes of the Israeli public."[2] This incisive review faithfully depicted the anti-Arab climate of hostility that infused Israeli society in the year following the collapse of the political process. Various spokespeople expressed surprise at Egypt's protest, some claimed that it showed that Egyptians did not understand that humor and satire are part of freedom of expression in a democracy.[3]

As the intifada continued, public opinion polls showed that most Israelis considered it to be a war initiated by the Palestinian leadership that rejected Israel's right to exist. The wide support for anti-Israel terror in Palestinian society attested to a deep-seated opposition to the very existence of the state of Israel. In short, the basic principle underlying Oslo, mutual recognition, was thoroughly shaken. High-ranking officers also tended to describe the confrontation with the Palestinians as an "existential threat" to the state of Israel. The chief of general staff, Moshe (Bugi) Yaalon, certainly made waves when he bluntly remarked that the Palestinian danger was a threat "of cancerous dimensions and characteristics" (25 August 2002). He was asked to clarify the remark in a wide-ranging interview some days later, at which point he again chose provocative words:

> The characteristics of the threat are latent, like cancer. When you are attacked from the outside, you see it. Cancer, on the other hand, is from the inside. Which is why it disturbs me more because in this case the diagnosis is vital. If the diagnosis is wrong and you're told it's not cancer, it's a headache, the response is irrelevant. But I claim that it is cancer. My professional diagnosis is that we have here a phenomenon that is an existential threat.

Referring to the desired treatment, he enlarged on the oncological prescription: "There are all sorts of solutions to cancerous phenomena. Some would advise amputation. But at the moment, I am applying chemotherapy."[4] It had been a long time since any senior Israeli figure had made such appalling remarks. Many faulted the chief of general staff for the metaphor. But others congratulated him on his courage in speaking his mind (notably, Ehud Barak, who lauded his diagnosis of the "nature of the conflict"). Few in Israel paid attention to the theme underlying Yaalon's words about the Palestinians as an existential threat, namely the discourse of "no partner" and a return to existential struggle—a discourse constructed with the help of many hands since the summer of 2000 and largely consistent with Yaalon's statements. Its pervasive nature may explain his astonishment at the harsh reactions he sparked ("People from your own side come and simply dig a hole under you. It drives me mad at times"—this was the headline of the published interview with him). Yaalon again reiterated the narrative that had taken root in Israel and beyond, that Palestinian rejectionism at Camp David had shown "that it's not about occupation. It's about not recognizing Israel's right to exist as a Jewish state." Arafat, he said, "sees Oslo as a Trojan horse that enabled the Palestinians to get into the country, and September 2000 as the moment of emerging from the horse's belly. Today, too, PLO ideology seeks to undo Israel from within. They are not interested in reaching an end to conflict but in making the state of Israel the Palestinian state."[5] Yaalon's words showed that such rhetoric was not the sole preserve of the right.

In this context, the conception that there is currently "no partner" on the Palestinian side became pervasive. These ideas and images dovetailed nicely with the narrative propounded by Israel's political-security spokespeople as to the failure of the Camp David summit: Israel, led by Barak, had made the Palestinians a most generous offer for permanent settlement, but the negotiations had failed because it transpired that Arafat and his people were not interested in peace with Israel but in its destruction. Moreover, when the PA leadership failed to achieve its goals at the negotiating table, it turned to violence and terror. This about-face rested on the premise that Israeli society would be unable to endure the heavy toll extracted by escalated armed confrontation for any length of time and the belief that the longer the violence continued and daily life was disrupted, the more pressure would mount in Israel for the government to modify its positions on permanent settlement. The confrontation with the Palestinians was defined in Israel as an "offensive of terror" and an "existential war." Since it was eminently clear that Arafat orchestrated the violence and terror, there was no point in cooperation, communication, or negotiation with the PA under his leadership.

These claims were intensively disseminated in the Israeli media. Day by day, readers, listeners, and viewers were exposed to a formidable stream of reports and analyses on the confrontation with the Palestinians and its implications. The pictures of killing and destruction wrought by terror perpetrated by various Palestinian groups were a frequent and shocking reminder that the front had moved to public buses, cafés, malls, and entertainment sites, venues that frame the daily lives of millions of civilians. Widespread suicide bombings, booby-trapped cars, and mortar fire at locations within Israel; numerous cases of shooting and detonation of explosives against soldiers and settlers in the Occupied Territories; and the strident incitement of Arab spokespeople—all these affected Israeli public opinion. More and more Israelis demanded tough action against the Palestinians. A few, even in the dreadful reality of violence and terror, called for a return to the negotiating table.

The information and analyses supplied by the media had a palpable effect on the positions of the Israeli public. The weak link in most of Israel's media offerings was an exaggerated, uncritical reliance on information stemming from the political-security establishment. The fact that journalists are deluged by reports emanating from interested parties is not unique to Israel. Reliable sources are the branch on which journalism sits. Media professionals maintain a complex relationship with their sources, and on the whole, a journalist's professional and intellectual integrity, along with the media's critical faculty, are what distinguish between conveying reliable information and analysis and serving as a mouthpiece.[6] During the al-Aqsa intifada, news broadcasts were overloaded with items deriving from "security sources," "a senior officer," and "a political source." The watchdog of Israeli democracy was stuffed with gobs of tendentious information. At the crucial stage, the longstanding proficiency of Israeli media makers was found wanting.

This failure was not the fault of individuals, nor, as far as Arab or Palestinian issues in Israel's media discourse were concerned, was it a single occurrence. It was partly the result of the frequent information and assessments taken from intelligence sources, even though these were collated and analyzed with tools devised for military needs, notably, evaluations of the threats Israel faced. This practice gave a negative tone to journalism regarding Arabs. It is not my intention to criticize journalists for relying on these sources in their ongoing reportage of news in the mass media (primarily television), where their work is based on real-time information inflow, and the pace of events often does not permit careful sifting. The criticism is aimed mostly at the overreliance of analysts and reports on assessments and items leaked by security sources, which, in the al-Aqsa intifada, was the basis for much of the information given the public. The airing of these sources in a format desirable to the leaking party achieved two main results: a tendentious dissemination of information or appraisals in the public media and legitimation from an independent party ("our political correspondent," "our Arab affairs analyst," etc.), whose conclusion was ostensibly corroborated by additional sources and professional talents. Beneath this cloak of vague attribution ("a senior security source confirmed. . . ," "our correspondent has learned . . ."), biased information stemming from the security-political establishments was spread every day. In many instances, it was impossible to verify or back up evaluations and information from nameless sources. Only rarely did one find a journalist who possessed such information and complemented his or her report with searching questions and supplementary details that did not originate in the corridors of power. The upshot was that the intelligence discourse trickled—undisturbed—into the public discourse and became indistinguishable from it.

The security orientation of Israel's media discourse was uniquely enhanced by TV editors and producers who deliberately peopled their programs with senior officers in either active or reserve service. Radio programs exhibited a similar propensity, as did the press, though to a lesser degree. The approach was underpinned by two controversial working assumptions. One held that the role of the mass media is to give the public what it wants. The other held that career officers have an invaluable viewpoint on military and security matters. The presence of security spokespeople in the media discourse only increased as the intifada persisted. Senior officers in active service were featured in all their rank and uniform, sometimes alongside former comrades-in-arms who now sported suits and ties. Both were invited day and night to analyze for the public the "conduct" of the Arab states and the PA. They—who for decades had been trained for warfare against the Palestinians—were now regarded as supremely fit to explain the considerations of the enemy leadership and the various groups that comprised enemy society. This militarization of Israeli society has been going on for quite some time. Senior reserve officers are deemed natural candidates for a whole range of executive jobs in major companies, municipal authorities, and prestigious education institutions as well as public service, politics, and government. In a climate of emergency, in which the whole nation is the army, the military voice reverberated predominantly in the media course, so much so that certain journalists at times seemed to merely echo the tunes composed by miscellaneous official parties.

Rarely did senior government officials publicly denounce the harmful effect of the military discourse on the functioning of the political echelon and the public discourse. Only after his stint as director general of the Foreign Ministry did Avi Gil address the influence of military personnel on political decisionmaking, stating with unveiled criticism: "[In Israel], the army is charged also with explaining the political conduct of people like Arafat, President Mubarak and Bashar Assad. Military intelligence, in its capacity as 'national evaluator,' is not meant to merely count cannon and tanks and assess the imminence of war, but it also has to explain to the cabinet the political conduct of players such as the US."[7] Yossi Beilin, who had served as a minister in a number of governments, protested the decisive role accorded the security establishment in the public discourse, which found expression also in deliberate leaks of military intelligence appraisals. "Military intelligence assessments reach the media immediately and are taken as unadulterated truth despite the many assessments to the contrary," he noted, adding that "military intelligence assessments on the Palestinians, their intentions in negotiations, the chances of violence erupting, and more, have become public domain, whether or not they are presented to the government. They have played a detrimental role in Israeli-Palestinian relations because they were understood as 'Israel'—rather than its military intelligence—constantly ascribing negative intentions to the Palestinians."[8] Gilead Sher, who served as Prime Minister Barak's right-hand man, identified the source of the problem; namely that Israel's national interests are not necessarily identical with military needs.

The books by Beilin (*Madrikh le-yona petzu'ah* [Guide for a Wounded Dove]) and Sher (*Bemerhak neggi'ah* [Within Hand's Reach]) furnish a number of examples of the problematic relationship between the military and the government with regard to the Israeli-Palestinian confrontation. Both state that in many cases, senior officers did not simply give their opinions but acted as if they owned the copyright to their analyses, trying at times to force their positions on the political echelon and the public. On the IDF view of the Palestinian designs, conduct, and leadership, Sher writes: "One of the most salient IDF approaches was a quasi-prophecy of doom that, almost inevitably, would be self-fulfilling one day: there would be a confrontation; the ever deceiving—not to say, lying—Palestinians are preparing for armed confrontation. The conception of force, whereby Palestinians could be subdued by means of pressure and even more by force, made too many inroads into the IDF." Sher imparts his sorry impression of senior officers conducting "direct dialogue with the public, as though it were their duty to account to the public at large rather than to the political echelon. Intelligence evaluations and analyses found their way to the media even before they were presented to the government and prime minister." The worrisome consequence was that "some of the prime minister's summations and commitments, passed on to the army by his military secretary, 'evaporated': tanks were not pulled back; commanders contented themselves with diverting the [tank] gun-barrels. The Gaza fishing area was not opened. Contrary to explicit instructions, Palestinian workers were allowed to cross [into Israel] in paltry numbers. Check posts were not dismantled."[9]

Shlomo Ben-Ami, a senior member of Barak's government, had similar complaints. Upon learning of certain matters during the intifada, he protested against the political echelon's piecemeal control of the IDF:

> The IDF acted in this crisis in its own spirit, not always in the spirit of the political echelon's guidelines. . . . The IDF command had a different agenda, and its commanders effused an outburst of rage that led, at times, to the cycle of violence being widened rather than narrowed. . . . Merchandise, which, it was explained, had to reach the Palestinian population, was held up at check-posts on the instructions of field commanders; bulldozers uprooted hot houses, plant nurseries, and other crops for security reasons, raising the Palestinian level of rage to unprecedented heights. The policy of collective punishment and economic hardship, which clearly did not serve the political echelon's endeavoring to achieve calm, was an agenda conducted by the military while turning its back on, and ignoring, the political echelon's guidelines and intentions.[10]

The influence of the IDF senior command on policy in the confrontation with the Palestinians was felt outside the cabinet as well. One unusual instance was supplied by Ami Ayalon, the former head of Shin Bet, who, in a newspaper report (February 2002), described the dynamics at work: "Israeli intelligence experts feed the US an assessment that additional pressure will

[have] Arafat crawling back to the negotiating table. Because of this, the [Bush] administration gives Israel a green light to act against the Palestinians as it sees fit."[11] Efraim Halevy, the former head of the Mossad, also recently joined the critics of the intelligence community's overinvolvement in setting policy vis-à-vis the Palestinians. At a lecture in Jerusalem (21 May 2003), Halevy warned against what he defined as "the perfect circle": that is, the insupportable situation whereby "the force operating in the field evaluates the political significance of its own actions, it conducts the dialogue with the adversary and it exerts the greatest influence on how leaders grasp reality."[12] It may further be argued that in a state of affairs where so many decisionmakers are military and security personnel and their media presence is so prominent, it is little wonder that the security-oriented outlook dominates Israel's public discourse. Security needs become entrenched as the paramount consideration. To the reasonable criticism voiced by Gil, Sher, Beilin, and Halevy, one may also add that the IDF and military intelligence are accustomed to appraising the dangers and threats facing Israel and to assessing the (chiefly military) capability of its adversaries. In these appraisals, analysts are barred from dealing with or examining Israeli politics or policy vis-à-vis Arab parties. We thus see an attempt to weigh the complex relations of a multidimensional conflict by subjecting them to a daily scrutiny that ignores the conduct of one of the main sides—Israel.

On the first anniversary of the al-Aqsa intifada, Israel's media was steeped in "progress reports" with the concomitant deluge of reports and analyses by officials and journalists adding up to a troubling uniformity. One of the few to take issue was Aviv Lavie, then *Haaretz*'s TV critic, who wrote: "Shlomo Ben-Ami and Gilead Sher unfurled their personal testimonies in the various weekend supplements; Emanuel Rosen tried to get to the root of the matter in a overarching report on *Ulpan Shishi* [Friday Studio], and Amnon Abramowitz acquitted himself of an address bursting with firm opinions on *Yoman* [News Magazine]. Unsurprisingly, they all arrived at the same conclusion: Arafat is to blame. He is unable to finalize a permanent settlement with Israel." Lavie, of course, did not rule out the possibility that this conclusion might be valid. His chief concern was reserved for the last sentence: "A close look at the journalistic product they created raises doubts as to their having come to the job with clean hands, meaning, with a real effort to neutralize their natural tendency to adopt the Israeli version."[13]

Some months later (February 2002), readers of *Haaretz* could again appreciate the difficulty of Israeli journalists and commentators in freeing themselves from the entrenched narrative in the corridors of power. In a report headlined, "I Was Right," the Arab affairs correspondent of Channel Two TV patted himself on the back: "I no longer have to convince anyone with eyes in his head that it was Arafat who lit the flame—[by giving] an order!" The Palestinian leader under siege in Ramallah was described as "a feeble-minded old man" whose views hadn't changed since the PLO's establishment. Arafat was a pyromaniac who set fire to anything across his path. His behavior was predictable, since he has a "tendency . . . to think in the direction of escalation."[14] In June 2002, more than a year after his term of office ended, Ehud Barak cited information that Israel had possessed as to Arafat's intentions following the Camp David summit: "We know, from hard intelligence, that Arafat intended to unleash a violent confrontation, terrorism." According to Barak, at the end of whose term the al-Aqsa intifada broke out, Sharon's visit to the Temple Mount and the ensuing riots provided Arafat with "an excellent excuse, a pretext." The intifada, he summed up, was planned in advance and prepared well beforehand, even if Arafat did not know the exact September day on which it was to start.[15] With these pronouncements, the simplistic hyperfocus on Arafat's personality by both officials and highly esteemed correspondents reached its climax: Arafat played all the chords of the Israeli-Palestinian confrontation, minor as well as major.

The idea that Arafat has sole control was adopted too lightly and propagated energetically by political spokespeople and media personnel (journalists, analysts, editors, and talk show hosts). All painted him as the Pied Piper, sounding the tune to which the West Bank and the Gaza Strip danced. This eclipse was broadcast by Israel's media, including those identified with an independent, critical discourse. *Haaretz*, for one, has long enjoyed such a reputation, and some of its journalists did keep a sense of proportion and their professional integrity even at the most difficult moments of the al-Aqsa intifada. Not a few of its writers, however, on occasion joined the national choir, uncritically singing the official narrative. The tendency was particularly conspicuous after Palestinian terror reaped Israeli life, as happened, for example, after Jerusalem's Sbarro restaurant was blown up (9 August 2001), an act for which Hamas took responsibility. A suicide bomber discharged a large explosive device he carried in downtown Jerusalem during the lunchtime crush. The toll was fifteen dead and about 100 wounded. Apart from outright rage at the brutality against Israeli civilians, the editorial board apparently wished to situate the event in a number of broader contexts, all controversial. On 12 August 2001, the *Haaretz* editorial ran the headline, "Arafat Is Responsible for the Terror." The piece itself said:

> If Israelis could trust Palestinian intentions, they would be prepared to evacuate the territories and concentrate on developing their state within agreed borders on the basis of the Green Line. This hasn't happened, largely because of Palestinian behavior: Arafat and his people threaten Israel's very existence [their demand for a right of return] and demonstrate by their conduct the aggression embodied by their approach and the inability to rely on their promises. Under these conditions, they should not be surprised by the passions aroused in the Israeli public at the sight of the blood spilt in Jerusalem.[16]

The blurring of the lines between media outlets identified with "right" or "left" also emerges from a close examination of cartoons in Israel's daily press. After the summer of 2000, both right-wing and left-wing media portrayed Arafat as the enemy and Israel as the victim of his evil designs. Israel was depicted as purely defensive, as having no choice but to use more force in its war on Palestinian terror (in this context, the naming of one of the IDF's wider actions "Defensive Wall" was an apt choice). At times, both also described Arafat as the epitome of the Palestinian experience: Arafat was the Palestinians, and the Palestinians were Arafat. The clear difference between the two lay in the left's portrayal of Arafat as having deceived Israel, as a liar and a terrorist who was not a partner for peace, whereas the right, which agreed wholeheartedly with this depiction, added that it was the Palestinians—not merely Arafat— who sought to destroy Israel. Arafat was portrayed as the greatest enemy of Israel and the Jews—on a par with the Nazi foe.[17]

In the first year of the al-Aqsa intifada, Arafat was featured in *Haaretz* cartoons as intensively involved in acts of terror against the state of Israel and its citizenry. These cartoons were all the work of Ze'ev, one of Israel's most esteemed caricaturists. In this period, he tended to draw Arafat's famous headgear, the kaffiyeh, as concealing bombs; thus, for example, in a cartoon showing the Israeli and Palestinian leaders exchanging blows, Barak is poised with fists up, and Arafat is armed. Barak is wearing a suit and bowler hat, but Arafat is wrapped in a kaffiyeh patterned with grenades and is wearing hobnailed shoes. From the side, Barak is also being attacked by Mubarak, who appears as a sphinx, his right fist striking Barak's back.[18] Another cartoon shows Arafat as a villain offering the new prime minister, Ariel Sharon, a huge dove of peace that is really a Trojan horse concealing variously armed terrorists. In reaction, Sharon is seen to be deflecting the offering with the words, "We are not allowed to accept gifts"[19] Yet another motif in *Haaretz* cartoons depicted Arafat as preferring violence to any sort of discussion with Israel. Thus, even when invited to talks by Minister of Foreign Affairs Shimon Peres, the salient spokesman of Israel's "peace camp," he prefers to continue to clutch a large bomb.[20]

The Crisis of Israel's Left

One of the by-products of Camp David's failure and the eruption of the intifada was "the crisis of the left" in Israeli society. Focusing on the left is critical to an understanding of the fundamental change wrought in Israeli society during the course of the al-Aqsa intifada. The right was always opposed to the "peace process." A look at the positions of acclaimed spokespeople of various Zionist leftist parties plainly shows that almost all blindly swallowed the narrative devised by Barak and robustly implanted it in the media discourse.[21]

This development was not surprising in view of the courtship between Barak and most of the members of the Zionist left, particularly from the period when he campaigned for prime minister as Labor's candidate. The left had pinned enormous hopes on him, mostly fearing that Netanyahu, a man whose opinions, policies, and traits revolted them, would remain in office. One indication of this appreciation of Barak is Beilin's dedication in his book, *Madrikh le-yona petzu'ah* (Guide for a Wounded Dove): "For Ehud Barak, who had the temerity to pursue peace," along with the chapter titles, which do not mask his opinion of the leaders. The chapter on Netanyahu's reign was titled "The Netanyahu Years: Killing the Process Softly." The chapter on Barak's term had the neutral rubric, "The Days of Barak."

When Barak returned from the failed Camp David negotiations and listed his reasons for faulting the other side, the Zionist left discovered not only that the partner for peace had been lost but also that the Palestinian leadership sought to destroy the state of Israel. As this "revelation" sank in, the dividing line between the rationale of Israel's "waking left" coming to its senses blended in easily with that of the Israeli right.[22] Both, of course, acted under the impact of the extraordinary rash of violence, but both also alienated themselves from Palestinian complexities. This tendency can be seen in the statements following acts of terror committed by Hamas and Islamic Jihad. Like a mantra, right and left repeated the hackneyed assertion that Israel held the PA and Arafat responsible for the terror. The differences between Palestinian groups and their radically different agendas were obscured beyond all recognition. Moreover, in the ranks of the Zionist left as well, statements could be heard to the effect that, in the prevailing circumstances, "there is no one to talk to and nothing to talk about." This is not to say that the contrasts between left and right on the Palestinian question or the possible resumption of the political process utterly vanished.[23] It merely shows that all that was revealed after the failed summit were a number of simplistic claims shared by left and right that, taken together, made up the consensus in Israel's political discourse. Few were the voices that called for a serious public review to sweep away the fog consistently spread by official spokespeople: What were the details of the proposals Israel made at Camp David? What exactly were the reactions of the Palestinian and US sides? Why did Barak refuse to meet with Arafat for any significant talks, despite the counsel of most of his advisers and the US hosts? What effect did Israel's statements and actions have on the positions of the Palestinian camp? And exactly which Palestinian groups resorted to violence and terror against Israelis?

It is important to note that not all Oslo supporters disappeared, nor were Oslo opponents on the radical left (most of whom do not define themselves as Zionist) silenced. In this context, it is worth noting author David Grossman's reasoned statement, warning, at the height of the incitement in the public discourse, against the damage caused by the hegemonic narrative. If Israel wished to end the dangerous situation, he noted, "she had to wake up and re-store to the larger story of the conflict the parts that had been wiped out and suspended from belief in the past two years. If we fail to replant the recent in-tifada in its historical context, no mutual understanding will sprout here, and without this we will not truly recover."[24] At the same time, the large public that defined itself as leftist and as the voice of support for Oslo vanished from the landscape. The media now furnished breast-beating leftists with a capa-cious podium. People who only a day before had strutted about like pure white doves suddenly and from every possible stage confessed to a rude awakening: peace with the Palestinians was a delusion. All at once they sub-scribed to the wonderfully accurate rhetoric and arguments that had domi-nated Israel's media and establishment discourse since the summer of 2000. The resulting medley of voices was now made up of the waking left, state leaders, and media analysts. Former minister Shlomo Ben-Ami summoned all his talents as a historian to situate the attitude toward Arafat in a wider con-text. In mid-July 2002, in a personal note appraising the dire crisis, he stated: "I agree that it was a historic mistake to bring him [Arafat] here; it almost cost us the state of Israel. At several points in time, we should have caught our-selves." With a pinch of criticism, he added: "But as a historian, I say that only now have the conditions ripened for Arafat's de-legitimization."[25] A few days earlier, the *Haaretz Friday Magazine* had run an interview with author Amos Oz, long regarded as the left's ideological compass. Oz was visibly shaken by Camp David's failure. For years, he had wholeheartedly supported partition-ing the disputed land; now, he sounded most pessimistic about the chances of peace between Israel and the Palestinians. The fuzzy premise underlying his words was identical to the message that, in fact, Barak had hoped to convey: "I can speak for myself: I have unilaterally retreated from what I have been saying for thirty years, for I assumed that if the Palestinians were offered what Ehud Barak offered them at Camp David they would respond with a counter-proposal. I confess I never imagined that the proposed two-state and two-capital solution and the return of 92 or 95 or 97 percent of the territory would serve as a trigger for a wave of war against us. It has caused me the most pro-found shock."[26]

The symbiosis between Barak's narrative spin and the positions espoused by the waking Zionist left is best embodied in a series of articles and inter-views by historian Benny Morris. To the simplistic assertions of Israel's dis-course ("the Palestinians' true face has been revealed," "Arabs can't be trusted," etc.), Morris added assorted historical arguments and academic scholarship that continue to be debated in diverse frameworks. His ground-breaking studies on the Israeli-Palestinian conflict rightfully earned him the reputation of an impartial historian. In the autumn of 2001, he gave a number of lectures at US universities, marking the start of a personal journey to dis-cursive provinces both inside and outside Israel. For most of the audience that heard him speak at Berkeley's Theological Institute at the time, his words were like a bolt from the blue. To some, they tasted like honey. The two sides involved in the al-Aqsa intifada were waging a PR war, and Israel's press attaché in San Francisco reported on Morris's Berkeley talk to Jerusalem's Foreign Ministry, which rushed to release a juicy press communiqué: Morris, the white-winged Israeli dove, in no uncertain terms blames the Palestinians and their leadership for the deteriorating situation; straight talk that could well serve Israeli interests in the campaign for local and world public opinion. Morris, in fact, stirred the pot. Over the coming months, he was to devote a good deal of his time to a series of articles presenting the most coherent stance of Israel's waking left on the processes at work between Israelis and Palestinians. No longer a loose statement in an interview or an article, as many of his political camp had been apt to produce, but substantiated writing with lucid attitudes and arguments. The reactions of the critics, detractors as well as supporters, were not long in coming. Morris was soon asked for an article by the editor of Britain's newspaper, the *Guardian*, which is identified with the European left, devotes a good deal of space to the Israeli-Arab conflict, and takes a rather critical line on Israel.

"The rumour that I have undergone a brain transplant is (as far as I can remember) unfounded," was how Morris, with typical cynicism, opened the *Guardian* article that was to provoke further reaction.[27] He gave a number of reasons for the radical change in his view of Arab intentions toward Israel. One was Syria's rejection of far-reaching peace overtures made on various occasions by Rabin, Peres, and Barak. Syria's position represented a "basic refusal to make peace with the Jewish state," which was destined to suffer the fate of the crusader state in the Middle Ages. Not mincing his words, Morris said that the refusal to live in peace with the state of Israel had over the generations molded also the ideas and policy of Palestinian leaders. Barak ("a sincere and courageous leader") had exposed the rejectionism of Arafat (an "inveterate liar"). Israel's proposals in the course of 2000 had shown up the Palestinians for what they really were: adamantly opposed to any sort of recognition of Israel's right to exist as a Jewish and Zionist state. This outlook is shared by Israel's Palestinian citizens (a "pro-Palestinian irredentist time bomb"). The ineluctable conclusion is as clear as day: the Palestinians are not interested in ending the occupation, but want "all of Palestine and as few Jews in it as possible." Their insistence on a right of return faithfully reflects this attitude. The struggle is thus for control of the entire disputed land, and it will continue until one of the sides manages to crush the other and gain a demographic majority in the entire area between the Jordan River and the Mediterranean Sea. A blacker possibility is that the land will be home to neither of the two peoples, but will become a nuclear wasteland as a result of war.

In another *Guardian* article, Morris discussed at length the possibility that transfer would determine the future of the conflict over the disputed land.[28] The question of Zionism's approach to the idea and feasibility of transfer has interested him for years, and his writings on the subject are based on a painstaking reading of masses of documents. In contrast, Islam, Arab societies, and the policies of their leaders are not topics that fall within his scholarship, yet this has caused him no pause in issuing confident analyses of their ostensible influence on Palestinian society. In the *Guardian* article, he restated his research conclusions that transfer was imprinted on Zionism from its inception. The fathers of Zionism were persuaded that the success of the national enterprise in the end would displace the Arabs from the land of Israel. In the 1930s and 1940s, against the background of the Arab revolt—a Palestinian all-out revolt against both the British authorities and the Zionists—and the search for political solutions, Zionist leaders girded their loins and discussed the idea in earnest. According to Morris, at that stage in the closed talks, two prominent Arab leaders (Emir Abdullah of Transjordan and Nuri Said, an Iraqi minister) and senior British officials expressed support for the idea of population exchange as an accompaniment to a partition plan so as to ensure a solid Jewish majority in the area slated for a Jewish state and a definite Arab minority in the area to be allocated for an Arab state. Like the Zionist leadership, where consensus favored these principles, these leaders too doubted the feasibility of transfer and were, of course, wary of going public on the idea. Morris, in books that crowned him a "new historian," documented the uprooting of some 700,000 Palestinians in the course of 1948, although he made it clear that there had been no preconceived plan to execute transfer. On one occasion, when asked if he would be prepared to live in a state that transferred out some of its citizens, he replied: "I certainly wouldn't want to live in an Arab state," adding, "as for the other possibility [the transfer of Arabs], I would have to see."[29]

Some months later, Morris was invited to attend a lecture by Ehud Barak at a closed forum in Jerusalem. He believed that Barak should publicize his version of the failure of the Camp David negotiations in order to counter the narrative being spread by the Palestinians and their supporters. This encounter led to a number of meetings in which he interviewed Barak and soon transcribed hours of tapes into a long article that found its way onto the prestigious pages of the *New York Review of Books* (13 June 2002). The same issue also ran an article by Robert Malley and Hussein Agha, who presented a viewpoint that was entirely different from Barak's. Malley had been Clinton's special assistant for Arab-Israeli affairs and a member of the American delegation to the Camp David negotiations. Agah has been involved in Israel-Palestinian affairs for more than thirty years. In the article, Barak once again blamed Arafat for the Israeli-Palestinian predicament but added, as is evident from a close reading, a new charge to his carefully spun narrative, a charge that until then had not been uttered in public by Israel's Zionist left. The Palestinians had acted as they did because "they are products of a culture in which to tell a lie . . . creates no dissonance. They don't suffer from the problem of telling lies that exists in Judeo-Christian culture. Truth is seen as an irrelevant category. There is only that which serves your purpose and that which doesn't."[30] With this slanderous statement, Barak could easily join the unflattering list of people who wield religion and culture to explain the behavior of societies while blatantly ignoring the context of events, not to mention the determinist assumption that certain cultures are burdened by an irremovable millstone ruling out the possibility of their ever changing their outlooks. Two weeks later, all the same writers published reactions to the previous articles in the magazine. This time, the Israeli article bore the signature of both Morris and Barak. It was no longer an inquisitive historian's interview of a former prime minister, but a joint article attesting to a meeting of minds on the stated positions.[31] Morris, who for years had been identified as the prime mover behind the phenomenon of Israel's "new historians," with this article gave expression to his complete embrace of Barak's problematic thesis. The former prime minister could note with satisfaction that his stance had won the academic legitimacy of a respected historian in the study of the Israeli-Palestinian conflict.

In an article published in the *New Republic* some ten months later, Morris sketched a self-portrait, as it were, of the change his views had undergone. His studies on the Arab-Israeli conflict, he said, had left him with the feeling that Palestinian history is throughout accompanied by the "instinctive rejectionism that runs like a dark thread through Palestinian history—a rejection, to the point of absurdity, of the history of the Jewish link to the land of Israel; a rejection of the legitimacy of Jewish claims to Palestine; a rejection of the right of the Jewish state to exist."[32] Since the 1930s, he argued, the ideological positions of the Zionist and Palestinian national movements had developed asymmetrically. While Zionist ideology increasingly retreated from the maximalist idea that the land was "all mine," the Palestinian national movement continued to cling to it. He went on to consider the negative features of Palestinian society, describing as "signs of a sickness of the soul" the broad support pervading Palestinian society for suicide bombers sowing terror and destruction among Israelis. From his standpoint, the Oslo process was a huge ruse by Arafat to pull the wool over Israeli eyes. Palestinian statements in support of a two-state solution according to the 1967 borders were inconsistent with their repeated demand for "a right of return." Morris nevertheless ended on a somewhat optimistic note. In his estimation, the Clinton program (December 2000) defined the only possible framework for peace on the condition that the Palestinians relinquish "their dream of destroying Israel" and discard their insistence on "the right of return."

Most of Morris's declarations were published in English, attracting little attention from the Israeli public. This changed at once in the wake of an interview he gave to the *Haaretz Friday Magazine* (9 January 2004). Ostensibly a review of two of Morris's republished books, the interview dealt with them only partially. The books well reflect his field of research, namely the Arab-Israeli conflict from the perspective of Israel's leadership in the prestate *yishuv* and the state of Israel. Morris's studies do not deal with contemporary Arab society or with Islam, even though his categorical assertions (in both the interview and the articles cited above) might give the contrary impression. The many reactions to the interview in Israel and abroad did not concern any new revelations of Israeli massacres or expulsions in the 1948 war or Morris's resolute conclusion that "Ben-Gurion was a transferist," who erred in not having ordered "a large expulsion" that would have "cleansed the whole country—the whole Land of Israel, as far as the Jordan River." He drew sharp—and justifiable—criticism for his provocative and baseless depictions of Muslims and Arabs in general and the Palestinians in particular. Once again, Morris placed Palestinian hostility to Israel in the context of "Islam and Arab culture." Palestinian society today, he said bluntly, "is in the state of being a serial killer. It is a very sick society, mentally." As to an appropriate "prescription," his response was chilling: "Something like a cage has to be built for them. I know that sounds terrible. It is really cruel. But there is no choice. There is a wild animal there that has to be locked up in one way or another." Asked what caused the dramatic change in his views, Morris replied once again that Palestinian refusal to accept Barak and Clinton's offers in the latter half of 2000 had hardened his earlier doubts into certainty: Arafat had deceived Israel from the beginning. Worse than that, "the entire Palestinian national elite is prone to see us as Crusaders and is driven by the phased plan," which is why they will not yield on the right of return. It is difficult to determine to what degree these words reflect a widespread mood in Israeli society, including the Zionist left. Nonetheless, one cannot ignore the possibility that Morris merely said out loud what others are already thinking. It is worth noting that, immediately after likening Palestian society to a "wild animal," Morris told his interviewer, who seemed to be somewhat taken aback by both the substance and style of his words: "I still think of myself as left-wing. I still support in principle two states for two peoples."[33]

The thumping that Palestinian society and the Palestinian leadership took in Israel's public discourse was only one side of the coin; the other was the measures Israel resorted to in order to destroy the PA's infrastructure of control. As the intifada intensified, the IDF stepped up military action against targets identified with the PA and redoubled its efforts to degrade the leadership, especially Arafat. Israeli spokespeople repeated the refrain that the PA was no partner for a political process, that its leadership and apparatus dealt in terror, and that accordingly Israel would oppose it consistently. The latent assumption was that the IDF's ongoing strikes would bring the Palestinians to the necessary realization that Arafat and the PA were harmful to the interests of the Palestinian people and the Palestinian people had best be rid of them. The obsessive focus on Arafat ignored the different agendas of various Palestinian organizations and groups and the fact that they—Hamas, Islamic Jihad, and the PFLP and PDFLP—had long protested the PA and its political policy. Similar

criticism was sometimes heard from activists who filled the ranks of organizations under Arafat's leadership. The conflict of interests between the veteran
leadership cadre and the new generation of leaders that had sprung up in the
Occupied Territories since the 1980s had left a palpable mark. This process did
not receive the notice it deserved in analyses and assessments of positions and
policies in Palestinian society. Nor did Israel's media discourse pay sufficient
attention to the repercussions for Palestinian society of the ongoing clashes between the IDF and the Palestinian population or of the expansion of settlements, even though it was widely understood that they have a significant effect
on the attitudes and actions of various groups. Attention to these processes
might have balanced the common impression in the public discourse that Israel
is the injured party, merely reacting quite naturally and even with relative restraint to unprecedented Palestinian violence.

Notes

1. On this trend, see: Dor, '*Itonut tachat hashpa'ah*. For a study on similar trends
in Israel's media news coverage, see Cohen and Wolfsfeld, *Framing the Intifada*.
2. *Haaretz*, 14 June 2001.
3. Within a few months, these same claims were put to the test except that, this
time, the circumstances were reversed. In mid-November 2001 Abu Dhabi TV presented a satire on Sharon as Dracula enjoying Arab blood. Israel's Ministry of Foreign
Affairs soon protested to the UN, and official Israel soon got hold of the footage for a
costly PR campaign. The incident was reported at length on the online version of
Yedioth Ahronoth, drawing a most interesting Israeli response; almost a quarter of the
66 reactions related to Yatzpan's satire. See www.ynet.co.il/articles/1,7340,
L-1321789,FF.html (in Hebrew). It is not difficult to discern the manipulation of the
significance ascribed by the public to the substance of the satire. As in the case of Yatzpan's satire of Mubarak, so too in the Abu Dhabi program, most of the public related
indulgently to the mockery of the other side's leader and angrily to criticism of it.
4. *Haaretz*, 30 August 2002. Yaalon's statement was preceded by no less harsh
words uttered in an interview with Major General Dan Halutz. *Haaretz Friday Magazine*, 23 August 2002.
5. Ibid., 30 August 2002. A similar conclusion was also put forward by Ben-
Ami, who contended in his memoirs that the Camp David summit had failed because
of, among other things, "the opposition [of the Palestinian leadership] to the very
moral right of a Jewish state to exist, the refugee ethos, and Islamic fundamentalism
that in principle repudiates any claim or historic Jewish right to the Holy Sites." Ben-
Ami, *Chazit lelu oref*, p. 461.
6. Reich, "Reporters and Sources."
7. *Haaretz*, 12 November 2002.
8. Beilin, *Madrikh le-yona petzu'ah*, pp. 256–257.
9. Sher, *Bemerhak neggi'ah*, p. 368. In his book on Barak, Drucker devoted a
chapter to this phenomenon (*Harikiri*, pp. 324–336). He concluded, "Barak is con-
fused and to a large extent allows the army to conduct policy." Ibid., p. 330.
10. Ben-Ami, *Chazit lelu oref*, pp. 319–320.

11. In Ayalon's view, this "green light" would not necessarily help Israel and the United States force conditions on the Palestinian leadership. In his words, "at most we will lose the only partner on the other side able to conduct negotiations with us." *Haaretz*, 8 February 2002.

12. *Haaretz*, 23 May 2003.

13. *Haaretz*, 28 September 2001. Lavie's review dealt only with leading programs of Israel's Channel One (public television). *Ulpan Shishi*, "Friday Studio," is a weekly roundup, and *Yoman*, "Journal," is a weekly news magazine (both air on Friday prime time).

14. *Haaretz Friday Magazine*, 1 February 2002. I offered a critical rebuttal of the arguments of this influential correspondent a week later in the same magazine. See *Haaretz Friday Magazine*, 8 February 2002.

15. Benny Morris, "Camp David and After: An interview with Ehud Barak," *The New York Review of Books*, 13 June 2002.

16. My translation of *Haaretz*, 12 August 2001.

17. In a *Jerusalem Post* ad by Women for Israel's Tomorrow (7 December 2001), Arafat is seen speaking to the media ("I have ordered 100 per cent effort to end the attacks on Israel"), together with Goebbels (who headed Nazi propaganda), pointing to him and saying, "This man is a bigger liar than I was." The fact that the ad speaks of Arafat but aims at a wider political target is evident from the text under the cartoon. Here, the public is invited to sign a petition entitled "No to a Palestinian state."

18. *Haaretz*, 22 November 2000.

19. *Haaretz*, 6 June 2001.

20. *Haaretz*, 10 August 2001. After one of Peres's talks with Arafat, Ze'ev somewhat modified his depiction of the Palestinian leader. Arafat is shown speaking on the phone with Peres while shooting in every direction. The words placed in his mouth by the cartoonist ("Speak up! There's shooting here!!!") are meant to expose Arafat's obvious duplicity. Ibid., 31 August 2001.

21. This is not the place to discuss the characteristics of the Israeli left. It is worth mentioning, however, that the dividing line between left and right corresponds almost exactly to support for or opposition to a peace process with Arabs and Palestinians. With regard to the leftist discourse, one must distinguish between the Zionist left (all of whom vote for Labor, Meretz, and, to some extent, Shinui) and citizens who, in one form or another, define themselves as non-Zionists, lending their support to the various Arab parties (Balad, Hadash, Ra'am). Most of the latter's activities, however, take place outside the party and parliamentary framework.

22. The "waking left" describes a common tendency among Israel's left (after the failed negotiations at Camp David) to reject their traditional stand, and even to admit that they were wrong and naive.

23. Amnon Lord, editor of the right-wing weekly newspaper *Makor Rishon*, in his book on the Israeli left claimed that this camp lived in a state "of conscious, political schizophrenia," marked "to a large extent by its commitment to the Palestinian struggle to the point of lending moral and political support to acts of terror." Lord, *Ibadnu kol asher yakar haya*, p. 8. In his words, "the centralization of the regime in Israel," the left's dominance in the media and the economy, enabled its elites to consolidate an "Oslo regime—a new regime in fact, not a peace agreement," that vigorously quashed its domestic opponents and blindly instituted a policy based on the illusion that real peace is possible with the Palestinians led by the PLO. Ibid., p. 133.

24. David Grossman, "Kibus ha-kibush" [Laundering the Occupation], *Haaretz*, 2 October 2002. Criticism of the Israeli narrative as to responsibility for the failure of the "peace process" and for the violence was voiced also by a number of senior jour-

nalists; for example, by B. Michael and Sylvie Keshet in their columns in *Yedioth Ahronoth*; by Gideon Levy, Amira Hass, Doron Rosenblum, Aviv Lavie, Meiron Benvenisti, and Itzhak Laor in *Haaretz*; and by Haim Hanegbi in *Maariv*. These voices went virtually unheard in the electronic media.

25. Interview with Shlomo Ben-Ami, www.bitterlemons.org/previous/bl150702 ed26.html.

26. *Haaretz Friday Magazine*, 10 January 2003 (my translation). An example of the "sobering up" of a key media figure may be found in the statements and writings of Ari Shavit, a senior *Haaretz* journalist. In an article (*Haaretz*, 15 October 2000) and TV appearance on "Tik Tikshoret" (Media File, 14 October 2000), Shavit contended that he and many of his colleagues had been led astray by the leaders of the Oslo process, that he and his colleagues had been blind, and they and Israeli society were now paying the price.

27. Morris, "Peace? No Chance," *Guardian*, 21 February 2002.

28. Morris, "A New Exodus for the Middle East?" *Guardian*, 3 October 2002.

29. See *Yedioth Ahronoth*, *Sheva'ah Yamim* (Friday Magazine), 23 November 2001.

30. Morris, "An Interview with Ehud Barak," *New York Review of Books*, 13 June 2002.

31. *New York Review of Books*, 13 June 2002, 27 June 2002.

32. Morris, "The Rejection." On Arafat as a peace rejectionist, see Judith Miller, *New York Times*, 11 November 2004.

33. Two weeks later, Morris published a response to the *Haaretz* interview to soften the tone of the interview, which he felt misrepresented him, and to retract some of his more provocative statements and generalizations. "I admit, I slipped here and there," he noted. Attempting to clarify his position, Morris added: "I do not support and did not support the extermination of the Indians, and I regret the use of the word 'cage.'" His main claims regarding Palestinian society in the past and present remained unchanged. Morris's response: "I Do Not Support [expulsion]," *Haaretz Friday Magazine*, 23 January 2004. For the original interview with Morris, see Ari Shavit, "Survival of the Fittest? An Interview with Benny Morris," *Haaretz Friday Magazine*, 9 January 2004.

8

September 11 and the Middle East

As the intifada continued, Israel sought to separate it from regional and global developments. The suppression of the Palestinian uprising was the top Israeli priority. But it soon emerged that US Middle Eastern policy after 9/11 could not be detached from the Israeli-Palestinian conflict. The collapse of the Twin Towers shook the earth, first in New York and then in Washington. The shockwaves sped through the United States and reverberated all around the globe. The attacks of 9/11 and its ghastly climax, broadcast live and aired over and over again, bore indelibly into the minds of billions of viewers worldwide. The sight of the aircraft flying toward the towers and the buildings collapsing like a house of cards became fixed images. An addictive virtual experience climaxing in interminable moments despite the known denouement and riveting viewers to the screen in disbelief. The soundless gliding of the two hijacked passenger planes headlong into the towers, the figures trapped inside swaying skyscrapers and waiting for help never to reach them all, the occupants who chose to leap to their death, the deafening roar of the toppling buildings, the huge clouds of dust over Manhattan—all became unforgettable scenes. An enormous mass of concrete and steel buried the victims deep beneath Ground Zero. The death toll, in New York, the Pentagon, and southwestern Pennsylvania, was 2,998 people. Even after the rubble was cleared, Americans, for months, went about as if still under the heavy cloud that had smothered the Big Apple. And even after emerging from the initial, all-embracing shock, they continued to show signs of the trauma of 9/11.

All eyes looked to Washington. In the White House, Capitol Hill, and the Pentagon, senior positions had been filled by neoconservative Republicans, and the conservative worldview left its fingerprints on the policies promoted by President George W. Bush, Vice President Dick Cheney, Secretary of Defense Donald Rumsfeld, and National Security Adviser Condoleezza Rice.

The collapse of the Twin Towers in New York and the havoc wreaked on Pentagon headquarters in Washington, D.C., did not bring down the strongest power on earth, but the blow to these symbol-laden targets caused considerable material and figurative damage, prompting the United States to reshape its security, foreign, and domestic policies. Under this administration, the attacks of 9/11 became the catalyst for a dramatic turning point in the policy of the one remaining superpower. The effects were felt first in North America and then in other parts of the world—in particular the Middle East. President Bush proclaimed "a global war on terror" even before the rubble stopped smoldering at Ground Zero. In principle, the fight against terror in all its forms was justified. But US diplomatic and military measures, as it soon transpired, were marred by faulty planning and evaluation stemming from the simplistic worldview of the administration's top brass. Its false assumptions and measures invited critical scrutiny of its course of action and intentions. The dissension began with the sweeping interpretation given by Bush and his senior aides to the term "terror" and the list of groups and regimes defined as terrorists. US resolve to let loose a global campaign and massive force before exhausting all other options brought it into confrontation and crises with other countries, including key Western states. The UN Security Council turned into an arena for diplomatic battles. The need to fight terror still enjoyed broad consensus, but the way to do so fueled increasing controversy.

On the whole, the mass media (notably TV's CNN, Fox News, and Sky, as well as the *New York Times* and *Washington Post*) presented a simplistic picture of the campaign, the forces involved, and their interests. Moral, cultural, and political divisions were soon marked out. The controversial thesis of a "clash of civilizations" authored by Harvard University's esteemed scholar Samuel Huntington was, in retrospect, taken as prophetic by broad sections of the public both within the United States and outside. A range of publications and studies on Islam and its extremism furnished ostensible corroboration for the campaign's religious and cultural roots.[1] The media discourse gorged on baseless assertions about Islamic extremism and Arab terror. Bush, early on, termed the campaign a "crusade," leaving an impression that would not fade away even after he included North Korea in the axis of evil, alongside Iraq and Iran. Administration leaders and supporters were hard put to eradicate the notion that the campaign was aimed primarily at Arab and Islamic groups and regimes. As the world war on terror got under way, the peoples of the Middle East found themselves in the eye of the storm. Driven by uncontrollable fury and compulsion, the Bush administration opened the Pandora's box of the twenty-first century. Protests and demonstrations against the US initiative were drowned out in the campaign tumult and ocean of words supplied by supporters of administration policy.

Overall, US policy was revamped to give priority to the global war on terror declared by Bush. The Middle East took shape as a main battle arena, significantly affecting US policy for the region. The United States reviewed its relations with Arab regimes, as well as its approach to the Israeli-Palestinian conflict. Although the adverse effects of continuing violence between the two sides were noted by US spokespeople, Washington clearly regarded other issues on the new American agenda as more important. Nonetheless, US leaders found themselves increasingly preoccupied with the Middle East from which they had previously sought to distance themselves. As the days passed, the Americans clearly tried to make the best of a bad situation. The 9/11 blow brought new clarity to "America's role in the world," Bush wrote on 11 September 2002 in the *New York Times*. The overriding goal of the war on terror was, he said, "America's greatest opportunity . . . to create a balance of world power that favors human freedom. We will use our position of unparalleled strength and influence to build an atmosphere of international order and openness in which progress and liberty can flourish in many nations. A peaceful world of growing freedom serves American long-term interests, reflects enduring American ideals." He ended the article by lending a universal dimension to the role of his country and, indeed, of his own leadership: "Today, humanity holds in its hands the opportunity to further freedom's triumph over all its age-old foes. The United States welcomes its responsibility to lead in this great mission."[2] The war on terror spread out over broad areas of the globe, but its repercussions became increasingly focused on the Middle East, particularly on Arab states and the toll of blood reaped by the lasting Israeli-Palestinian confrontation.

The reaction of official and unofficial Arab spokespeople to the events of 9/11 attested to the predicament they found themselves in. Invoking a wealth of religious, moral, and political reasons, the large majority condemned al-Qaeda's acts of terror and the attack on thousands of innocent victims. Harsh censure was voiced also by nonestablishment Islamic groups, including the Muslim Brotherhood. Two days after 9/11, Yusuf al-Qaradawi, one of the movement's more prominent spokesmen, lashed out at the terror act—while still finding fault with the United States and its Middle East policy—in a ruling that began: "We greatly regret what has happened as a result of the attack on the World Trade Center and other places in the United States, despite our opposition to American policy which tends to favor and support Israel."[3] Others objected to Osama bin Laden's call on Muslims to join the jihad he had declared. "Jihad against whom and for what purpose?" asked al-Hamid al-Ansari, dean of the faculty of Islamic law at the University of Qatar. In an article in the important Arabic newspaper *al-Hayat*, he lambasted bin Laden and his followers, questioned their authority to hand down (religious) rulings, and accused them of striking a blow not only against innocent people but also against Arabs and Muslims. He concluded by calling for a serious review of the Arab media discourse and school curricula, which together helped create an atmosphere where such extreme views could flourish.[4] A few days after

9/11, Mahmoud Darwish, the prominent Palestinian poet, wrote in *al-Ayam*, published in Ramallah: "There is only one name for the catastrophe that struck Washington and New York: the madness of terror. . . . Nothing can justify terror that melts down human flesh with metal, concrete, and dust. Nor can anything justify the division of the world into two camps that can never find a meeting ground: the one of absolute good, the other of absolute evil. Civilization is the sum total of all the world's cultures."[5]

There was no lack of support for al-Qaeda and Osama bin Laden, although the reports and pictures of large-scale, angry demonstrations across the Arab and Islamic world gave a false impression of the extent of support for bin Laden and for the use of terror as a legitimate means to promote goals. Still, there was no disguising the glee felt at US misfortune. The knockdown to the United States was chalked up as bin Laden's "success" and undoubtedly helped enhance his following. This point may help somewhat explain the pattern of Arab and Muslim identification: alongside those who cried "bin Laden, our leader," more people by far carried slogans denouncing the United States and its allies. On the face of it, it would appear from the Arab media discourse that a tiny minority identified with the acts attributed to al-Qaeda (even if we allow that not many would have dared to declare their public support). According to the most common claims raised, most of the Arab public did not look on bin Laden as a role model. Broad Arab sectors spurned the religious fanaticism that he stands for. They rejected the "Islamic agenda" advocated by the militants and pointed to the failure to institute it in Sudan, Iran, and, of course, Afghanistan. Arab countries have been grappling for years with the multiple challenges posed by Islamic movements, parties, and groups—including militant groups. Since the start of the twentieth century, a struggle has been waged across the Middle East over the character of the modern Arab state. One key factor in this ongoing debate is the place of religion in the political, constitutional, and social order, and the longer the debate lasts, the more evident the different goals and positions held by the various groups. Although the various Muslim Brotherhood movements have sought to promote an Islamic state and society from within the existing establishment and via legal means, militant groups opposed to this approach have chosen armed struggle instead and do not shrink from using terror against citizens and tourists alike. In Egypt alone, they have killed more than 1,000 people since 1993. The crumbling of the regime in Algeria, which began with the national elections in December 1991, quickly deteriorated into civil war. According to one estimate, the battle over the fate of Algeria has resulted in more than 100,000 dead, many from stark acts of terror.[6]

The Arab public discussion took place in various forums, notably on satellite television and first and foremost on al-Jazeera. The TV station's star shone ever more brightly against the background of the US-led war on al-Qaeda and Afghanistan's Taliban regime, under whose mantle bin Laden had operated undisturbed.[7] In the early stages of the US-British offensive against Afghanistan, the planners had obviously thought that this time, as in 1991, they would be able to filter the information transmitted to consumers of the electronic media. As in the war to eject Iraq from Kuwait, the US government (especially the Pentagon) hoped to keep control by having generals brief the press with approved information and close-ups of exact hits on military targets. Their experience in the Gulf War apparently led them to assume that leading international media would willingly cooperate. They were right. The Western media, apart perhaps from BBC World, presented the official positions. Military and terrorism analysts filled TV screens and press columns, and the descriptions and claims made by senior members of the Bush administration and their supporters were not really subjected to criticism. Their credibility was rarely questioned.[8]

It was left to leading Arab satellite stations to present the Arab and Muslim viewpoint, including that of the sworn enemies of the United States. The broadcasts were also an opening for a searching discussion of professional and ethical questions. Thus, for example, al-Jazeera's management tackled the issue of whether bin Laden and his adherents should be provided with a podium or whether his actions should be termed "terror." Ultimately, they decided to air the taped interviews with bin Laden's people, which were relayed to the station from the Qatar capital, Doha. Al-Jazeera first broke the US media taboo in deciding to broadcast an interview with bin Laden that had been recorded three years before 9/11, after the bombing of US embassies in Tanzania and Kenya (7 August 1998). Bin Laden had been allowed to expound on his worldview, on the goals of his organization, and on holy war (jihad) as the modus operandi of his choice. The Americans, at the time, had made the connection between the embassy bombing and al-Qaeda and, in reprisal, had fired missiles at his base in Afghanistan. Following 9/11 and the fingerprints that again led to al-Qaeda, al-Jazeera decided to air the interview once more. The broadcast, "Osama bin Laden Speaks," broke all viewing records of major Arab televisions stations. It was rerun the next day, with English subtitles for the benefit of viewers who did not know Arabic.

The broadcast, predictably, unleashed a torrent of reaction. Millions of viewers were eager for a glimpse of the man whose group had plotted the awesome crime. The interview enabled bin Laden to unfurl his fanatic doctrine before millions of Muslims, who were the chief target of his words. In an era in which the medium is often the message, bin Laden proved a master at marketing a dark, extremist doctrine. Calm, self-confident, and profoundly convinced of the justice of his moral path, the zealous, charismatic warrior expounded his ideology. Like the leaders of similar radical groups, he distinguished between the faithful of Islam and the infidels (headed by Christians and Jews), and described the United States and the West as the embodiment of evil and world exploitation. In many cases, he said, the faithful are ruled by an oppressive regime wherein religious leaders, who fail to institute Islamic law, derive their legitimacy from the establishment. The ruling elites collaborate with the infidel West, particularly with the United States, in order to secure their rule. The technological, military, and economic power of the United States allows it to do anything it pleases, including to support the oppression of Muslims. The plight of the Palestinians under Israeli occupation is a blatant expression of this dreadful state of affairs. Only jihad against the domestic and foreign exploiters can deliver the faithful from this impossible situation.

The Arab public and media discourse revolved around two ostensibly separate and penetrating issues. First, what is it about bin Laden's message that causes so many Muslims to identify with him? Second, what is it about the United States that causes so many (and not only fanatical Muslims) to oppose it, even in the sorry straits it has found itself since 9/11? As said, a large share of the expressions of support *for* bin Laden was really a protest *against* the United States and its symbols and policies; that support also bore the tokens of protest against Arab regimes and their policies. In the Western and Israeli media at times, the protest against US policies was presented simplistically as the identification of entire societies with terror against civilians—such as 9/11—and as advocacy for a fanatical Islamic order as championed by the radical group al-Qaeda and its ilk. Writers and interviewees in the Arab media frequently noted that the United States should carefully probe the reasons for the widespread abhorrence and objection inspired by its policies. Varied explanations (and often accusations) were offered. Most pointed to a connection between its unbalanced policy on the Arab-Israeli conflict and its negative image among substantial Arab and Muslim sectors. Arab commentators reiterated that reflexive tendency of the United States to side with Israel harmed the chances of reaching a just settlement of the Palestinian problem or Israel's further evacuation of occupied Arab territories. Egyptian Nobel Prize laureate in literature Naguib Mahfouz put forth a more comprehensive explanation: "The main lesson of what we saw on 11 September is that, in order to really be the master of the world, you need not weapons but justice." He, too, thought the Americans would do well to ask themselves: "How did we become so hated? And what should we do to become worthy of this leadership role by right? This, instead of merely attributing the causes solely to the evil of the perpetrators."[9]

The simplistic presentation by the Western media of legitimate Arab or Palestinian national struggles as terrorism provoked Arab criticism. And the well-known poet Nizar Qabani pointed out the absurdity of this in a poem entitled "I Am in Favor of Terror":[10]

> We are accused of terror
> if we defend rose
> and woman
> and glorious *Qasida*

and blue of sky
and homeland left without water
without air
without tent. Or she-camel
or black coffee!!

*   *   *

We are accused of terror
when we write of the remains of a homeland
in ruins.
Dismantled, dismembered
its rent limbs scattered all over
a homeland seeking its address
and a nation without name

*   *   *

We are accused of terror
when refusing to die
by the hand of Israeli bulldozers
digging in our land
digging in our history
digging in our new testament
digging in our Qur'an
digging in the land of our Prophets

Later in the poem, the poet describes the "new world" that the United States wishes to institute. An order hostile to Arabs ("Inherently loathing . . . the scent of desert dwellers"). Qabani concludes with the defiant cry of Arab spokespeople that, if to defend legitimate goals such as freedom is a sin, then they have no problem expressing support for this kind of "terror":

Because of all this
I shall raise my voice high.
I am for terror!
I am for terror!
I am for terror!

Other intellectuals, in contrast, were caustic about Islamic fanatics in the Arab camp. Egyptian playwright 'Ali Salem had sharp words for Islamic fanatics in the Arab camp who, he said, for years had cultivated a climate of animosity toward the West while cynically exploiting the media. In a satirical piece on al-Hayat's op-ed page (5 November 2001) titled "New Curriculum to Teach Extremism to Our Children," Salem declared that he was hunting for funding to set up a kindergarten to turn out tomorrow's extremists, the cleverest of whom will take their place as journalists, intellectuals, and thinkers, serving as newspaper editors, broadcasters, and officials in all walks of life.

The curriculum in the imaginary kindergarten would expose the ingrained duplicity of the "others," the foreigners and infidels who on the surface advocate only such values as freedom, democracy, human rights, and progress. Sparing no sarcasm for the self-avowed supporters of suicide bombers, he wrote: "You [the kindergarten children] will easily see that they [the "others"] love life, and that is their weakness, which we will exploit; while we love death, and guard it. Don't believe that Allah, blessed be he, created life for us so that we might live it and enjoy its beauty; Allah created life and us to test our ability to rebel against it, not to submit to it, he created life for us so that we would despise it and shed it at the first opportunity." Hatred of the "other" will ultimately lead to hatred of nature, of life, and even of self. The absurdity of this blind hatred, against which he has protested for decades, speaks from the closing sentence: "Hate the seashores, hate the flowers and roses, hate the wheat fields, hate the trees, hate the stars, hate music, hate all forms of art, literature and science, hate refinement and sensitivity, hate logic and understanding, hate your families and your compatriots, hate the others—all the others—hate yourselves, hate your teachers, hate me, hate this kindergarten, hate this life and all it contains."[11]

The realities challenged by Salem's piece are undeniable: recent decades have seen growing public support in Arab society for the proponents of an Islamic agenda. The controversy over "the Islamic current" lies at the heart of the public discussion in all Middle Eastern societies. But it has become much more intensive since 9/11 and the ensuing crises. Many have addressed the connection between the growth of militant groups and Arab political realities. The discussion turned the spotlight on tough issues, namely the interaction of religion and state, the values of democracy, and their implications for Arab societies. A call went out for Arab regimes to put their house in order, and it resonated. Pressure mounted to accelerate democratization and wide-ranging reform, especially in politics and the economy. Arab liberals, leftists, and Islamists demanded "democracy now." The unique circumstances of the period since 9/11 have led to similar proclamations by members of the ruling elites, including people in official positions. Thus, following Arab public discussion of "the day after" the war in Iraq, Hassan bin Talal, Jordan's former crown prince and today the head of a prestigious Arab institute, published an article that made waves. He aimed his words not at any specific Arab regime but at the ruling elites. Using language that was terse and to the point, he called on Arabs to look inward to their own societies and systems of government, weigh the lurking dangers of radicalization, institute reform, and speed up democratization.[12]

At the same time, there were enough other voices that spoke in slogans, pointing an accusing finger at "the West," "imperialism," and "Zionism," spokespeople who, with the flourish of a pen, strove to evade domestic problems and describe 9/11 as a conspiracy concocted by the United States or Israeli secret services. False charges were spread to the effect that the "Jews had had a hand in the foul deed because at the moment of impact, there were not many Jews in the Towers" or that it was inconceivable that bin Laden's crowd was responsible for the deed since it was so sophisticated that it required the sort of information and capabilities commanded only by state intelligence services and crack military units. Edward Said, writing two months after 9/11, cautioned the Arabs against falling into the dead-end trap of "anti-American" rhetoric. The article, headlined "Suicidal Ignorance," was sealed with a barb at what looked like a growing trend at the time: "It is not acceptable to sit in Beirut or Cairo meeting halls and denounce American imperialism (or Zionist colonialism for that matter) without a whit of understanding that these are complex societies not always truly represented by their governments' stupid or cruel policies." Legitimate Palestinian and Arab resistance must distance itself from the ignorance and belligerence directed at entire societies.[13] About a year later, 'Abd al-Muneim Sa'id, director of the al-Ahram Center for Political and Strategic Studies (Cairo), wrote: "Building is a long and arduous process; blaming others has always been easy and costs nothing. Denial is easy, whereas assuming responsibility is extremely difficult. After all, who wants to look at themselves in the mirror and see the truth?"[14]

Between Iraq and Palestine

The administration of George W. Bush set its sights on Iraq in the early stages of the global war on terror.[15] During the search for the fingerprints of the 9/11 assailants, leaks to the US media noted that intelligence information had uncovered a connection between Iraq and al-Qaeda. Administration officials began to cite the reports with greater frequency, though they were never proved. Iraq under Saddam Hussein was marked as a menace because of its long-range missiles and weaponry that had to be dismantled in the interests of the "free world" and the stability of the Middle East. As time wore on, the Bush administration and Britain under Prime Minister Tony Blair appeared more and more resolved to topple Saddam Hussein, claiming that, apart from the direct and indirect assistance his tyrannical regime extended to terror organizations, its possession of weapons of mass destruction (WMD) constituted a real threat to many countries.[16]

The unilateral moves by the United States and Britain on the Iraq question and the statements of their leaders drew sharp criticism from governments and public sectors all over the world. The leaders of France, Russia, and China, along with most Arab leaders, voiced their objections to military measures against Iraq, certainly before exhausting diplomatic and other avenues to resolve the crisis. Moreover, opponents of the war demanded that any action to be taken against Iraq follow discussion and majority approval by the

UN Security Council. The Bush administration viewed these demands as useless and not constructive, dubbing them yet another endeavor to appease a despot. The allusion was clear: Saddam Hussein was Adolf Hitler's double, and Iraq's Ba'ath regime was the contemporary Nazi Germany. The Security Council devoted several months to the Iraq crisis, the delegates of its permanent and temporary members carefully reviewing the reports of the UN weapons inspectors headed by Hans Blix and of the director of the International Atomic Energy Agency, Muhammad al-Baradei.[17] Meanwhile, US and Iraqi leaders resorted to verbal fisticuffs. In mid-February 2003, several weeks before the US-British offensive against Iraq, there were huge antiwar demonstrations as millions of protesters took to the streets in London, Paris, Rome, Los Angeles, and Tokyo. According to public opinion polls, there was 57 percent opposition to the war in France and 52 percent in Britain. Most of the words and banners of the protesters ranged themselves against US aggression and Britain's tendency to follow suit. A very small minority voiced support for Saddam's regime. Both, of course, served the Iraqi public relations campaign.

Among the Arab public, criticism of the United States and Britain rose steadily, in the main corresponding to the Western antiwar message. The opposition did not necessarily reflect support for Saddam Hussein and his government but did express a genuine concern for the Iraqi people and fear of the consequences for the civilian population. One prominent claim in the Arab public discourse was that the impending war was not motivated by lofty ideals of liberating the Iraqi people—as most American spokespeople would have it—since the Bush administration could not care less about Iraqi living conditions. The main goal of the United States was to cause an earthquake in the Middle East, replace regimes inhospitable to the United States, and take over the vast oil fields. Iraq was merely the first stop on an expedition by US administration hawks, who did not even bother to conceal their megalomaniac ambitions but showered threats on Arabic and Islamic governments and groups. By gaining control of Iraq's mighty oil reserves and maintaining an enormous military presence on Iraqi soil, the United States would make Iraq the vanguard of US forces in the Middle East. This massive presence was to serve as a warning to any group or government that sought to undermine the new order desired by Washington.

Various Arab spokespeople demanded that Arab leaders take a more forceful stance against the United States and oppose the Iraqi offensive in every way possible. Many also objected to the Bush administration's sweeping definition of "terror" and the doggedness of its leaders to put unprecedented military might into the field without having substantiated the touted cause for the offensive and while contemptuously minimizing the heavy toll to be exacted from the Iraqi people. As discussion swelled, the United States took on an ever-darker image in Arab and Islamic eyes. In the months leading up to the offensive and even more so during the military action itself, US conduct struck broad public sectors as the imperiousness of an empire, spurning no means to achieve its goal. The US vision for "the day after" the invasion appeared appallingly simplistic and aroused both concern and rage. Arab public opposition to the world's strongest power hinged on two key issues: the toppling of existing regimes and the coercion of values and norms alien to the local population. These apprehensions were voiced even by those who felt disgust with Saddam's rule, people who had not hesitated to blast Iraqi policy for years prior to the current crisis. They feared that Iraq was not the final stop on the Bush expedition, fueled by superpower resources, to promote a new world order. The United States hoped to lay the foundations for this long expedition by remaking the Middle East.

The connection the Americans made between bin Laden's al-Qaeda and Saddam Hussein's Ba'ath regime was rejected by the Arabs. In addition, Arabs emphasized that US claims of Iraqi WMD were baseless. Unofficial spokespeople noted that the very charge exposed the longstanding double standards of US policy in the Middle East, in which US governments, whether Republican or Democrat, treated Israel with kid gloves and the Arabs with an iron fist. The United States chose, for example, to ignore the fact that Israel was the only state in the region with nuclear weapons. Wide media coverage was given to the constant persecution (since 9/11) of Arabs and Muslims living in the United States or wishing to travel there, contributing indirectly to the blackening of the United States and the questioning of its image as the bastion of democracy and freedom of speech. With a mixture of rationalism, demagoguery, and simplistic presentations, Arab interviewers and interviewees asked: Where is the freedom of speech that is supposed to be so characteristic of the American media? What happened to CNN and other leading television networks that they so quickly enlisted on the side of the Bush administration? "You are either with us or against us," Bush said; is that kind of remark consistent with democratic values? Is the United States in favor of allowing criticism only when it, itself, is not the butt of it? Is all criticism of the current Bush administration to be taken as identification with terror? Are not the administration's reactions to its critics a form of intellectual terror? Is the demand that Arab governments stand alongside the United States—and ignore the opinion of their own public—a thrust for democratization or the reverse? The long-term struggle for democratization, numerous opposition groups reiterated, must be fought domestically, not at foreign dictates. "Democratization is in our hands, not in American hands," wrote Na'aman Jum'ah, the editor of Egypt's oppositionist newspaper *al-Wafd*, in early July 2003. Almost no one in the Arab media came to the US defense except, of course, US spokespeople; they occasionally continued to be invited to voice their opinions in leading Arab media channels, even at the height of the Iraqi offensive.

Most of the Arab regimes had a fair assessment of their limited ability to take a tough stance against the Americans in the given circumstances. Weighty interests hung in the balance, certainly from the perspective of the governments of Egypt, Jordan, Saudi Arabia, and most of the Gulf and North African states. For years these states had been forging closer ties and cooperation with the United States. The civilian and military aid that the United States was prepared to grant them, in addition to commercial and economic advantages, had no substitute. For many Arab rulers, these relations were the main guarantee of their continued rule. Their policies, in the new crisis, were aimed first at preventing any significant damage to their ties with the superpower. However, these governments were highly conscious of the substantial public criticism clamoring for firm action against the United States. Most of the Arab regimes found a way out of the predicament by stepping up "quiet" communication with the United States, including on intelligence and military matters, by liberally scattering declarations of support for the Iraqi people, and by permitting oppositionist groups to hold protest demonstrations without, however, letting them run amok.

The tensions between Arab oppositionist groups and Arab regimes continued to build up, and the wave of antiwar demonstrations in major cities around the globe intensified the internal Arab public debate. The complex situation was widely covered by leading satellite channels (e.g., al-Jazeera and Abu Dhabi) and the independent press (headed by *al-Hayat,* published in London). Ostensibly, the Arabs should have been pleased by the worldwide protest wave. But these demonstrations highlighted the stark contrast with their own countries, the overall Arab stance, and that of the Arab governments. The relatively small number of domestic demonstrations that did take place earned the dubious epithet of "the silence of the grave," and the language of diplomacy adopted by decisionmakers was written off as "burying their heads in the sand." The source of the trouble, according to oppositionist circles, was the denial of freedom of organization and freedom of speech. A sense of gloom and doom stole through Arab society; the Arabs had been caught up in a vicious cycle from which they would be hard put to extricate themselves. Edward Said gave expression to the oppressive atmosphere of the Arab discourse at this stage in an article titled, "An Unacceptable Helplessness." Like other Arab intellectuals, the Palestinian thinker wondered:

> How can a region of almost 300 million Arabs wait passively for the blows to fall without attempting a collective roar of resistance and a loud proclamation of an alternative view? Has the Arab will completely dissolved? Even a prisoner about to be executed usually has some last words to pronounce. Why is there now no last testimonial to an era of history, to a civilisation about to be crushed and transformed utterly, to a society that despite its drawbacks and weaknesses nevertheless goes on functioning? Arab babies are born every hour, children go to school, men and women marry and

work and have children, they play, and laugh and eat, they are sad, they suffer illness and death. There is love and companionship, friendship and excitement. Yes, Arabs are repressed and misruled, terribly misruled, but they manage to go on with the business of living despite everything. This is the fact that both the Arab leaders and the United States simply ignore when they fling empty gestures at the so-called "Arab street" invented by mediocre Orientalists. But who is now asking the existential questions about our future as a people?[18]

These and many other questions deluged the Arab media. The criticism was aimed mainly at the ruling elites, who were blamed for the unbearable Arab dependency on the United States, and it of course bemoaned the absence of democracy, which would have compelled the regimes to adopt an entirely different policy in the Iraqi crisis. Religious oppositionists censured Arab regimes for not listening to the rising voices. During the Iraqi crisis, this charge was made repeatedly by Yusuf al-Qaradawi, popular sheik and prominent spokesman of the Muslim Brotherhood, on al-Jazeera's prime-time weekly talk show, *al-Shari'a wal-Hayat* (Islamic Law and Life), where he features regularly. Nor did the Arab media, particularly the press, mince words about Saddam Hussein and his Ba'ath government. He was portrayed as a dictator who, in his twenty-five years at the helm, had embroiled his people in a series of wars, notably against Iran and Kuwait, and had employed horrible measures against Iraqi civilians and groups. Another key topic raised by official and unofficial Arab spokespeople throughout the crisis was the direct link between the worldwide campaign against terror and the Israeli-Palestinian crisis. Israel was pictured as the Middle Eastern state standing to gain the most from a prolonged global antiterror campaign. The United States and Britain, after all, were leading an unremitting war against regimes and groups that Israel regarded as a serious threat. Again and again, various Arab spokespeople said that Israel was exploiting the situation that had developed as a result of 9/11 to forcefully quell the intifada and impede the chances of resuming an earnest political process. The IDF's policy of targeted killings and strong-arm policies against the Palestinian population, especially intifada activists, was "state terror." Anyone interested in achieving stability in the Middle East would do well to restrain Israel.

At the end of February 2003, the die was cast. The United States and Britain decided that diplomacy had been exhausted, and two weeks later, President Bush issued Saddam a vague ultimatum to disarm or else: he and his regime would be responsible for the consequences. The Iraqi offensive had become a certainty. The Bush-Blair decision was unusual. The Security Council had not lent them the legitimacy they sought; millions of protestors all over the world (including in Britain and, to a lesser extent, in the United States) had demonstrated opposition to the war; and the cause for the offensive, Saddam's ostensible possession of WMD, had not been proved. On Thursday, 20 March,

US and British forces launched a massive assault on Iraqi installations. In the coming days and—mainly—nights, various points were targeted by the cruise missiles and "smart" bombs unleashed by the strike forces. The campaign's progress was the talk of the day all over the world. Billions of viewers became virtual participants in a faraway war, following the massive bombings by US and British troops, the movement of forces along different attack routes in Iraq, and the occasional opposition they encountered from locals.

Israel took the approach that others were to be commended for doing the work of the just. In the weeks preceding battle, the question of security took over the media discourse, with TV channels falling over themselves to sign up new stars—reserve generals in the role of regular commentators. As if that were not enough, a major general was appointed "national commentator" (dubbed by the media as the "national pacifier," although, as it soon transpired, his every appearance only raised the anxiety level of the public, which feared that Scud missiles would again be launched at Israel, as had happened in the Gulf War). There was no need for sophisticated analysis in order to arrive at a highly predictable conclusion. The elucidations fed the public so intensively were based on recycled information and assessments emanating from the security and political establishment, as well as from American media channels, most of which embraced official positions as an impartial depiction of developments in the Iraqi campaign. There was no real attempt to examine the ensemble of causes behind the war. Traditional loyalty to Uncle Sam found expression in a perfect identification with every US move and statement and an utter lack of wonder or probes. Official assertions, almost without exception, were received as a full, objective reflection of the actual situation. After the commentators established that there was no doubt that Iraq possessed WMD, the focus turned to another issue: when would Saddam Hussein release his Scuds at Israel, what warheads would they carry, and what would be the IDF reaction? The wider aspects of the war became marginal. Military analysts had a heyday. Apart from parroting uniformed and reserve generals who filled the TV studios, they tried to impress viewers with an array of visual stunts—computerized simulations of the movement of forces. The movements of Israeli correspondents, who had furtively gained access to the battle arena, were also eagerly followed—a sure giveaway of the provincialism of Israel's media discourse.

The US-British plan of attack was based on air, sea, and land forces and advanced weapons systems that landed Iraq a stunning blow. Iraq's takeover was accomplished quite quickly and with relatively few casualties for the aggressors. Iraq did not make good on its prewar promise "to set a fire" under the Americans and British in a campaign that would turn the country into a "cemetery for the invading forces." Its army was crushed beneath superior might, and Saddam failed in his two strategic goals, to preserve his regime and thwart the invading armies. Nevertheless, the one remaining superpower was about to learn that instant conquest is no recipe for stability or a new order. Bush's declaration of victory (1 May 2003), delivered against a background poster reading "Mission Accomplished," soon proved to be wishful thinking.[19] Certainly, the US-British offensive achieved its main goal to the maximum, putting an end to Saddam's regime and capturing Saddam himself (13 December 2003). But getting a handle on daily life in Iraq proved far more difficult and complex than the planners had conceived. After the battle dust settled, it turned out that the conquering forces had no real program for "the day after." The express US aim, like the code name for the offensive, had been to bring "freedom to Iraq." Soon, however, it found itself enmeshed in the daily face-off typical of a conquering force and a local population, becoming the object of all civilian demands and, worse still, of violence committed by remaining Ba'ath loyalists. The ranks of the opponents were apparently inflated by an unclear number of non-Iraqi Islamic militants. The number of American and British casualties rapidly outstripped their losses in the two weeks it had taken to seize Iraq.

In addition, the war in Iraq seriously dented the image of the world's sole remaining superpower. More and more people around the globe saw the United States on the threshold of the twenty-first century as a high-handed empire, as the police officers of a worldwide beat bent on establishing mastery. The rage aroused by US policies and leaders was no longer restricted to militant groups. Diverse public sectors joined in the censure, including within American society. On the second anniversary of 9/11, in 2003, as the international media focused on interim summations, searching questions were asked about Bush's global war on terror and US embroilment in Iraq. Headlines in leading US weeklies and dailies faithfully reflected a widespread feeling that the United States had lost its way. There was growing fear that three decades after the United States got out of the aimless Vietnam War by the skin of its teeth, Bush administration policies were creating a similar situation in Iraq. On a daily basis, the ongoing occupation was taking a heavy toll in human life as well as material resources, which, for the most part, are borne by the United States alone.[20]

Meanwhile, the US wars in Afghanistan and Iraq led to spreading recognition that there was a direct link between the global campaign to stamp out terror and the Israeli-Palestinian confrontation. The Arab public discourse renewed and reinvigorated charges of US double standards where Israel is concerned, citing this standpoint as the reason that the United States did not bear down heavily to have the conflict settled. The same argument featured in the announcements of Osama bin Laden and Saddam Hussein, publicized from their hideaways. The latter made the claim as an invitation to the masses to join the jihad against the United States and Israel; Arab state leaders, on the other hand, made it to urge the White House to halt the Israeli-Palestinian bloodbath and enforce the first phase of the Roadmap. One critical question overshadowed all: could a serious political process be promoted at all in the given circumstances? Apart from the tangled world war on terror and the ongoing Israeli-Palestinian cycle of violence, the Palestinians were plagued by a severe leadership crisis, and in Israel and the United States, the reins of state were in the hands of leaders who found the political process designed by their predecessors repugnant. From the start, the main personalities in Bush's administration had endeavored to deprioritize the Israeli-Arab conflict in US foreign policy. They had lambasted the Clinton administration for its overinvolvement in the Israeli-Arab political process, maintaining that in consequence of its mismanagement, the efforts and resources invested over years had gone to waste.

Speaking with one voice, Sharon and Bush claimed that there could be no progress in the political process until the terror stopped. Sharon, for his part, had attacked Oslo from every possible podium and, for years, had advocated the position that Jordan is the Palestinian state. An interview he gave in mid-April 2001, about two months after being ensconced as prime minister, provided rare insight into his political worldview and its evident modifications: "I have not changed my outlook," he declared, "the only thing that has changed is my opinion on the matter of Jordan being Palestine. And this, too, simply because a fact has been established here. I never intended for there to be two Palestinian states."[21]

Notes

1. Huntington, *The Clash of Civilizations*; Lewis, *What Went Wrong?*
2. *New York Times*, 11 September 2002.
3. See his official website, www.qaradawi.net. A month after the terror attack, *al-Hayat* (11 October 2001) carried a number of articles in this vein. Especially prominent were one by the Lebanese philosopher Radwan al-Sayyid ("Retrieving Islam from Its Kidnappers") and an article by Tunisian thinker Abu Ya'rib al-Marzuqi. Other writers directed piercing criticism at the impact of terror on the political and social situation in Arab states and its support of radical militants. See, for example, the articles by Lebanese sociologists Wadah Sherara and Salim Nasser (*al-Hayat*, 16 September 2001, 22 September 2001). One could not ignore, some noted, that the objective of the zealots was to establish an Islamic state based on their radical interpretation of Islam. Bin Laden was not to be glorified, and he was certainly not to be seen as an Arab national leader, Egypt's Wahid Abd al-Maguid argued in an article entitled "Abd al-Nasser—Saddam Hussein—Bin Laden," in *Al-Ayam*, 3 November 2001.
4. *Al-Hayat*, 29 November 2001.
5. *Al-Ayam*, 17 September 2001.
6. Esposito, *Unholy War*, p. 104; Kepel, *Jihad*, pp. 159–176.
7. El-Nawawy and Iskandar, *Al-Jazeera*.
8. For a critical scrutiny of US media politics in the Iraq war, see Artz and Kamalipour (eds.), *Bring 'em On*.
9. *Al-Ahram*, 27 September 2001.

10. Qabani's poem was published in various places. For the full version, see *al-Kawakeb* 2701 (6 May 2003): 66.

11. *Al-Hayat*, 5 November 2001.

12. *Al-Ahram*, 28 March 2003.

13. Said, "Suicidal Ignorance," *Arabic Media Internet Network*, www.amin.org/eng/edward_said/15nov2001.html. The conspiracy theory was sharply condemned in an article by Saudi publicist Suliman al-Nakidan, *"Nazariyyat al-Mu'amara wal-qasd"* [The Conspiracy Theory and the Purpose], *al-Sharq al-Awsat*, 25 October 2001. For a written example of the conspiracy theory, see the article by Mustafa Mahmoud, who contended that American and Israeli parties were behind the attack. According to him, Islamic militant groups did not have the capability to carry out terror acts of such scope and coordination. The attack was part of the plans of Western and Zionist elements to lash out at the nation of Islam, especially at Arabs. *"'Ala Hafat al-Zilzal"* [On an Earthquake Edge], *Al-Ahram*, 3 November 2001.

14. "Confronting the Conundrum," *al-Ahram Weekly*, 31 October 2002.

15. In the decade following the Gulf War (1990–1991), the United States and Britain headed the list of states demanding that international sanctions continue against Iraq. Their forces firmly prevented the Iraqi army from operating in extensive regions of the republic, especially in the north where Kurds make up most of the population. The Gulf War did end with the exit of Iraqi forces from Kuwait territory and a grave blow to the capability of the Iraqi army, but in the United States, as in a number of states in the region—primarily Kuwait, Saudi Arabia, Egypt, Iran, and Israel—Saddam's regime continued to be regarded as a threat to varying degrees.

16. Richard Clarke, a security expert for more than thirty years, gave detailed testimony of how senior officials in the Bush administration leveled serious, though unfounded, accusations at Saddam Hussein's regime. Clarke, *Against All Enemies*.

17. Blix, *Disarming Iraq*.

18. Said, "An Unacceptable Helplessness," *al-Ahram Weekly*, 16 January 2003. Further on, he says: "The task cannot be left to a cacophony of religious fanatics and submissive, fatalistic sheep. But that seems to be the case. The Arab governments—no, most of the Arab countries from top to bottom—sit back in their seats and just wait as America postures, lines up, threatens and ships out more soldiers and F-16's to deliver the punch. The silence is deafening."

19. "Iraq: Special Report," www.whitehouse.gov/news/releases/2003/05/iraq/20030501-15.html.

20. According to a CNN report, by 21 January 2005, 1,372 US soldiers had been killed in Iraq. See www.cnn.com/SPECIALS/2003/iraq/forces/casualties.

21. *Haaretz Friday Magazine*, 13 April 2001.

9

The Arab Peace Initiative
and Bush's "Vision"

Escalating Israeli-Palestinian clashes stained the early months of 2002 with blood. Israeli military pressure was out to "destroy the terror infrastructure," though mainly it wreaked havoc on civilian and governmental infrastructure in the West Bank and Gaza Strip. Israeli cabinet ministers and both uniformed and retired generals day and night tagged the PA as "supporting terror" and portrayed Arafat as fully controlling "the height of the flames" of the violence and terror set by various Palestinian groups. IDF actions injured large numbers of Palestinians, but the armed struggle against Israel did not let up for a moment. The terror infrastructure, moreover, was motivated by the desire to take revenge on Israel and lash out at everything and anything connected with it or representing it. Israel's bearing down harder on the Palestinian population—via utter control, supervision, and disruption of daily life—constantly fueled the desire for revenge. Palestinian groups for years had advocated dogged struggle against Israel. Now, the unprecedented spiraling of the al-Aqsa intifada and the incessant IDF actions created an atmosphere of public support for armed struggle against the occupation.[1] Citing these trends, Khalil Shikaki, a renowned pollster of Palestinian public opinion, noted:

> Public support for violence and the belief that violence pays have risen to unprecedented levels during the second Intifada. . . . However, the increase in support for the Islamists and violence does not necessarily reflect an ideological transformation—toward radical positions—that would be difficult to reverse. Rather, it demonstrates an angry response to the pain and suffering inflicted by Israeli occupation policies and retaliatory measures since the start of the second Intifada. The anger led people to demand revenge and to support all types of violence against Israelis, including suicide attacks against civilians inside Israel.[2]

147

In Israel, a distinction was no longer made between the PA's armed forces and Hamas, Islamic Jihad, and the PFLP and PDFLP. Many civilians—mostly Palestinians—were caught in the fire between the IDF and these groups. This was the deadly price of doing battle in densely populated areas, and in no few instances, also of striving for results without really considering the danger to innocent civilians. As far as the Palestinians were concerned, all the factions and groups fought in the same trenches. All took part not only in armed struggle against the IDF but in acts of terror against civilians in the Occupied Territories and deep inside Israel. New names were added to the harvest of blood almost daily. On both sides, a lack of faith in the desire or ability of the existing leaderships to extricate the peoples from the tangled web added to the climate of despair.

Meanwhile, the United States continued its unyielding pursuit of terror groups and regimes it had defined as hostile. The wider the United States cast its net, spreading over five continents, the greater was the motivation of these groups to hit US targets. At this stage, the main question preoccupying the media was whether the Bush administration really meant to go on toppling anti-American regimes as it had done in Afghanistan. If so, which regime would be next in line? And could it be prevented? Bush's "Axis of Evil," in which he fingered the enemies of his country or, as he put it, of Western civilization, appeared to be the basis of a pretentious scheme to bring about a new world order. Since the fall of the Taliban, however, various Arab spokespeople had been calling on their leaders and peoples to vigorously oppose the dismantling of regimes by foreign forces. It was commonly believed that the hawkish line promoted by Bush's top brass would eventually lead to an offensive both against Arab regimes (first, Iraq and Syria) and against militant groups (such as Hizbollah and Hamas). Many people demanded in the Arab media that the summit scheduled for the end of March 2002 in Beirut formulate a united Arab stand on these critical issues. There was swelling domestic criticism of the wishy-washy position displayed by most Arab regimes. More and more, Arab leaders were apprehensive about the hot potato that the deepening US-Iraqi crisis had become. The steps they took showed almost daily that they had no intention of making decisions that might be welcomed at home but would exacerbate the tensions already existing with the Bush administration.

The sense conveyed by most of the spokespeople was that "the Arabs" were too weak to influence either post-9/11 US policy or Israel, which did in the occupied Palestinian territories almost everything its extremist leaders saw fit. Attendant on these feelings, the leaders of Egypt, Saudi Arabia, Qatar, and Kuwait tirelessly lobbied via diplomatic and political channels to promote the vital interests of their regimes. Very gradually, the US administration began to realize the interconnectedness of the Israeli-Palestinian conflict and the worldwide campaign against terror, especially the confrontation with Saddam Hussein's regime on which the United States wished to focus. As a result, for the first time, Bush and his secretary of state began to make public reference to the vision of a Palestinian state. In early March 2002, the IDF embarked on its most far-reaching measures, deep inside Palestinian territory. On Tuesday, 12 March, thirty-one Palestinians were killed by Israeli fire. That same day, the United States submitted a singular proposal to the UN Security Council. Adopted unanimously by all council members (Syria abstained), Resolution 1397 affirmed the vision that "two States, Israel and Palestine, live side by side within secure and recognized borders." It also called for immediate cessation of all acts of violence, including all acts of terror, provocation, incitement, and destruction between the parties.[3]

It is these tensions that spawned one of the most important peace initiatives of the Arab-Israeli conflict. The move was heralded by a small press item published in early February 2002 by Thomas Friedman, the foreign affairs correspondent of the *New York Times*. Whether it was his own initiative or the fruit of a sophisticated leak remains unclear. One way or another, Friedman suggested that the upcoming summit of the Arab League adopt a straightforward resolution proposing a solution to the Israeli-Palestinian conflict; it would revolve around Israel's complete withdrawal to the 4 June 1967 lines and the establishment of a Palestinian state, in exchange for which all the Arab states would offer Israel full recognition and peace. A few days later, the renowned columnist was the guest of the crown prince in Riyadh as part of Saudi efforts to repair its image in American eyes after having come under the penetrating gaze of US spokespeople. At dinner, Friedman reiterated his proposal to the crown prince. By his account, 'Abdullah bin 'Abd al-Aziz al-Saud shot him an astounded glance and asked: "Have you broken into my desk?" The Saudi ruler said that he had on his desk a draft of the address he was to deliver at the Beirut summit, which matched the framework of Friedman's proposal to a T. "I wanted to find a way to make clear to the Israeli people that the Arabs don't reject or despise them. But the Arab people do reject what their leadership is now doing to the Palestinians, which is inhumane and oppressive."[4] As the summit drew nearer, there were more leaks about the Saudi proposal and a flurry of diplomatic activity aimed at transforming it into a pan-Arab peace initiative. Just before the publication of the proposal's details, there had been a sense of helplessness; now, suddenly, almost every day brought with it anticipation of a political breakthrough. A chance to stabilize the situation and put the brakes on any further deterioration. Political channels buzzed with communication by Arab delegates to their European and US counterparts, and a number of amendments were introduced into the Saudi proposal with a view to ensuring broad Arab agreement and the world support it would require.

Above all, the importance of the Beirut summit resolutions stemmed from the components of the unprecedented Arab proposal for peace with Israel and the timing of the proposal's publication. The Arab League's adoption of the initiative confirmed the thinking of key leaders—Saudi Arabia's and Egypt's—

that the continuation of the Israeli-Palestinian conflict was inimical to the interests of Arab states. In their view, though the armed conflict inflicted pain on Israeli society, it nevertheless played into the hands of Israel's hawkish government, whose goal it was to void Oslo and bring down the Palestinian leadership headed by Arafat. For the first time, Arab leaders publicly laid out both the principles of a permanent settlement between Israel and the Palestinians and an overall peace framework for the Arab-Israeli conflict. Their action opened up a new political prospect, aimed at propelling the sides toward a serious political avenue. The framework's chief points were full Israeli withdrawal from all the Arab territories it had conquered after 4 June 1967; a just resolution of the refugee problem consistent with UN Resolution 194; recognition for the establishment of an independent sovereign Palestinian state with its capital at al-Quds; and a clear call to end the Israeli-Arab conflict and to sign peace treaties between the Arab states and Israel, which would include unconditional mutual recognition, good neighborliness, and blanket normalization. The summit's closing statement contained formulations not included in the original Saudi initiative, such as: "The Arab leaders praised the steadfastness of the [Palestinian] people in face of Israeli occupation, and paid respect for the Palestinian martyrs and supported the legitimate struggle of the Palestinian people until fulfilling the demands of the right of return, the right of self-determination and the establishment of their Palestinian state with Holy Jerusalem as its capital." The statement also reconfirmed the "suspension of establishing any relations with Israel in view of the setback to the peace process and the reactivation of the Bureau of the Arab Boycott of Israel until Israel responds by implementing the resolutions of international legitimacy," particularly the retreat from all Arab occupied lands to the lines of 4 July 1967.[5]

The summit resolutions were not a detailed peace plan but a common Arab statement of principles for a political settlement of the Israeli-Arab conflict. It was clear to all that the principles would have to be clarified in complex negotiations. The initiative was meant to send one basic message to the public and administrations in Israel and the United States: this is the Arab vision for achieving peace in the Middle East. The message, of course, was also intended for the general Arab public, including the Palestinians. Support for the idea of a "just and comprehensive peace in the Middle East" had, from time to time, surfaced in Arab League discussions since the Cairo summit in June 1996.[6] The Beirut initiative was unique both in its outline of the principles for peace and in the manner in which it was received by the public discourse. The adopted blueprint called on Israel "to reconsider its policies and declare that a just peace is its strategic option as well." The resolution by the Arab League called "upon the government of Israel and all Israelis" to support this peace initiative and thereby put an end to the bloodshed and to enable Arabs and Israelis "to live in peace and good neighbourliness and provide future generations with security, stability and prosperity."[7]

These singular statements were followed up by the address of Saudi crown prince 'Abdullah at the opening session of the Beirut summit. In appealing to his fellow leaders and the millions of viewers who followed the summit proceedings on live television, Saudi Arabia's acting leader noted:

> Allow me at this point to directly address the Israeli people, to say to them that the use of violence, for more than fifty years, has only resulted in more violence and destruction, and that the Israeli people are as far as they have ever been from security and peace, notwithstanding military superiority and despite efforts to subdue and oppress. Peace emanates from the heart and mind, and not from the barrel of a cannon, or the exploding warhead of a missile. The time has come for Israel to put its trust in peace after it has gambled on war for decades without success.

Reminiscent of Sadat's address on his historic visit to the Knesset, the closing statement noted that Israelis must accept the fact that peace is unthinkable so long as Arab lands continue to be occupied. At the same time, should Israel choose to return the Occupied Territories to their owners, which would show Israel's desire for true peace: "we will not hesitate to accept the right of the Israeli people to live in security with the people of the region."[8]

The Israeli government was not overly impressed by the Beirut summit's initiative nor by the public statements of Saudi's crown prince. In contrast to the Arab vision for a political settlement of the Israeli-Arab conflict, the lack of vision of Sharon's first government was exposed in all its nakedness. The direct public appeal made by the crown prince to the people of Israel fell on deaf ears. Israeli officials hastened to pour cold water on the Beirut formulations, dismissing the call to recognize Israel and Israel's right to live securely in the region as mere blather. Other Arab leaders—Jordan's King 'Abdallah and Egypt's President Hosni Mubarak—also appealed directly to Israelis in interviews on Israel television and elicited a similar reaction. The same was true of Arafat's public calls. On one occasion (20 July 2001), Arafat wrote an "open letter to my Israeli friends." On another, he appealed to Israelis and world public opinion in the *New York Times* in an article headlined, "The Palestinian Vision of Peace." All had one common message: to act in consort to stop the cycle of violence without ignoring the political price involved in achieving a just, comprehensive, and lasting peace.

The efforts to revive the political process were accompanied by a series of grisly terror acts carried out by Palestinian suicide bombers, members of Hamas, inside Israel in the last week of March 2002. The most appalling incident took place at Netanya's Park Hotel (27 March), where some 250 Israelis were celebrating the Passover Seder. The occasion and timing were symbolic and had been carefully chosen by the bomber, 'Abd al-Basat Odeh. Shortly after 7 p.m., as Israelis sat around festive holiday tables reading from the *Haggadah*, the story of the Israelite exodus from Egyptian bondage, he detonated a suitcase of explosives he was carrying. Twenty-nine people were killed and about 150 injured to varying degrees. Millions of Israelis were glued to television screens, and the holiday atmosphere gave way to expressions of pain, rage, and calls on the government to clamp down with an iron fist. Censure of the base act of terror perpetrated in the middle of the Passover Seder poured in from all over the world. Four days later, another Palestinian Hamas suicide bomber walked into a Haifa restaurant. The weeklong Passover festival was still going, so Israelis were out on the streets in full force. Virtually everyone inside the Matza Restaurant was injured. Fifteen Israelis were killed and many others wounded. The many victims of the Netanya and Haifa terror incidents joined a grim and mounting toll begun with a suicide bombing at Jerusalem's Moment Café on 9 March. More than 130 Israeli citizens died in the reign of terror that Black March, and hundreds of others were injured.

Following the Park Hotel bombing in Netanya, the IDF launched Defensive Shield, a meandering, blood-soaked operation, based on a "bank of aims" that was simply an endless list of targets in the West Bank and the Gaza Strip. The government gave the IDF a green light to greatly step up combat against the Palestinians and set no time limit for employing a wide range of means against all armed Palestinian groups. The question of Arafat's personal fate preoccupied many. On a daily basis almost, commentators, politicians, and career and reserve soldiers put in their two cents on the subject. The IDF blockade of the Muqata'a, the PA's headquarters in Ramallah, where the Palestinian leader was holed up, grabbed most of the media attention. Arafat and his supporters waged a battle of survival for both their persons and their government. The everyday hardships imposed on the lives of 3.5 million Palestinians were barely covered.

The suicide bombings at Netanya's Park Hotel and Haifa's Matza Restaurant, like the launching of Defensive Shield, took place against the backdrop of the Arab summit in Beirut, its discussions of the Saudi proposal, and the publication of an Arab peace initiative that was the first of its kind. Given the escalation in Israel and the Occupied Territories, there was little chance of embarking on a political process. Nor did it look as though the situation was about to calm down, a bleak outlook feeding despair. Israel, according to the views of the IDF, the cabinet, and the media discourse, had no choice but to summon all its might against Palestinian fanatics intent on its undoing via terror. Once again, there was an outcry to achieve what cannot be achieved by force alone: to root out the infrastructures of terror. Over the next three months, the air rattled with the din of bombs, gunfire, and ambulance sirens; hideous sights from various arenas in Israel and the Occupied Territories; and the high passions of Israelis, Palestinians, and Arabs. The cycle of hostility was fueled daily by mutual killings and blows, while accusations were flung at both internal and external adversaries. Public pressure, Israeli and Palestinian alike, gave the impression that the entire region was on the edge of an abyss. One direct consequence of the escalation was the burying of the extraordinary peace initiative put forward by Arab leaders at the Beirut summit. In both societies, Israeli and Palestinian declarations that incite violence—against a ghastly backdrop of hostile acts—removed discussion of this all-important initiative from the public discourse.

No small share of Arab fury and censure was directed at the Egyptian and Jordanian regimes for not doing enough to save the Palestinians from Israel's strong arm. Arab nationalists and Islamists repeatedly urged Arab states that had signed peace treaties with Israel to shut down Israel's legations and expel its envoys. Some even called on Arab leaders, notably Mubarak, to instruct the military to take action to defend Palestinians.[9] In response, Egypt's president noted: "I am not in the habit of making decisions only in order to satisfy the man on the Egyptian or Arab street. . . . I am not looking for applause from people who would make us move backward. I have no interest in the media attacks waged by agitators against me and against Egyptian policy for I know better than they what is harmful and what is beneficial to Arab interests." Asked about his reaction to the call that Egypt begin a war against Israel, Mubarak said: "The people sounding these calls do not know what it means to open war. . . . With respect to what is happening between the Palestinians and Israel, war will not help and will not achieve the necessary security and peace. . . . The Egyptian army has no interest or goal other than to defend its country, guard its borders, and warn against any aggression toward Egypt."[10]

Israel, too, had harsh words for Arab governments, especially the leaders of Egypt and Saudi Arabia. Official spokespeople claimed that Cairo and Riyadh could do much more to check the Palestinians and simply chose not to, simplistic claims that ignored meaningful political measures. Egyptian and Saudi leaders had in fact stepped up their efforts to resolve the crisis as the escalation spiraled. In most instances, Israel suspected their motives and rejected their intercession. That is how it reacted, for example, to the Egyptian-Jordanian initiative (April 2001) and the Saudi initiative, which became the basis of the Arab peace plan adopted by the Arab League at the Beirut summit (28 March 2002). In both cases, Israel's government spurned opportunities to seriously discuss ideas put forth by Arab leaders. There is no doubt that the Arab positions were far removed from those of the Israeli government. But a readiness to weigh new ideas and participate in joint forums does not oblige Israel to accept unfavorable positions. To roundly dismiss initiatives submitted by regional leaders, however, is detrimental to Israel's interests and image and to the chances of bringing about a real change in its dealings with the Arabs, particularly the Palestinians.

After the adoption of the Arab peace initiative at the Beirut summit, while all eyes looked to Washington and the ground rumbled with violence and hopelessness, Egypt decided to roll up its sleeves and get down to business. For anyone following Egyptian policy since the outbreak of the al-Aqsa intifada, this decision came as no surprise. The snowballing Israeli-Palestinian confrontation had amplified the popular cry for Arab leaders to toughen their stance toward Israel. Calls were issued to go to war or, at the very least, to recruit and dispatch volunteers to the Occupied Territories, where they could fight alongside the Palestinians. This bellicose choir of Arab extremists was joined by the presidents of Yemen, Syria, and Iraq. Mubarak, in an address on the twenty-seventh anniversary of the 1973 war, lambasted the warmongers. The people clamoring for war, he said, are people who have no experience of war and do not know what it means. "War" the Egyptian president concluded, "is no simple matter."[11]

The Arab League's summit (Cairo, 21–22 October 2000) framed another scene of open confrontation. Arab public opinion was incensed by the many Palestinian casualties in clashes with the IDF, which had activated its superior military capabilities against the Palestinian insurgency. In the summit's opening addresses, as in the media, a number of spokespeople demanded action on behalf of the Palestinians, even if only the dispatch of arms and volunteers. President Emil Lahoud of Lebanon, who chose to speak rather than read out a written statement, noted that if the leaders don't take steps, the populace will rise up and those who do not act will pay dearly for their silence. The summit must therefore adopt tangible resolutions in the direction that the Arab street wants. Yemen's President 'Ali 'Abdallah Salah urged his counterparts not to fear Israel, "the cancer in the body of the Arab nation," a rhetoric that had long been absent from league deliberations. Mubarak responded this way: "We were surprised to see threats that could abort this [political] process and pull back the region into an atmosphere of violence, despair, and anarchy." Both before and after the summit, Mubarak warned that menacing language does not necessarily serve Arab interests. He told his colleagues that though "expectations of this summit are sky high," it is their role as leaders to identify interests and what was best for all and to act accordingly, in other words not to be swept up by extremist voices, even though "we are all angry and full of resentment due to the accumulated events."[12] In so saying, Mubarak displayed leadership and aligned Egypt's weight against escalation and chaos. The tone taken by the leaders of Jordan, Morocco, and Tunisia was similarly moderate.

The summit proceedings and resolution called on world opinion and international bodies to intervene more actively in the crisis and come to the aid of the Palestinian population. Israel's policy of might makes right drew censure and was portrayed as an additional sign that it was Israel who was the real rejectionist in the conflict. Furthermore, it was claimed, Israeli policy posed a danger to peace and regional stability. The imposition of collective punishment on the Palestinians and the daily injuries inflicted on innocent people eroded

Arab faith in the peace process, while the current crisis threatened pan-Arab national security and could well sink the Middle East into dire anarchy. In an effort to link the crisis to normalization, Arab states that had signed peace treaties with Israel were urged to reexamine their ties. States that had opened common interest offices in Israel were urged to sever all bonds and shut down the legations.

Egyptian involvement in the search for a way out of the crisis rested primarily on the assumption that the continuous Israeli-Palestinian confrontation gravely threatened the interests of regional states, including its own. Mubarak's main goal was to change the status quo of ongoing escalation and create the necessary conditions for resuming the political process. Egyptian experience itself showed that the negotiating table was the only place to achieve goals vis-à-vis Israel. Decades of Arab boycott and attempts to overcome Israel in armed struggle had failed. Peace with Israel was the prior condition for stability and, in fact, for the tackling of a whole range of internal problems that had plagued Egypt in recent decades. Regimes and groups advocating armed struggle against the Zionist entity played into the hands of Israeli leaders, who could use this policy as an excuse to perpetuate the status quo or apply the concept of the "iron wall" originally advocated by Ze'ev Jabotinsky and later by most Israeli leaders. Bellicose remarks against Israel's existence, and certainly terror, only reinforced Israeli public opinion that nothing had changed in the Arab position, that the Arabs continued to seek the destruction of the Jewish state.

More than two decades of peace have not softened the mutual suspicions of the Israeli and Egyptian populations and leaders. For years, many Israelis would paint Egypt as putting spokes in the wheels of peace. This simplistic premise has found faithful expression in the stance adopted by Prime Minister Sharon, most of his cabinet, and most of his party. True, the decisionmakers in the two states have not always seen eye to eye on many issues. Egyptian leaders often blamed Israel for the lack of progress in the political process. The attitude toward Israel in the Egyptian press was highly critical and, unfortunately, not free of mendacious reports and even outright racism. Egypt convicted an Israeli citizen, 'Azam 'Azam, of espionage and sentenced him to a long prison term, despite Israeli remonstrations that he was innocent and Israeli demands that he be released.[13] And yet none of these problems detract from the fact that peace with Israel remains one of the cornerstones of overall Egyptian policy. Peace with Israel is also the foundation of the unique relationship Egypt enjoys with the United States and the special status it has acquired as the main thread in the fabric of the Middle East; as a contributing factor to stability and moderation; and as firmly committed to extending the political process to include other Arab parties, specifically the Palestinians. In the circumstances that developed since 9/11 and in light of the Israeli-Palestinian escalation and the Iraqi embroilment, there seemed to be a real danger of growing instability and with it, an increasing threat to all the Arab regimes.

Right after the Beirut summit in 2002, Egypt formulated its steps for the months ahead. After examining a number of scenarios to move out of the crisis and clarifying matters with the Americans and the Palestinians, it decided on a new, two-pronged approach, aimed at the Bush administration and the internal Palestinian arena. Egypt acted in different ways to persuade the US government that the Egyptian leaders were true partners in the campaign against Middle Eastern extremism and for measures to promote stability, freedom, and peace in the region. It urged Bush and his staff to open a new political avenue for re-solving the Israeli-Palestinian conflict by explicitly supporting a settlement based on partitioning the disputed land into two states to live in security and peace. In a long series of working sessions and exchanges with the Bush ad-ministration and the State Department, Egyptian leaders were conscious of the high price to be asked of the Palestinians, notably, stopping the al-Aqsa intifada and neutralizing Arafat. During Mubarak's visit to Washington in June 2002 in the company of a large entourage, detailed talks were held on advancing the po-litical process on the basis of the Arab peace initiative and the directions de-manded by the United States for moving forward. Prior to setting out for Wash-ington, Mubarak had told the *New York Times* of the proposal he meant to put before Bush and his administration. The Egyptian president informed the news-paper that his proposals "would be far more detailed" than those outlined by Crown Prince 'Abdullah of Saudi Arabia. Mubarak suggested recognizing a Palestinian state in all the territory that the UN had recognized as Palestinian be-fore settling all the outstanding problematic issues: permanent borders, refugees, the division of Jerusalem, and the settlements. Such a declaration might revive Palestinian "hope of achieving a state," a hope that had recently been "dashed by the actions" of Sharon's government. External intervention was the call of the hour, for "to leave the problem of the Middle East to Arafat and Sharon alone, you will get nowhere," Mubarak said. "It should be a heavy-weight country like the United States that should try to interfere, try to listen to this and that and in the end make the two parties make a conclusion."[14] At the same time, Egypt took the position that despite Arafat's mistakes, Israel's claim that he was no partner and irrelevant to the deliberations was to be rejected. Some of the suggestions Mubarak put forth in Washington, D.C., were consis-tent with the ideas that were soon to be included in what became known as "Bush's vision." Concurrently, Egypt's increasing role in the internal Palestin-ian discourse soon became apparent, especially in an attempt to reach an over-all Palestinian ceasefire with Israel. This delicate task was entrusted to Omar Suleiman, head of Egypt's intelligence services and Mubarak's personal envoy for special missions. The highly charged relations with Sharon's government cast a pall over cooperation with Israel on a footing of mutual trust and respect. Still, Israel could not prevent Egypt from acting in the political arena.

Bush's Vision

Although the Bush administration welcomed the resolutions and peace initiative of the Arab summit in Beirut, it believed that, at that stage, there was no point in promoting a political process unless it was preceded by a number of significant steps, primarily on the part of the Palestinians. The Americans sought to focus on regime reforms in the PA (first of all, a new constitution, free elections, and the appointment of a prime minister empowered with the necessary authority). In connection with security, they demanded firm action by the elected regime to bring the armed groups into line and rout out terror. Of Israel, the United States demanded that it cease its operations deep within Palestinian territory (Area A) and improve the life of the local population. As the days passed, Bush, although apparently concerned about the tough measures employed against the Palestinians, nevertheless showed understanding for Israel's motives, in effect allowing it to continue its policy.

Like Sharon's government, Bush and his aides began to portray Arafat as the cause of all the troubles. In Israel and the United States, the leader who had headed the Palestinian national mainstream for thirty years was defined as irrelevant to political talks. Nor did Israel's blockade of Arafat's quarters arouse US objections. The IDF had for months surrounded the building sheltering Arafat and his associates, demanding the surrender of some of the latter. In a move aimed solely at humiliating the Palestinian leadership and Arafat, bulldozers razed the buildings next to the office in which he and his aides were holed up. Media speculation was rife as to the possibilities of killing, arresting, or exiling the Palestinian leader. Meanwhile, US officials took to cultivating figures they had tagged as suitable replacements for the top PA job, and, after months of domestic political struggle, their efforts seemed to bear fruit. Mahmoud Abbas (Abu Mazen) was chosen to fill the newly created post of prime minister. He put Muhammad Dahlan in charge of security and Salam Fiad in charge of the treasury.

Following these developments, the Americans resolved to embark on a comprehensive political move to point a way out of the imbroglio for all the parties involved and to infuse their peoples with new hope. On 24 June 2002, in short, measured sentences punctuated by gestures and facial expressions, President Bush presented his initiative for resolving the Israeli-Palestinian conflict.[15] "My vision," he stressed, "is two states, living side by side in peace and security. There is simply no way to achieve that peace until all parties fight terror. . . . Peace requires a new and different Palestinian leadership, so that a Palestinian state can be born." Bush, in fact, was asking the Palestinian people to cast off Arafat's leadership, embrace a new leadership, and institute significant reforms ("more than cosmetic change"). His blueprint comprised two chief phases. The first was the more elaborate, and here he referred to the guiding principle of the "Roadmap" then taking shape in discussions of the

Quartet (the United States, Russia, the European Union, and the UN). His vision for this stage spelled out the following: after changing the Palestinian leadership, which is "encouraging, not opposing, terrorism," and inaugurating new governmental, security, political, and economic institutions, "the United States of America will support the creation of a Palestinian state whose borders and certain aspects of its sovereignty will be provisional until resolved as part of a final settlement in the Middle East." As for Israel, its forces must "withdraw fully to positions they held prior to September 28, 2000. And consistent with the recommendations of the Mitchell Committee, Israeli settlement activity in the Occupied Territories must stop. . . . freedom of movement should be restored." Bush called on Israel to "release frozen Palestinian revenues into honest, accountable hands." The second phase of the Bush vision was outlined in more general terms. It was to revolve around negotiations between Israel and Palestine on all the issues in dispute and be sealed by a final-status agreement that would see an end to the conflict.

Israel, once again, was dragged into the political arena. Bush's vision could be heard reverberating in the background, along with leaks about the upcoming publication of a Roadmap to resolve the crisis as a first step that might lead to establishing an independent Palestinian state. According to the leaks that appeared in the press, senior officials in the Bush administration were now singing a new tune for Israeli ears, and they missed no opportunity to repeat the refrain: the United States was perturbed by the continuing deterioration in the Palestinian arena but supported Israel's right to defend itself against the murderous terror directed at its citizens. The Bush administration expected Sharon's government to embrace a political program rather than make do with military action alone. Public opinion polls showed that most Israelis supported a political settlement and even the establishment of a Palestinian state. Most of the public also judged correctly that the degenerating economic situation was due to the confrontation with the Palestinians and the lack of political prospects. These trends were repeatedly cited by economists, the Finance Ministry, and the Bank of Israel, and dealt with by economic and political analysts, although the media did not give them the attention they deserved. From 2001 to 2003, Israeli economic growth had been at an ebb, the gross national product had fallen to an all-time low, the standard of living had plummeted, a fearsome number of people were now classified as living below the poverty line (more than a 1.25 million citizens, including 500,000 children), unemployment was breaking new records, and the deepening recession had translated into a sharp drop in consumer indices and a worrisome rise in the government deficit. The stock exchange was hard put to raise public capital, and foreign investments had dwindled. Israel had requested US guarantees for billions of dollars it sought to raise overseas, and it was far from certain that the United States would be forthcoming.

Given these circumstances, Sharon adopted a new modus operandi resting on the Bush vision as a reasonable program to resolve the Israeli-Palestinian confrontation. The "new Sharon" was marketed intensively by the Israeli media and portrayed as moderate and ready to reach a political settlement with the Palestinians under their new leadership.[16] He and his aides had carefully formulated the address he delivered before the Herzliya Conference (4 December 2002), and it became his professed political platform (see Appendix 3).[17] It began by stating that for more than two years, Israel had "been confronting a ferocious battle against a culture of bloodshed and murder." The campaign of terror had been "meticulously planned and prepared" by Arafat, who assumed that because of "the high regard for human life in Israeli society," he would be able to force on Israel's government "additional political concessions, concessions with nothing in return." Sharon noted that Israel's war against Palestinian terror derived from "our political understandings with the United States." He lauded Bush's vision, which he accepted "in principle" and defined as "a reasonable, pragmatic and practicable [plan], which offers a real opportunity to achieve an agreement." The progression toward peace would be accomplished in phases and "on the basis of performance," first and foremost the complete cessation of terror, violence, and instigation and the institution of regime reforms in key spheres. He indicated that IDF actions in the Palestinian territories were not aimed at politically controlling these areas ("Israel will not re-control territories from which it withdrew as a result of political agreements"). Choosing his words with care, Sharon formulated a shrewd political statement about the Palestinian state and its characteristics. Like President Bush, he declared that Israel would permit the establishment of a Palestinian state "with borders yet to be finalized," and immediately he emphasized that these borders "will overlap with territories A and B, except for essential security zones." Israel, he said, would not only insist on the demilitarization of the Palestinian state but also would control all its exits and entrances. He summed up with the negotiations on final status. After sharing with his audience his "doubts, reservations and fears," he again declared that "Israel is prepared to make painful concessions for a true peace." The centrality of the Herzliya speech was reflected by its inclusion in the basic guidelines of the second Sharon government (Clause 2.6) as one of the pillars on which Israel was to base its political activity.[18]

A slow but sure change marked the rhetoric of Israel's hawkish prime minister, who, until very recently, had been considered one of the fathers of settlement policy in the Occupied Territories, a rabid opponent of the establishment of a Palestinian state between the Jordan River and the Mediterranean Sea, and a firm exponent of the idea that "Jordan is Palestine." Sharon, in his second term of office, could note with gratification that he had managed to put brakes on the course of Oslo launched by his predecessors and to neutralize Arafat, whom he viewed throughout as a bitter enemy intent on Israel's destruction. The tough questions were still on the agenda: Did Sharon's acceptance of the vision of a Palestinian state and his statements, which seemed to indicate that it was infeasible to go on ruling the Palestinians by force, show that he was ready to conclude a permanent settlement on all outstanding issues between the two sides? Or was his political outlook far more limited—did he envision a Palestinian state in only half the area of the West Bank, its independence and sovereignty subject largely to Israel's will?

Bush's vision, especially his remarks about the need to elect a new Palestinian leadership to take resolute action against terror and violence, rekindled Palestinian and Arab public discussion about the continued course of the al-Aqsa intifada and the status of the Oslo process. Since the summer of 2001, the absence of pubic discussion of the intifada's martial nature and the murder of Israeli civilians had drawn criticism from Palestinians. But, at the time, criticism by Palestinians had been a whistle in the wind; the violence was everywhere, and critics feared the long arm of the PA and other militant groups. Israel, at that stage, appeared determined to topple the PA and strike at its leadership, even at the cost of further deterioration. The IDF policy of targeted killings, including of political leaders, undermined the arguments against Palestinian violence. By the time a year had passed, the critics had been buttressed by widespread support as reflected in the media. A few days before the announcement of the Bush vision, a manifesto was published in the Palestinian press, sponsored by the European Union and signed by some 300 Palestinians from all strata of Palestinian society, including such public figures as Hanan Ashrawi and Sari Nusseibeh. It called for a stop to the suicide missions aimed at the wholesale killing of Israeli civilians "since we do not see that they have any results other than to heighten hatred."[19] At the bottom of the manifesto, a fax number was given for those interested in lending their support to make contact. The manifesto raised a hue and cry. Oppositionist groups accused the signatories of defeatism and of turning a deaf ear to the public will. The verbal fracas lasted months. Critics of the political process, especially oppositionist groups, claimed that "Oslo is dead," and that the leadership should pay the political price for having steered the Palestinian people down the wrong road.

Public doubt over the effectiveness of violence for realizing Palestinian national interests was also voiced by senior PA officials, including Mahmoud Abbas and Muhammad Dahlan. They said that that the oppositionist groups, primarily Hamas, had no alternative to offer that could translate all the movement's empty slogans into practice. On the second anniversary of the al-Aqsa intifada, al-Ahram Weekly, the most important Arab English-language newspaper, devoted a special issue to the uprising. It ran long interviews with representatives of the various Palestinian currents and groups, providing a window onto their serious differences regarding Oslo and the intifada. A Palestinian minister, Hassan 'Asfur, noted:

The attacks that target Israeli civilians are not receiving the same public support, especially after 11 September. There is a wide Palestinian debate about the usefulness of such attacks. Resisting the occupation in Palestinian lands is our legitimate right, but military operations inside Israel that target civilians are a controversial subject. Emotionally, such attacks attract people because of the Zionist crimes, but from the political point of view, there is an awareness that these attacks don't serve our struggle.[20]

Hamas took a thoroughly different position, represented in the anniversary edition of *al-Ahram Weekly* by 'Abd al-'Aziz al-Rantissi. The Gaza doctor believed that the PA clung to Oslo, refusing to acknowledge its demise, because its entire existence was based on its agreements with Israel. "Oslo and the PA are inextricably entwined. The PA is the Oslo Agreement."[21] The biggest mistake the Palestinians had made in negotiations, he said, stemmed from their repeated futile attempts "to build a state without ending the Israeli occupation first." The preoccupation with reforms and the empowerment of a Palestinian prime minister were fruitless, he added, for they had no place so long as the occupation continued and the Palestinian people were not free. "The real task facing the Palestinian people is ending the occupation, not building a state," he concluded; meaning, there was no choice but to continue the armed struggle toward this longed-for goal.[22]

Gamil Majdalawi, spokesman of the PFLP, also noted that it would be impossible to get Israel out of the territories "without terror and crimes and massacres." Israelis, he said, would change their attitude toward the Palestinians only when they appreciated the high price they would have to pay for continuing to rule over them. Suicide missions, despite the controversy they aroused, had to go on so long as Israel persisted in its all-out war against the Palestinians. The Palestinian goal, he said, was and is to liberate the entire West Bank and Gaza Strip, to establish a sovereign Palestinian state with its capital at al-Quds, and to ensure the refugees the right of return. His organization believed that the Oslo Accords had been born in sin and, in fact, no longer applied because they had failed to realize the minimal national demands of the Palestinian people. "Israel never really viewed the agreement as a peace plan, but rather as a security arrangement."[23] Furthermore, his words implied that the PFLP favored significant regime and constitutional reform, spurning cosmetic changes that would allow one person to retain power. The way to achieve this goal was to establish a joint leadership with the participation of all the political forces in Palestinian society.

Notes

1. These trends were well reflected in the polls of the Palestinian Center for Policy and Survey Research. See www.pcpsr.org/survey/cprspolls/index.html. Similar re-

sults were obtained in polls by Birzeit University's Development Studies Program. See http://home.birzeit.edu/dsp/opinionpolls/list.html#2k2.

2. Khalil Shikaki, "Palestinian Public Opinion and the Peace Process: Changes Before and After the Second Intifada," Symposium at Ben-Gurion University, 11 May 2004.

3. For the text of the resolution, see www.un.org/Docs/scres/2002/sc2002.htm.

4. "An Intriguing Signal from the Saudi Crown Prince," *New York Times*, 17 February 2002. Friedman's editorial at the beginning of the month was titled "Dear Arab League," *New York Times*, 6 February 2002.

5. For the official Arabic version of the summit resolution, see the Arab League website, http://64.77.65.168/arableague/A2816News1.html.

6. For the resolutions of the Cairo Summit, June 1996, see www.saudiembassy .net/1996News/Statements/StateDetail.asp?cIndex=461.

7. See the Beirut summit's resolution at http://64.77.65.168/arableague/ A2816News1.html.

8. For the statement by the Saudi crown prince at the Beirut summit, see www .saudiembassy.net/2002News/Statements/SpeechDetail.asp?cIndex=141.

9. In early April 2002, this forceful line was rife in the Arab media, for example, in articles in *al-Quds al-Arabi* (a newspaper published in London) and on a number of programs aired simultaneously on al-Jazeera TV and Abu Dhabi TV.

10. *Akhbar al-Yum*, 13 April 2002. A similar position appears in an article by Samir Rageb, editor of *al-Gumhuriyya*, 10 April 2002. In both, the editors took a dim view of the provocative policies of the presidents of Yemen and Syria. The editorials of *al-Sharq al Awsat* (appearing in London) also supported the Egyptian line and criticized its opponents. See, for example, the editorial, "Have the Critics of Jordan and Egypt Considered the Consequences?" *al-Sharq al Awsat*, 9 April 2002.

11. *Al-Ahram*, 6 October 2000.

12. For Mubarak's statements at the Cairo summit of the Arab League, see www.al-bab.com/arab/docs/league/mubarak00a.htm.

13. 'Azam was released from prison on 4 December 2004 as part of the efforts to re-energize the political process and increase Egypt's involvement in it.

14. *New York Times*, 4 June 2002.

15. For the full, official text of the Bush vision, see the White House website, www.whitehouse.gov/news/releases/2002/06/print/20020624-3.html.

16. For a critical discussion of these widespread trends in the Israeli media, see Kimmerling, *Politicide*, 148–153.

17. The Herzliya Conference is an annual three-day discussion of Israel's national security with the participation of key figures from Israeli politics, security, economics, and academia. More details are on the conference website, www.herzliyaconference.org/ Eng.

18. See Appendix 3 of this book. For the basic guidelines of Sharon's second government (26 February 2003), see the Knesset website. For the Hebrew text: http:// www.knesset.gov.il/docs/heb/kaveiyesod2003.htm; for the English link: http://www .knesset.gov.il/allsite/mark02/h0213381.htm#TQL.

19. *Al-Quds*, 19 June 2002.

20. *Al-Ahram Weekly*, 26 September 2002. Abbas's critical address before the popular councils of refugee camps in Gaza were widely publicized; see *al-Hayat*, 26 November 2002.

21. *Al-Ahram Weekly*, 26 September 2002.

22. Ibid.

23. Ibid.

10

From the Roadmap to the Geneva Initiative

The Bush vision for resolving the Israeli-Palestinian conflict by the end of 2005 was welcomed by most Arab states, especially Egypt, Jordan, Saudi Arabia, and Morocco, as well as the international community, including Europe. This broad international support was translated into practical terms in mid-July 2002 at a parley of the policymakers of the Quartet—the United States, Russia, the European Union (EU), and the UN—which had been created shortly before to formulate a resolution of the Israeli-Palestinian crisis. That conclave decided to adopt the Bush vision as the basis for a phased program to stop the cycle of violence and terror and settle the Israeli-Palestinian/Arab conflict by peaceful means. And so the Roadmap was launched. The tactic was to progress gradually from the situation in the present toward the anticipated overall peace in the future. The Quartet spent about half a year drafting ideas and testing the reactions of the adversaries. The final version of its program was completed on 20 December, though all the parties were careful to still call it a "draft."

The draft comprised three phases (see Appendix 4). In the first phase, with an unrealistic time limit of six months, hostilities were to cease, establishing a new basis for communication between the sides. Israelis and Palestinians were supposed to meet a long list of obligations requiring no small dose of commitment. The Palestinian leadership was to "declare an unequivocal end to violence and terrorism and undertake visible efforts on the ground to arrest, disrupt, and restrain individuals and groups conducting and planning violent attacks on Israelis anywhere." In addition, it was to carry out significant regime reforms that would necessarily lead to the transfer of most of Arafat's powers to a prime minister and senior ministers appointed on the strength of a new constitution. Concomitantly, Israel was to gradually pull back its forces to pre-intifada positions, to dismantle dozens of settler outposts in the West Bank and put a freeze on "all settlement activity (including natural growth of settlements)," to halt its military operations (including targeted killings), and to allow the Palestinians freedom of movement within the Occupied Territories. The implementation of the obligations of both sides and the transition from phase to phase were to be supervised by the Quartet, which would decide if conditions were ripe for proceeding to the next phase. All Quartet decisions were to be adopted by consensus.

The second phase, capped by the title, "Transition," was also allotted a mere six months. It was to commence after Palestinian elections for the institutions of government and continue processes begun in the previous phase, including reform, stabilizing the security situation, and normalizing everyday Palestinian life. Its chief goal was defined as exploring the possibility of "creating an independent Palestinian state with provisional borders and attributes of sovereignty." This possibility would first be studied by an international conference, to be convened following consultations with the two parties; its details, however, were to be left to Israel and the newly elected Palestinian leadership in negotiations. The conference would also discuss the goal of achieving "a comprehensive Middle East peace (including between Israel and Syria, and Israel and Lebanon)," as well as regional issues (water, environmental quality, economic development, refugees, and arms control). In addition, during this transition, members of the Quartet would take steps to promote "international recognition of a Palestinian state, including possible UN membership." To remove all doubt and misgivings, it was further stated that the second phase of the Roadmap was not meant to be a substitute for permanent-status negotiations. Should a Palestinian state be proclaimed within provisional borders, the transition phase would come to an end, and the sides would immediately embark on the third phase, which revolved around negotiations on permanent status.

Like Oslo, the Roadmap deferred permanent-status issues to the final phase, titled, "Permanent Status Agreement and End of the Israeli-Palestinian Conflict." At the heart of this phase, which was to last two years, negotiations were to be conducted on the taxing questions of the Israeli-Palestinian conflict (borders, Jerusalem, refugees, and settlements) and on the conclusion by Israel of peace treaties with Syria and Lebanon. This phase, too, was to begin with an international conference to garner legitimization for an independent Palestinian state within provisional borders, to set an agenda for permanent-status negotiations between Israel and Palestine, and to drive forward a political process between Israel, Syria, and Lebanon. This intensive activity was to be bolstered by the "active, sustained, and operational support of the Quartet."

Initially, when the Roadmap was announced, the Bush administration chose not to declare US support even though US representatives, led by Secretary of State Colin Powell, had been involved in every stage of its drafting. The US decision to formally endorse and announce the Roadmap was due to mounting pressure on the Bush administration and the escalating violence between Israel and the Palestinians. The document was officially presented to the adversaries on 30 April 2003, and the two sides were asked by the Quartet to submit their reactions before the Bush administration stated its own position.[1] It was a foregone conclusion that it would be up to the United States to decide whether to promulgate the Roadmap as is or to introduce changes. Israel's prime minister and most of the cabinet considered the Roadmap dangerous and waited expectantly for the US reaction to the plan. They were gratified to note that US officials kept saying that US policy derived from President Bush's. Senior Israeli ministers in Sharon's first government—including Shaul Mofaz (Defense), Sylvan Shalom (Finance), and Benjamin Netanyahu (Foreign Office)—made no bones about their open opposition to it. Nevertheless, ramped-up lobbying by states both in the Middle East (Egypt, Saudi Arabia, and Jordan) and outside the region ultimately led the Bush administration to declare that it accepted the Roadmap. The acceptance was, at the time, attributed simplistically in Israel's public discourse to the desire of the United States to reward British prime minister Tony Blair for his stalwart support in the war on Iraq. Once again, national state interests (including those of the United States) were ground into a superficial narrative and swallowed whole. There was no attempt to challenge the hollow analyses, most of which regurgitated evaluations prevalent in the Israeli establishment.

Israel's government and prime minister were now faced with tough decisions, for which Sharon invoked his abundant political savvy. Armed with a declaration from the Bush administration that, at the implementation stage, the United States would fully and earnestly take into account Israel's reservations to the Roadmap, Sharon announced his support for the measures outlined therein. On 23 May 2003, the government convened to discuss the matter, and at the end of the long, stormy debate, most of the ministers appeared to oppose the document. But Sharon's experience stood him in good stead, and he managed to squeeze out a majority support for it. The government press release noted that the Roadmap would be implemented subject to fourteen political and security reservations that Israel had submitted to the United States. For most of them, adequate provisions could be found in the Quartet's three-phase program. On three issues, Israel's demands diverged significantly from the Roadmap. It demanded that the establishment of Palestinian institutions of government and Palestinian reforms be supervised "by the Americans" (rather than by the Quartet); that at the launching of the Roadmap, the Palestinians publicly declare their "renunciation of a right of return" and Israel's right "to exist as a Jewish state"; and, finally, that neither the Saudi initiative nor the Arab initiative adopted at the Beirut summit serve as a basis for the political process.[2] Hereafter, the phrase used in the prime minister's statements was that Israel supported the implementation of "the measures called for" by the Roadmap. Sharon generally sandwiched this support with a commitment to

Bush's vision, carefully and consistently ignoring the stipulated target date of that vision—2005—for a final settlement between Israel and the Palestinians.

It was vis-à-vis his own party that Sharon ran into embarrassing situations, some of them under media spotlights. At a particularly turbulent session of Likud's Central Committee (8 June 2003), Sharon's address was drowned out in catcalls and challenged by brandished placards reading, "Map of Illusions."[3] The protest was led by Moshe Feiglin of the rightist Zu Artzeinu (This Is Our Land) movement, whose founders had shrewdly and legitimately brought thousands of voters into Likud ranks with the clear intent of swaying leadership positions from within. The Roadmap was criticized also by bona fide Likud members and not only at the Central Committee Convention, but at Sharon's Knesset appearances before his own faction. Most Likud voters, old and new alike, expressed disappointment at Sharon's about-face. Some of the reactions flung at the prime minister at these meetings included such choice phrases as "Israel's destruction," "document of surrender," "giving up everything," and "hell." Rightist parties and movements were of one mind that the mere publication of the Roadmap conferred a "reward for terror" and that the far-reaching obligations Sharon's government had undertaken were harmful to Israel. These arguments were written up and published by fluent spokespeople, such as Minister Uzi Landau ("a map that will lead to national disaster"), former minister Moshe Arens ("the map's fine print"), and essayist and right-wing activist Yisrael Har'el ("a Roadmap to stamp terror as kosher"). Harel defined the Quartet's program as "the fruit of an eclipse," which, if adopted, "could lead to the gradual elimination of the state of Israel."[4]

In Israel's major cities, sprayed graffiti and pasted public notices displayed uncomplimentary messages about the Roadmap, Sharon, and Abbas. One placard featured at numerous roadside stops and on information boards read: "Stop the Roadmap to Auschwitz." The words, in English and Hebrew, were set against a yellow background with a picture of the entrance into the death camp and the railway tracks leading into it. A shocking visual analogy meant to draw a parallel between the Quartet's Roadmap and the tracks conveying trains into the infamous camp. A number of banners opposing the establishment of a Palestinian state—one of the pillars of the Roadmap—were clearly aimed at Sharon: All over the country, dangling banners read "Jordan is Palestine" and "They mustn't be given a state." There was no need to mention Sharon explicitly. The very words, "Jordan is Palestine," were meant to remind the public of what the prime minister had preached for years. From time to time, the minds behind the placards underscored the dangers the Roadmap posed to Israeli society: "Dismantling settlements = civil war." As noted, the Roadmap called on Israel to dismantle "outposts" and freeze "all settlement activity (including natural growth of settlements)." This demand and the very terms it employed was abhorrent to the right. There is nothing more galling to settlers than to have their communities labeled "settlements" *(hitnahluyot)* or "outposts" *(ma'ahazim).*

For the majority, the places in which they chose to make their homes are bound up with the names and sites of the Bible. There is no substitute for Sabbath prayers at the Tomb of the Patriarchs or rejoicing in the festival of the Torah (Simhat Torah) in Hebron, one of four traditional holy cities. Every day, their children are taught to make the connection between the verses in the Book of Joshua and their doughty struggle to settle regions of the homeland that, in their eyes, were never open to debate. In their eyes, the local Palestinians are mere foreigners, occupying land that is not their historical patrimony but the eternal land of the Jewish people.

The prime minister's laconic response to his detractors rocked Israel's public discourse. "It is important to reach a political settlement," he began, adding in the same breath, "the idea that it is possible to keep three and a half million Palestinians under occupation is wrong for Israel, for the Palestinians and for the Israeli economy."[5] "Occupation" is a dirty word in the Zionist public discourse, especially on the right. In citing the immorality of continued occupation, Sharon shook his public following to the core. It took just one sentence from Sharon to initiate an extraordinary public discussion of one of the basic issues of the confrontation with the Palestinians. The left was quick to pounce on this godsend, cynically congratulating Sharon for having finally adopted their outlook. In the media discourse, analysts recycled their opinions in favor of the "new Sharon." The prime minister's statements on "occupation" were presented a further sign of the change he had undergone, at least since forming his second government. Unfortunately, the opportunity to deal with fundamental issues died down as fast as it had been ignited. On the advice of close associates, Sharon offered a "clarification." His words had not been properly understood. He had not been talking about Israel's control of the Occupied Territories but of the state of occupation under which millions of Palestinians live. The storm abated somewhat, and Sharon's government survived the inevitable political crisis with its right wing, including some Likud ministers.

The Roadmap also sorely tried the new Palestinian government that had been established on 30 April 2003. Israel and the United States demanded that the prime minister, Abbas, and the minister charged with security, Dahlan, vigorously combat every individual or group attempt to continue the intifada. The new government leaders asserted that they would not allow individuals and groups who were not part of the government apparatus to carry weapons, statements in line with the inflated expectations of Israel and the United States that Abbas and Dahlan would or could disarm the militias. Hamas, Islamic Jihad, and the al-Aqsa Brigades hurried to declare that they would not hand over their weapons so long as the occupation continued. In Palestinian society, there were high hopes that Abbas's gestures toward Sharon would soon bring about significant change, easing the unbearable burden of daily life and seeing a release of thousands of security prisoners from Israeli jails. Abbas's placating statements at the 'Aqaba summit (4 June 2003) were regarded by many as unnecessarily obsequious. Others believed that he had acted with wisdom, setting Sharon a honeyed trap. All were perturbed by the words of the US president at the time, who emphasized, "Today, America is strongly committed, and I am strongly committed, to Israel's security as a vibrant Jewish state." This, as the Palestinians saw it, was a repudiation of their historical bond to their homeland and showed a one-sidedness on the refugee question even before permanent-status negotiations had begun.[6]

The Palestinian government enjoyed few days of grace, facing numerous challenges from its very inception. Arafat and his people, on the one hand, and oppositionist groups, on the other, watched them like hawks and every now and then swooped down with talons at the ready. The struggle for authority of Abbas's government was bound up with Arafat's last stand over the previous three years for the leadership of the Palestinian people. During this period, many had been ready to attend the political requiem of the leader who had led the Palestinian national struggle for a generation. More often than can be counted, Israeli and US spokespeople had declared Arafat "irrelevant," a diagnosis copyrighted by Ariel Sharon. As the chorale for his removal grew louder, the extent to which his baton conducted the music of internal Palestinian politics became increasingly clearer. His battle for personal and political survival against domestic rivals and foreign opponents was waged day by day, with an amazingly simple tactic: he supported the resumption of the political process and the call for reforms, subject to the new Palestinian constitution and PLO institutions. He had not, of course, become a champion of law and order overnight. His newfound constitutional devotion was aimed first and foremost at preserving his dominant position in shaping the path of the Palestinian people.

Abbas's government hoped to bring about a dramatic change in the confrontation with Israel and to carry out structural reforms in government and the rule of law in Palestinian society. The promotion of these two major aims was contingent on the cessation of violence and terror. The Palestinian prime minister took advantage of the political credit granted him around the world to explore the possibilities of reaching a cease-fire with Israel or at least an understanding with the various Palestinian groups to halt their military actions against Israel and give normal life a chance in both societies after three years of fierce engagement. Discussion was resumed with the main Palestinian factions on the possibility of a *hudna* (an Arabic and Islamic term, meaning a pause in fighting that could lead to peace). The proponents of the *hudna* were well aware of Israel's opposition to a cease-fire with militant Palestinian groups. The position of Sharon's government was that a cease-fire could be agreed only with the PA, whose job it was to suppress the militant groups, not to compromise with them. To break the vicious cycle of argument and counterargument, the Palestinian government tried to arrive at an internal *hudna* between the various Palestinian factions. Abbas and his senior aides believed that a halt in the violence from the Palestinian side would compel Israel to stop using military force in the Occupied Territories and create the necessary conditions for executing reforms in a variety of spheres. Egypt played a key role in the internal Palestinian talks, a team under Omar Suleiman heavily pressuring the different groups that participated in what was known as the Cairo dialogue. These efforts spurred more intensive Palestinian and Arab debate on continuing the al-Aqsa intifada. The Arab media voiced criticism of Hamas, Islamic Jihad, and the al-Aqsa Brigades more than at any time in the past. Armed struggled against Israel was presented as doing more harm than good since the deadly blows dealt Israeli civilians served chiefly the hawkish line of Sharon's government and were thus detrimental to the Palestinian cause. The oppositionists responded that, despite their reservations about the proposed *hudna*, they would support it out of a sense of national and religious responsibility and to prevent civil war. They would abandon their actions for three months and in exchange Israel would release the security prisoners it held and stop its operations against the Palestinian people and their fighters. Israel was to desist from closures and blockades, remove the checkpoints that denied Palestinians freedom of movement in the West Bank and the Gaza Strip, and cease its policy of targeted killings of prominent intifada activists. Should Israel not meet these conditions, there would be no preventing a return to the intifada and armed struggle. Furthermore, all the spokespeople of the militant groups reiterated that they would resist any attempts to disarm them.

At the end of June 2003, after months of teetering talks, the *hudna* went into force as agreed to directly by the main Palestinian factions and Abbas's government and indirectly by Israel. It was not a formal cease-fire but a series of understandings between the parties involved, not all of which were publicized. The Israeli government was not a direct party to the declaration; it nevertheless expressed its satisfaction at the measure, though it noted that a halt to hostilities did not guarantee immunity for members of terror groups. The US State Department toyed with the idea of exploiting the momentum created by the anticipated pause in violence to embark on the first phase of the Roadmap. The White House and Defense Department, in contrast, warned against raising hopes about US involvement at a time when attention was focused on Iraq, where things were becoming more and more messy.[7] The *hudna* thus set out on an uncertain road, and though there was soon a sharp drop in violence and terror, it did not stop completely. The Israeli and US establishments were gratified by the move that they had initiated and had long been cultivating: Abbas's government would take a tough stand against the armed Palestinian militias and consolidate its rule in the face of Arafat and his supporters. This self-satisfaction was not accompanied by any significant Israeli or US steps that might have contributed toward overall change. Public sectors and governments inside and outside the Middle East demanded that Israel, in light of the relative calm, ease up on the pressure to which it had subjected the Palestinian population for three years and do its share to resume the political process. In particular, there were increasing calls for Sharon's government to implement its obligations according to the Roadmap and make goodwill gestures to bolster the image of Abbas's government in the eyes of the Palestinian public. Israel's government responded only partially to these developments and demands. In a number of towns and regions, it transferred control to the PA, dismantled several checkpoints, and released hundreds of security prisoners, tight-fisted measures made with an undisguised suspicion that the *hudna* would not lead to calm and peace but would primarily provide the terror organizations with an opportunity to recoup.

The hopes for a dramatic change nourished by most Palestinians in the Occupied Territories were extinguished by the familiar realities of life under occupation. Thousands of security prisoners remained under lock and key, freedom of movement had improved only slightly, and Israel's government did not act as if it really meant to dismantle all the outposts and resume the political process. The Palestinian government and Abbas, in particular, drew unsparing domestic criticism. Abbas and his senior ministers failed, in meetings in Jerusalem and Washington, D.C., to convince the Israelis to take meaningful steps that would give the Palestinian public hope and strengthen the new government against its political rivals. Israel's response was that more meaningful steps would be taken only after Abbas's government did real battle with the Palestinian terror organizations. The parties shared a common goal, to halt hostilities and resume the political process, but they remained divided over the sequence of measures that would get them there.

The political hourglass of Abbas's government soon ran out, and with equal speed, hopes dissolved of a breakthrough to rescue Palestinians and Israelis from the cycle of violence unleashed since the failed negotiations of the Camp David summit. The chances of renewing a political process were trampled by two acts of terror on 9 September 2003, perpetrated by Hamas in Jerusalem and at the Tzrifin army base near Tel Aviv, and in a series of targeted killings carried out by Israel against Hamas leaders that preceded these acts and continued more forcefully in their wake. The Roadmap adopted by the adversaries after great exertions, along with the *hudna*, suffered a mortal setback. Once again, Israeli and Palestinian societies became caught up in the horribly familiar web of violence and terror. Arafat accepted Abbas's resignation from the top post in the Palestinian government and charged Ahmed Qureia (Abu 'Ala)—chairman of the National Legislative Council and one of the prime movers behind the Oslo process—with forming the next government.

Israel again sought to turn the spotlight on Arafat and place the blame squarely on him for the failure of the course on which so many hopes had been pinned. The more that Israel and the United States described him as "irrelevant" and "an obstacle to peace," the more relevant and popular he seemed to be in the eyes of the Palestinian and Arab publics. Israeli security services, the government, and the public discourse dusted off the timeworn discussions of what was to be done about Arafat. Politicians and generals re-examined a range of options, most of which amounted to either expelling or killing him. A minority held that Arafat's expulsion would only backfire. It was supposedly an internal Israeli debate, but Israeli decisionmakers looked to Washington. It was clear to all that from the White House would go forth the word on the fate of Arafat, the man who, until not so long ago, had been "the partner," and who still could preen over the distinction of being a Nobel Peace Prize laureate.

The Geneva Initiative

In the latter half of 2003, Israelis and Palestinians met on numerous occasions (generally under the patronage of a third party) in an attempt to come up with a formula to extricate the sides from the cycle of violence. One such endeavor, later referred to as the "Geneva Initiative," aimed to rekindle support for the peace process inside and outside the disputed land. Like other "track two" channels, the Israeli participants (led by Yossi Beilin) acted on their own, without the approval or guidelines of the Israeli government; participants on the other side, in contrast, included senior officeholders in the Palestinian Authority who reported to and solicited guidance from the leadership. The Palestinian side was also buttressed by professional PA auxiliary staff under Yasser Abd Rabbo, a minister in the Palestinian cabinet. Both groups included public and academic figures, as well as retired senior army officers; all supported the Oslo process and a two-state solution.[8] For some time, one of the questions facing the initiators was when to go public with the step they had taken. They were aware that other programs had been tabled in unofficial channels (primarily the "Statement of Principles" concluded by Ami Ayalon and Sari Nusseibeh, formally launched on 25 June 2003), but most of all they were concerned about news of Sharon's intention to come out with a political plan on the presumption of there being "no partner" for peace and advocating unilateral measures.[9] As opposed to this widespread view of "no partner," the Geneva group claimed the opposite, that "there is a partner" and that a whole slew of final-status issues could be agreed on if negotiations were to the point. In a meeting in Amman (12 October 2003), at the end of a two-hour discussion, the final version of the initiative was approved. It was formally launched at a glittering, high-exposure ceremony in Geneva (1 December 2003). The detailed document signed by representatives of both sides was most ambitious: it presented a model for a final-status agreement and an end to the Israeli-Palestinian conflict. A good deal of intellectual effort had gone into it, aimed at translating into the language of treaties the principles drawn up by

President Clinton at the end of December 2000 and to broaden the understandings reached in the Taba talks.

An enormous amount of thought and resources went into the marketing of the Geneva Initiative. Copies of the document were dispatched to the homes of millions of Israelis and Palestinians. Internet sites were set up in Hebrew, Arabic, and English (with links to French, Spanish, and Portuguese translations). The document contained detailed maps, background material, and comments.[10] Ample funds paid for huge ads in the press. The personal undertaking of the signatories to promote the initiative was evident in countless interviews granted the local and international media. The Geneva Initiative soon became a familiar subject in Israeli, Palestinian, Arab, and international public discussion.

The assertive marketing emphasized the benefits to be reaped by both Israelis and Palestinians if the initiative were adopted. The cover of the Hebrew version listed them against a blue-and-white background: an end to the conflict, recognition of Israel as the state of the Jewish people, acknowledgment that most of the settlers would remain in Israeli territory, a resolution of the refugee problem, a new era based on peace, and the acknowledgment of Jerusalem as Israel's capital. The attached commentary noted that the Palestinian state would be demilitarized and its leadership would fight terror and incitement. An international control mechanism would supervise the implementation of the commitments of both sides. The Hebrew booklet also came with a short piece by author David Grossman, who since the publication of *Nochahim nifkadim* (Present Though Absent) and *The Yellow Wind* had become one of the foremost spokespeople of Israel's "peace camp." In his words, the advantages of the Geneva Initiative was that its formulators had managed to discuss all the issues in dispute and to recommend solutions based on compromise by both sides. Adopting the initiative as an official agreement would give a real chance to achieving a durable peace. Moreover, the agreements and their public publication show, he said, "that on the Palestinian side there is a serious, reliable partner for a peace settlement, and that there is still a chance for an historic compromise between the peoples." Just how widespread was the unfounded charge that the Palestinians alone were responsible for the collapse of the peace process comes to light in a reading of Grossman's piece. "Do the terrible mistakes that the Palestinians made in the past three years," he wonders, "doom also the Jewish people to a helpless descent into the abyss?"[11]

The proponents of the Geneva Initiative depicted the plan as a lifesaver for anyone worried about Israel's existence as a democratic Jewish state, suggesting that continued Israeli control over the Palestinian people would upset the demographic balance in the territory between the Jordan River and the Mediterranean Sea. It was not the failure to embrace one or another political initiative that was up for public discussion, but something far more critical:

Israel's continued existence as a democratic Jewish state. In this light the marketers brandished the concord on the refugee question, presenting it as the crowning achievement of the Geneva Initiative. Aptly enough for a document submitted before the Israeli-Jewish public, the "right of return" was not mentioned at all in the agreement; instead, it stated, the possibility of Palestinian refugees entering Israel would be subject to the approval of Israel alone. The recommended solution "would make it possible for Israel to continue to exist as a Jewish and democratic state."[12] In an attempt to attain legal legitimacy for these arguments, the Israeli proponents rested on the opinion of Ruth Lapidot, a professor of international law at Hebrew University well versed in various political agreements concluded between Israel and Arab parties. Lapidot's position on the refugee issue was no secret: there was no legal basis for the Palestinian claim of "right of return." UN Resolution 194 was merely a recommendation to Israel "to facilitate the return of refugees." Accordingly, the Geneva Initiative did not recognize a "right of return." Israel was simply asked "to permit the absorption of certain refugees at its discretion, setting the number in comparison with different third countries." The numbers talked about were "small," and a mechanism would be created to deal with the matter, facilitating the "regulation of refugees" and thereby preventing pressure "on any specific alternative such as absorption within Israel." Lapidot concluded that the implementation of the procedure recommended in the Geneva Initiative might well put an end to the refugee problem.[13] These opinions and emphases emanated from the Israeli initiators. Palestinian commentators subscribed to different opinions, stressing what they saw as the main points: the border between Israel and the Palestinian state would be based on the 4 June 1967 lines with mutual modifications based on a ratio of 1:1, the West Bank and the Gaza Strip would be joined by a "corridor" to be under Palestinian management, Israel would recognize Palestinian sovereignty over al-Haram al-Sharif, and all Palestinian and Arab prisoners jailed in the framework of the Israeli-Palestinian conflict would be freed.[14]

The Geneva Initiative drew a wide range of criticism and attention. In this sense, its proponents achieved one of their chief aims, reopening public discussion on a concrete proposal for a settlement of final-status issues. Upon its publication, Prime Minister Sharon and most of his government attacked the Israeli initiators, claiming that in the prevailing circumstances the document put forth "is removed from reality" and could not bring about a resumption of the political process. Once it became clear that the initiative had caused quite a stir in the local and international media, the aforementioned critics rephrased their condemnation to refer to specific formulations and agreements that they depicted as damaging to the interests of the state of Israel. They claimed that in any future negotiations the Palestinians would cling to the Geneva document as the starting point and subsequently demand more and more concessions. The Israeli right accused the Geneva proponents of bringing on a fresh disaster. MK Arieh Eldad of the Moledet Party compared the Israeli side of the Geneva Initiative as an attempt to save the ship of the Jewish state by drilling a hole in its bottom. "The document," he said, "betrayed the principles of Zionism, retreated from the land of Israel, divided Jerusalem and relinquished the Temple Mount."[15] Other spokespeople faulted the recognition of Palestinian sovereignty over the Temple Mount and the return of refugees (albeit in limited numbers) to the state of Israel. The transfer of sovereignty over the Temple Mount to the Palestinians was seen on the right as a sign of the signatories' alienation from Judaism and the site's centrality in Jewish tradition. They saw it as an incomprehensible blow to the heart of Israel's existence as the state of the Jewish people.

Various Israeli spokespeople (not necessarily from the right) regarded the alternative solutions to the refugee problem as proposed in the Geneva Initiative in the same light. The alternatives were presented as indirect recognition of a "right of return," even if in the first phase the Palestinians consented to a limited number of returnees. In this case, the alternatives were likened to a crack in the dam of Israel's long-standing position. Once this position was breached to returning refugees, the latter's demands would turn into an overpowering flood.[16]

On the Palestinian side, the Geneva Initiative came in for scathing criticism from oppositionist groups, primarily Hamas, Islamic Jihad, and the PFLP and PDFLP, as well as among people identified with the Fatah and PA. On the whole, they contented that the proposal swept problems under the carpet and conceded to Israel "rights" that had been fought over by generations of Palestinians. Above all, they cited the problematic treatment of the "right of return," including Israel's exoneration from responsibility for having created the refugee problem. On numerous TV shows and in press articles, the Palestinian signatories were accused of having made far-reaching concessions on this crucial issue without the political or moral authority to do so. Reporters for Arab satellite television held interviews in refugee camps in Lebanon and Jordan and documented the criticism of the Geneva Initiative voiced by camp residents. The agreements reached on questions of sovereignty and security also came in for censure by Palestinian spokespeople. A common claim was that the initiative would lead to the establishment of mechanisms making the Palestinian state dependent on and subordinate to Israeli interests.

The criticism of Israelis and Palestinians did not discourage the architects of the Geneva Initiative. Opinion polls indicated steady support in both societies. Supporters drew much encouragement from the broad international backing won by the initiative. At the same time, on the ground, the cycle of hostilities continued. As the cannons roared, public discussion of the initiative subsided. Most Israelis and Palestinians sought relief from the unbearable immediate situation. The possibility of reaching an agreement on final-status issues took the back burner in the public discussion. The conception of "no part-ner" continued intact, and the efforts of the Geneva Initiative proponents to put a dent in it with a campaign of "there is a partner" did not change the ma-jority position in either society. There were signs, however, that an unprece-dented attempt had been made to come up with a new initiative to break the status quo. Prime Minister Sharon resolved to promote a plan of unilateral dis-engagement that was to bring about a dramatic change in the confrontation with the Palestinians. The Geneva Initiators claimed that it was their measure that had pushed Sharon to adopt the disengagement plan, including with-drawal from Palestinian areas and dismantling settlements. Many of the Is-raeli signatories rushed to lend their support to Sharon's unilateral initiative.

Notes

1. The official version of the Roadmap (30 April 2003) is on the State Depart-ment's website, http://www.state.gov/sr/pa/prs/ps/2003/20062.htm.
2. "The Full Version of Israel's Remarks on the Roadmap," *Haaretz*, 27 May 2003.
3. *Yedioth Ahronoth*, 9 June 2003.
4. *Haaretz*, 31 October 2002. The articles by Landau and Arens appeared in *Haaretz*, 8 April 2003 and 10 June 2003, respectively.
5. *Haaretz*, 27 May 2003.
6. For the different voices raised in the discussion, see *al-Hayat*, 5–10 June 2003. For Bush's statement at the 'Aqaba summit, see http://www.whitehouse.gov/news/releases/2003/06/20030604-1.html.
7. James Benet, "Sharon and Abbas Stand Side by Side, Then Begin Talks," *New York Times*, 2 July 2003; John Kifner, "Arabs View Cease-Fire with Cautious Opti-mism," *New York Times*, 1 July 2003.
8. Beilin's most recent book says very little about the road to formulating the Geneva Initiative, despite the title of the book. Beilin, *The Path to Geneva*, pp. 253–265.
9. For the Ayalon-Nusseibeh "Statement of Principles," see the website The Peo-ple's Voice, http://www.mifkad.org.il.
10. For the text, maps, and comments, see the website of the Geneva Initiative, http://www.heskem.org.il/default.asp.
11. "The Geneva Initiative," p. 5.
12. Ibid., pp. 8, 10.
13. Ruth Lapidot, "Be'ayat ha-plitim ha-falestinayim be-havanot Geneva—nituah mishpati" [The Palestinian refugee problem in the Geneva accords—a legal analysis], ibid., pp. 24–29. Lapidot drew attention to the fact that the Geneva docu-ment "does not contain a definition of who is a refugee having the right to benefit from the proposed arrangement" and expressed regret that there was no mention of "the rights of Jews who had been forced to leave Arab states, with all their assets remain-ing behind."
14. "The Geneva Accord—Open Forum with Yossi Beilin, Yaser Abd Rabbo, and Other Drafters" (3 December 2003), see Foundation for Middle East Peace website: http://www.americantaskforce.org/fmep_event.pdf.

15. Arieh Eldad, "Ha-hor b'karka'it ha-sfina" [The hole in the bottom of the boat], http://www.moledet.org.il/eldad-hor.html.

16. For a summary of the critics' positions—especially from the right—see Michael Oren and Yossi Klein-Halevi, "Emunat Geneva" [The Geneva credo], *Tkhelet* (Winter 2004): 25–33; as well as the address by MK Yuval Steinitz at Tel Aviv University (29 December 2003), http://steinitz.likudnik.co.il/Front/NewsNet/reports.asp?reportId=461.

11

High Fences
Make Good Neighbors?

The idea of unilateral separation from the Palestinians had been raised occasionally from the start of the Oslo peace process. At the end of January 1995, following a slew of terror acts against Israelis and at the recommendation of Police Minister Moshe Shahal, Rabin decided to explore the option. Thus was born the concept of a "security fence" to be situated along the "seam area" (*merhav ha-tefer*) between Israel and the West Bank. Like various proposals made during Peres's reign of government, Shahal's suggestion was not carried out. Referring to these notions as a whole, the report of the state comptroller (April 1998) determined that

> since January 1995, a number of programs have been put forth presenting systemic solutions to the problem of the "seam area." Committees were generally set up in the wake of terror acts, but no decision was ever taken to implement their recommendations. A look at these programs shows that they largely share similar principles as to the basic assumptions and security components of the suggested solution, which is based on maintaining control and supervision of the passage of Palestinians and goods.[1]

The idea took further shape under Barak's premiership. "We here and they there" was the slogan Barak and his supporters brandished on innumerable occasions, particularly during his electioneering for head of state. The critical question of the precise division between "here" and "there" was never specified, although the impression was that the route would be dictated by Israeli interests and leave Palestinians limited control of about half of the West Bank and all the Gaza Strip.

The failure of the Camp David negotiations, the eruption of the al-Aqsa intifada and the entrenchment of the "no partner" conception encouraged advocates from both right and left to take tangible steps to promote separation.

Toward the end of his term of office, Barak instructed the head of the National Security Council, Major-General Uzi Dayan, to work out the details of a fence partitioning Israel and the West Bank. In the course of protracted staff planning, the government changed hands, and Ariel Sharon was voted into his first term of office. In July 2002, Dayan submitted his recommendations on the security fence and the envisaged route to Sharon. The Ministerial Committee for National Security approved the plan in principle, but Sharon did not conceal his reservations. Like many on the right, he feared that the route would be seen as a political border and that Israel would come under international pressure to do something about the settlements. At the same time, the plan earned widespread support among politicians and the security establishment. Public opinion polls consistently showed that it was also supported by a large majority of Israel's Jewish population, who viewed it as an effective defense against terror; failure to erect it would expose Israelis to terrorism, and state leaders would be held accountable.[2] The Zionist left (especially the Labor Party) was enthusiastic about a separation fence between the two peoples, holding it up as an alternative to the inaction of Sharon's government. As a result, Sharon backtracked and had work begin on its construction, albeit at a snail's pace and amid modifications to the original route outlined. More importantly, the adoption of the fence plan induced Sharon to formulate the principles of his stance on Palestinian-Israeli relations for the coming years. And so began the unilateral disengagement plan, with the separation fence as a key component.[3]

The Israeli media covered the fence's progress extensively, although, as in the past, the microphone was more liberally offered to the supporters of the idea. As portrayed by the media, there was "no choice" but to erect a fence given the ongoing relentless terror; moreover, unilateral measures were necessary since there was no Palestinian partner with whom to reach a peaceful settlement of the conflict. Well-known commentators described the fence as a nearly magic solution, stressing that the sooner it was built the better. "The recommendation of the security forces must be adopted and a fence built also in Jerusalem," wrote Dan Margalit, a senior Israeli journalist who spared no zeal in advancing the project.[4] The security-oriented position for a fence was sounded too by retired senior officers, especially on television. The IDF "did its bit" as well: it directly encouraged interviews with officers in regular service who repeatedly noted how helpful they found the fence in their daily war on terror and who backed up their words with figures on how the number of terror acts went down as the "obstacle" (*mikhshol*) went up. Elaborate endorsements of the fence appeared on the Ministry of Defense website: The security fence, it said,

> is a vital component of defense to complement the coping [strategies] against terrorism. . . . The barrier does not constitute a defined border and its installation is therefore not based on one or another political demarcation. The car-

dinal interest is security. . . . in the future, when permanent arrangements will be put in place with the Palestinian Authority, a border will be determined and, if need be, the route of the fence modified. . . . One of the key principles guiding the planners of the fence route was consideration of [minimal disruption to the] daily lives of the population living along the "seam" and to the existing interaction of the Palestinian and Israeli populations. The erection of the fence was consequently carried out with maximum consideration for the Palestinian population, subject to the strictures of security needs.[5]

The security establishment thus became one of the major marketers of a separation fence. Nor was it by chance that its advocates called it a "security fence." In its original format, the "barrier" (Israel's official name for the separation fence) was to encircle the West Bank, not only from the west but also from the east. Various—and conflicting—data have been published to date on the final, total length. By the beginning of 2005, about one-third out of a planned 580 kilometers (360 miles) had been completed. For the most part, the "barrier" is a fence; in a few sections, it is a high concrete wall. The overall cost of the project is estimated at $1.5 billion.[6] It is a "separation" measure not achieved in negotiations, enabling its initiators to evade the basic problems of the conflict.

The construction of a separation fence won also the stamp of academic approval in a series of professional conferences and forums held by Israeli universities and research institutes. Gideon Biger, for example, conducted a study for the Ministry of Defense (the IDF History Unit) entitled, "Fences and Borders Around the World (August 2004)" that opens with the following statement: "The numerous attempts made over the years in Israel and around the world to fence off state territory, to erect fences along agreed-upon borders, and to demarcate sovereign states by means of barriers and ground construction requires scholarly examination. This paper presents cases of the construction of a wall or fence along a border in order to prevent the undesirable passage of people from one side to another."[7] Thus, virtually without any discussion of the context of the conflict, the "professional, scholarly literature" contributed to the portrayal of the separation fence as a universal phenomenon of fencing off "state territory." The scholar's conclusion was rather predictable: "For, almost always, the installation of a barrier leads to success at the site where it is properly built, properly maintained, and bolstered by the disposition of efficient human defense. A barrier is as efficient as the manpower responsible for its functioning. An unguarded barrier, no matter how obstructive or sophisticated—will always have people crossing it."[8] In the most comprehensive publication on the subject to date (in Hebrew), the author shows evident support for the project:

The construction of a security separation fence, which would prevent entry into Israel by the great majority of suicide bombers and booby-trapped cars, would seriously thwart the "strategy" of terror organizations, reduce their ability to carry out terror acts and encourage—the meanwhile few—elements, such as Sari Nusseibeh, who hopefully will be prepared to give up on the principle of a right of return or to reach a long-term interim agreement. . . . Preventing terrorism by means of a security separation fence would show the Palestinian public that the path of violence will not succeed.[9]

On the right, various groups opposed the building of a separation fence, especially along the suggested route. Their chief argument was that a fence would significantly undermine the Jewish right to settle anywhere in the land of Israel. They feared that a fence would become a permanent border dividing Israel from the Palestinian entity. And as for it being a partial solution to anti-Israel terror, it might possibly curtail the violence in certain areas, but it would only step up the violence against settlements remaining on the eastern side. Their spokespeople stressed that in the prevailing circumstances of continuing intifada, putting up a fence was both "submission in the face of terror" and a vain hope that a fence could meet Israel's security needs. Although it is understandable that many settlers held this view, it was also common outside the settlements. Environment Minister Tzahi HaNegbi, for instance, said on 19 February 2002: "I do not believe in defensiveness during war. The best defense is offense . . . the solution we believe in is to break the enemy. Not to shut ourselves away. . . . A society that says it is in despair cannot pursue and break the enemy."[10] Israel's right, of course, also found supporters in academe. The right-wing forum Professors for a Strong Israel claimed that the fence had become the "golden calf" worshipped by the media, but that it would not, in fact, enhance security. Only a massive IDF attack would quell terrorism. In the debate over the route, the forum chairman suggested rather that Israel would do well to fence off the Palestinian settlements "defined by the General Security Service (GSS) as foci of terror."[11]

On the Zionist left, opinions on the separation fence varied. The Labor Party, as I pointed out earlier, supported it enthusiastically, and some of its members—not without justice—even claimed copyright. Citing security reasons, they portrayed the fence as the call of the hour and an effective means to significantly slow down the terror assault on Israel. "Separation" à la Barak ("We here and they there") had long occupied an honorable niche in the party. Yossi Beilin, the leader of the Yahad Party, which succeeded Meretz and coveted the crown of the "real left" in the leftist camp, had to decide between party members who advocated a fence (even if reservedly) and members who were vigorously opposed. At times, Yahad spokespeople gave the impression that rather than deal with the essential issues at stake in the fence, they would yet again avail themselves of an opportunity to tout their own alternative—the Geneva Initiative. Few in the Yahad Party or the Peace Now movement considered the obvious contradiction between supporting a solution based on two states (and especially on the Geneva Initiative), which presupposes "a Palestinian partner for peace," and supporting a fence that significantly deviates from the Green Line (the 1949 Armistice line). The fence is based on a unilateral measure and for all intents and purposes assumes that the Palestinian leadership is not a partner for peace. The contradiction was inescapable in Yahad's stance: its leaders were the architects of the Geneva Initiative, yet they voted for Sharon's unilateral disengagement plan. In an unconvincing attempt to explain this political position, Yahad brandished a banner of "Stage two for disengagement—accord now!" Yahad's approach invited criticism from within the left because it was oblivious to the hardships the fence would cause Palestinians. A summation of this opinion can be found on the Left Bank website. The writer, Yigal Bruner, lists the ills of the fence in his conclusion:

> A change that will void all talk of programs, such as the Geneva program, and bring us to a new situation that already partially exists, a cruel state of enclosures. Apartheid. This is the last moment to stop the fence. We, on the Left and in the Center, stand before a historic choice. We can talk about Geneva while every day enclosures are already rising, just as we talked about Oslo while the settlements expanded, the outposts were doubled, and the roads of apartheid paved.[12]

In fact, there were appreciable short- and long-term repercussions. As construction of the fence proceeded, it became clear that for the first time since 1967, the lives of millions of Arabs and Jews were changing dramatically in a sizable chunk of the disputed land. In particular, for a large part of the Palestinian public, the fence made life unbearable. Considerable parts of the route had been drawn east of the Green Line and overnight turned dozens of communities with hundreds of thousands of Palestinians into isolated enclaves. To a great extent, it divided not only Palestinians and Israelis but Palestinians and Palestinians. The change in daily routine took countless expressions, including control over cultivated and uncultivated fields, water sources, transportation routes, and freedom of movement (to school, to municipal offices, to medical centers). Although most of Israel's left chose to ignore these grave results, the actions of groups such as Ta'ayush (Arab Jewish Partnership), Yesh Gvul, Gush Shalom, and Coalition of Women for Peace stood out. Their opposition was reflected in demonstrations and in field trips along the fence route and even in graffiti sprayed on sections of the "barrier" built as a wall ("Barrier to Peace," "The Bad Fence"). Rarely earning a hearing in the media, these groups spread their message on the Internet.

"Fence," "Wall," and Legal Proceedings

On a number of occasions, the question of the separation fence was brought before the High Court of Justice, where judges of the Supreme Court sit as the final court of appeals in criminal and civilian suits. The legal deliberations are fascinating because of both the fundamental and practical verdicts handed down and in light of their consequences for Israel's public and political debate. Sitting as the High Court of Justice, the judges were asked to rule on a basic issue: the legality of the fence. "Our task is difficult," Supreme Court president Aharon Barak noted, "We are members of Israeli society. Although we are sometimes in an ivory tower, that tower is in the heart of Jerusalem, which is not infrequently hit by ruthless terror. We are aware of the killing and destruction wrought by the terror against the state and its citizens. . . . As we sit to judge, so are we judged. . . . Only a separation fence built on a base of law will grant security to the state and its citizens."[13] This was Justice Barak's nod to the complex "location" of a legal system called upon to weigh questions in which legal and national-political aspects were not always sharply delineated and that obliged a principled, moral stance. A Sisyphean search for the golden mean between local law and national interests and between international law and the human rights of the inhabitants of the Occupied Territories. The court was asked to consider (1) Palestinian petitions against the state of Israel, claiming that the erection of the fence was damaging to rights, property, and freedom of movement; and (2) the danger that a discriminatory regime was being instituted against the large Palestinian population and would exacerbate their already difficult living conditions. The High Court of Justice thus turned into an extraordinary venue for the contesting interests and narratives of Israelis and Palestinians.

The legal discussion on the matter of the fence provided an enlightening review of the design and dissemination of the Israeli narrative on the necessity of the fence. The description by the state prosecution of the circumstances obliging the construction of a "security fence" was often a translation into legalese of common claims in Israel's hegemonic discourse. A discursive process thus took root with legal, political, and national discussions mutually feeding one another. Later, once the judges ruled, the decision affected also Israel's public debate. And vice versa. All drew on extensive references to the context of the decision of the heads of state to build a separation fence. Both the answer of the respondents and the rulings of the judges contained a chapter on "background" or "factual background" devoted to a description of the "essence of the current conflict between Israel and the Palestinian side." This chapter presented the common Israeli narrative as to exclusive Palestinian responsibility for the failure of Camp David negotiations (July 2000) and the decision of Palestinian leaders to "move over to an assault of cruel terrorism on Israel and Israelis."[14] The construction of the "barrier" was substantiated solely on the basis of security needs and the obligation of the government to protect the civilian population, given the background wave of acts of terror. One of the prosecution's responses (1 January 2004) stated that the decision to put up a barrier was "a natural, warranted step in the spirit of 'good fences make good neighbors.'" In common with the prevalent claim in the public debate, the prosecution argued that the fence constructed in the Gaza Strip was the best indication that the building of a "barrier" in the West Bank had a good chance of preventing terrorism against Israel's citizens: "The Gaza Strip is surrounded by a fence and, indeed, in the years that the fence has been operative, suicide bombers did not leave the Gaza Strip for Israel via the fence."[15] The fencing off of the Gaza Strip did greatly reduce the number of Palestinians who succeeded in perpetrating acts of terror in Israel. But at the same time, it spurred on commanders of the armed struggle to change their tactics of warfare. RPG rockets and Qassam short-range missiles soon became the hallmark of the Palestinian armed struggle. True, they caused relatively little damage to life and limb. Nevertheless, the failure of the IDF's countless attempts to thwart their launching created the impression that the Palestinians posed a serious challenge to Israel regardless of the fence around the Gaza Strip. Furthermore, the motivation of numerous Palestinians to inflict injury on Israel remained undisturbed.

In all high court discussions, the judges, without reservation, took the position that the fence was an obligatory defense measure in view of the unprecedented terror assault and stipulated that the route was not to be regarded as a political demarcation line. These principles, consistent with the government's position, were elaborated in a series of rulings. The court, however stated that legal determinations about decisions of the government (the "administrative body") should properly be made according to the "principle of proportionality," which "focuses, therefore, on the relationship between the objective whose achievement is being attempted, and the means used to achieve it." In keeping with this principle, the judges ruled that in certain instances, the route of the fence was to be modified, and they instructed the government to take such steps as to avoid injuring the Palestinian population. The high court thus accepted part of the petition submitted by the Beit Sourik Village Council and determined the orders issued "nullified since their injury to the local inhabitants is disproportionate."[16]

The Supreme Court thus gave its sanction to most of the government arguments. This sanction, however, was somewhat dented by the International Court of Justice in the Hague, in its Advisory Opinion (9 July 2004).[17] With undisguised criticism and virtually outright, the Hague judges rejected the reasons for the building of "the wall" (as they defined the separation fence) and Israel's interpretation of its control over the Occupied Territories. The Israeli occupation was portrayed as contrary to international conventions, primarily the Fourth Geneva Convention. Israel was called on to immediately cease construction of the "wall" and specifically to dismantle the portion built in deviation from the Green Line. In Israel, the opinion of the International Court of Justice was thoroughly dismissed, and the judges' handling of the complex issue was brought into question. Instead of directly confronting the specific arguments against the project, Israel had made do with submitting an affidavit to the court and devoted most of its energies to a public relations campaign. Once again, the Israeli media rose to the occasion; almost to a person it aired mainly critical views of the International Court of Justice's very authority to hear the matter and of the rulings handed down by the judges, who were unaware of the circumstances that made the erection of the "security fence" mandatory.[18] Construction of the fence continued, though very slowly.

Arab Reactions

The Arabic media tended to denote the Israeli project as "gedar al-fasel al-'unsuri" (the racist separation fence). The separation fence and numerous checkpoints scattered throughout the West Bank were portrayed as a severe blow to human rights and as collective punishment of the Palestinian people. Israel, many claimed, was cementing an apartheid regime in the Occupied Territories. More than once, the severe restrictions on Palestinian daily life were compared to the ills visited on other persecuted peoples, especially the Jewish ghettos of World War II.[19] Israel's contention that the fence was put up as a measure of defense against terrorism was described in the Arabic public discourse as a paltry excuse. Various Arab spokespeople rejected the forecast that the fence would better defend Israel's civilians and cited Israeli opponents to the project, including West Bank settlers. Abbas, in an interview with Israeli journalists during his presidential campaign, noted: "Last week I toured Qalqilya. I passed along the wall you built there. I saw one large prison house with one gate to the world. You've penned up an entire zone. When I was prime minister and I met with Sharon, I told him, the fence will not give you security. If you insist on continuing to build it, OK, but on your land, not ours."[20]

Arab spokespeople ascribed the building of the fence to a series of factors, chiefly to the continuing Israeli desire to separate from Palestinians along a route to be dictated by Israel. The difference between Sharon and his predecessors was the latter's resolve to carry out the program. "While the former prime minister, Yitzhak Rabin, did say 'get Gaza out of Tel Aviv,' the present prime minister, Ariel Sharon, is the first to lend the program a tangible character."[21] It was argued that Sharon was taking advantage of international and regional circumstances to revive his real plan: the establishment of a Palestinian state on 42 percent of the West Bank. Israel maintained that the fence was installed for security reasons, but in fact the route shows that it is a political fence that will enable Israel to control extensive Palestinian areas that will cut up the Palestinian state into cantons subject to full Israeli control; this, on top of the fact that the fence was diametrically opposed to the Bush vision and the Roadmap (calling for the establishment of an independent Palestinian state with territorial contiguity).[22] The "seam area" (including the fence) being created by Israel will be formed by annexing extensive, fertile farmland. That will deal a mortal blow to the income of tens of thousands of Palestinians and compound the constraints of the Palestinian economy, which is already in dire straits. The separation fence is thus a device to further burden Palestinian lives, with the aim of forcing them out of their settlements and into emigration. It is not expulsion in the traditional sense, but it is certainly "expulsion à la twenty-first century, meaning ostensibly voluntary emigration. Israel is not asking these people to leave, they will simply do so of their own free will—once they are stripped of sources of income in their villages."[23] Many of the Palestinian leadership declared that "the construction of the separation fence was a clear case of terrorism since it destroyed Palestinian lives."[24]

The Unilateral Disengagement Plan

The violence increased and the "no partner" conception spread with deleterious consequences in various spheres. Political talks and security coordination between the two sides ground to a complete halt. Only a handful of Palestinian workers were allowed into Israel, which meant a drastic drop in the standard of living of millions of Palestinians. Unemployment in the Occupied Territories swelled to unprecedented proportions. Political support for the PA leadership sank to an all-time low. Public opinion polls showed the growing strength of the oppositionists—especially Hamas, though there was still considerable support for a two-state solution. Khalil Shikaki, the head of a research institute studying the Palestinian population since the start of Oslo, related these trends (11 May 2004) in the overall context of the Oslo process: "The trend over the last decade, but especially during the last four years, has been negative on both counts: the Palestinian Authority has lost much of its popular legitimacy, and the balance has shifted in favor of the Islamists. . . . Support for the two-state solution and for reconciliation based on it ranges between two-thirds to three-quarters."[25]

The Israeli public stepped up pressure on the government to provide far more effective defense for the civilian population. A large majority of the Jewish population wanted a separation fence in the hope that it would greatly reduce the terror. It was the unilateralists' finest hour. Those Palestinians and Israelis who to begin with had not believed in a two-state solution on the basis of the 4 June 1967 borders now set the tone of the public discourse, which had an impact on policy. Settlers demanded that settlements be fortified and expanded. Most of Israel's political parties embraced the simplistic idea that a fence would bring relief from the harsh realities of conflict. Palestinian groups championing armed struggle demanded that the intifada be continued. The Palestinian leadership, headed by a besieged Arafat at his Ramallah headquarters, were hard put to move beyond the limited frame of action left them by Israel and the United States and, apart from uttering slogans, did not take any real steps to extricate themselves from the crisis. The attention of the Bush administration was focused on the battle for control in Iraq. Instead of embarking on significant measures to stop Israeli-Palestinian violence, the United States issued feeble statements.

Israeli prime minister Ariel Sharon recognized the extraordinary opportunity that had come his way and initiated a plan aimed, once more, at reshuffling the Israeli-Palestinian conflict. He hoped to utilize the unusual local and regional conjuncture to advance a national goal he regarded as supremely important: to derail and replace the Oslo blueprint. Sharon likely knew that this "window of opportunity" could close at any moment. After all, both the Bush vision and the Roadmap related to the contingency of a Palestinian state by the year 2005.[26] This is what influenced Sharon's position, although, ultimately, the course Israel adopted veered from his original motives. He was soon to find how difficult, if not impossible, it was to disentangle the two sides from the cycle of violence, unless the basic problems of the Israeli-Palestinian conflict were dealt with. As 2004 drew to a close, a mere year after Sharon came out with his unilateral disengagement initiative, it was patently clear to him that his plan was taking a new direction. This critical year started with the unilateral disengagement initiative (including a very limited withdrawal from the Occupied Territories and evacuation of settlements) and ended with the agreement on "coordination" with the new Palestinian leadership (under Abbas), Egypt, and the United States. Another key feature of this year was the titanic struggle waged between the opponents of disengagement on the one hand and Israel's security forces and government on the other.

Sharon first went public with his unilateral disengagement initiative at the Herzliya Conference (18 December 2003), the chief nongovernmental Israeli security forum. In recent years, it has furnished state leaders with a podium to air political theories. Sharon endorsed Israel's commitment to the Roadmap and undertook to ease the daily life of Palestinians and even to dismantle outposts, as he had told US president Bush he would. He assured Palestinians that he did not intend to use his policy to control their fate and added that Israel supported the establishment of "a democratic Palestinian state with territorial contiguity in Judea and Samaria." At the same time, Israel could not live under terror and wait endlessly for change: "if in a few months the Palestinians still continue to disregard their part in implementing the Roadmap—then Israel will initiate the unilateral security steps of disengagement." The deception Sharon constructed had it that only the Palestinians did not honor commitments and that only their leadership encouraged terror. In such a situation, it was incumbent upon Israel's government to take steps to protect its citizens. The disengagement plan, in his words, "will be fully co-ordinated with the United States" and, in line with it, the IDF will deploy along "provisional security lines. . . . This security line will not constitute the permanent border of the state of Israel."[27] In this address, as in later interviews, Sharon portrayed the plan as "a security measure, not a political one," which, in any case, did not defy the Bush vision and the Roadmap; it would be possible to return to the latter in the future with a new Palestinian leadership that had repudiated terror. Further details of the plan soon came to light. Israel's unilateral disengagement would include the full evacuation of the Gaza Strip (settlements and military forces alike) and of an area in northern Samaria—including a number of military installations and the settlements of Ganim, Kadim, Humesh, and Sanor. In addition, from remarks dropped by Sharon and his associates, one could fill in what had been left unsaid at the Herzliya Conference. In an interview for the Jewish New Year in the fall of 2004, the prime minister noted: "After all, we won't remain in Gaza, not according to any or anyone's political plan. On the other hand, thanks to this plan, there is a chance that Israel will keep strategic places in Judea and Samaria."[28] More than any other statements, those made by Dov Weisglass, Sharon's close adviser, revealed the prime minister's intentions. In an interview in *Haaretz Supplement* (8 October 2004), Weisglass described the aims and advantages of the disengagement plan thus:

> The significance is the freezing of the political process. And when you freeze that process you prevent the establishment of a Palestinian state and you prevent a discussion about the refugees, the borders and Jerusalem. Effectively, this whole package that is called the Palestinian state, with all that it entails, has been removed from our agenda indefinitely. And all this with authority and permission. All with a [US] presidential blessing and the ratification of both houses of Congress. . . . With the proper management we succeeded in removing the issue of the political process from the agenda. And we educated the world to understand that there is no one to talk to.[29]

The fact that Weisglass was faithful to Sharon's overall conception was confirmed by Sharon's feeble reaction when asked to comment.

Sharon's statements and the decisions adopted in the Knesset, the cabinet, and the IDF aroused stormy debate over unilateral disengagement. The Labor Party and a large chunk of the Zionist left (including Yahad and Peace Now) expressed support for the plan in one form or another.[30] The differences in the positions of the state of Israel under Sharon and of the left became a blur. The left hastily embraced the "new Sharon" and cursorily claimed that he had adopted their platform. Sharon's consent to dismantling settlements and withdrawing from Gaza were touted triumphantly as vindication of the left's path. The "victors," however, ignored the problematics of unilateral disengagement, Weisglass's statements about a long-term freeze on the political process, and, of course, the ongoing occupation. A few voices condemned the left's support for Sharon's policy; the left answered that disengagement could transform the realities and dynamics so as to facilitate resumption of the political process and to renew discussion of the Geneva Initiative. Public opinion polls at the end of 2004 showed that most Israelis supported unilateral disengagement and considered it "a first step towards extensive evacuation of Jewish settlements in the West Bank as part of a permanent agreement with the Palestinian Authority."[31] It is important to note that these assessments were based more on hope than on a sober view of Israel's political situation. The left's support was crucial to the survival of Sharon's government. But it was the rival political camp, Sharon's own party, that conducted the more interesting and penetrating discussion of disengagement.

The discussions, held in various party and government forums, were extensively covered by the media. Shortly after his Herzliya address, Sharon and his plan drew severe criticism at the Likud convention (5 January 2004), causing astonishment both in Israel and around the world. The prime minister's speech at the convention was greeted with catcalls, and the same thing happened at other party forums. Even stronger stricture came from spokespeople of right-wing parties and movements. The Judea and Samaria Council (J&SC) dubbed the initiative a "program of illusions" that constituted a "reward for terrorism" and could lead to the "transfer of Jews" and the "ruin of Zionism." The efforts of the right "to rescind the evil decree" gained momentum in 2004 and found expression in cabinet meetings, Knesset deliberations, and countless public events (demonstrations, torch parades, placards and stickers, press articles and media interviews locally and abroad, and even in complaints lodged with the police against the prime minister). The right hoped that the opposition of Likud members would compel Sharon to shelve the plan. These hopes soared when a special questionnaire (2 May 2004) showed that most Likud members opposed the plan. Much to their amazement, however, Sharon made it plain that he remained undeterred.

The opponents redoubled their efforts in anticipation of the plan's critical discussion in the cabinet and Knesset. Ministerial support was very thin; nonetheless, the initiative was finally approved after virulent arguments (6 June 2004). Sharon won a majority vote only after agreeing to a decisive formulation: "this decision does not mean [an automatic] dismantling of settlements."[32] In the next months, extraparliamentary groups on the Right (Gush Katif Campaign Headquarters, Women in Green, Terror Victims Headquarters, Gamla Shall Not Fall Again, A Different Spirit, Professors Forum for Political and Economic Power, and the Hebron Jewish Community Council) launched a wide range of protests. Thousands of demonstrators at Jerusalem's Zion Square (12 September 2004) lambasted Sharon, calling him names ("the dictator") and accusing him of suffering from delusions ("Sharon has disengaged from reality"), of adopting a policy that would lead to "civil war" and to an unprecedented "national disaster." A manifesto circulated on the eve of the demonstration and signed by prominent figures on the right called on the security forces to declare that "transfer and uprooting [of settlements] were a national crime and a crime against humanity, a sign of tyranny, wickedness and arbitrariness, designed to deny Jews their right to live in their land only because they are Jews." The manifesto asked settlers "not to accept compensation, to actively oppose uprooting, though without hurting anybody." Cabinet ministers were urged not to lend a hand to the "blatantly illegal" (evacuation) order and thereby to prevent "an irreversible breach among the people and in the army." Officials, soldiers, and police officers to be recruited to carry out the order were asked to "heed the voice of their national and human conscience, and not to take part in acts that would taint them to their lifelong regret."[33] The signatories thus supported a nebulous sort of opposition, which, however, they were careful to stress, objected to violent confrontations with police and military forces. This was the opening volley of a debate that was to widen into a call for refusal—the refusal to carry out military orders. Right-wing public figures, especially rabbis, published manifestos adjuring soldiers and officers to desist from lending a hand to the evacuation of settlers. According to the impression given by the Israeli media, the potential compliance with the call was broad indeed.

Outdoor placards and press advertisements placed by right-wingers grew increasingly incendiary against Sharon and the advocates of disengagement. The Rabbinical Congress for Peace took out a full-page ad under the title, "Stop! Stop! God preserve us from the terrible destruction," the gist of which was a *halakhic* ruling, in accordance with Jewish law, "forbidding the transfer of any part of the Holy Land, which was signed by 300 distinguished Israeli rabbis."[34] Against the backdrop of right-wing opposition and heated public debate, the Knesset had to process the Law on the Implementation of Disengagement (27 October 2004). The version brought to the vote stated that "Israel had concluded that there was no Palestinian partner for peace today with whom progress could be made in a bilateral peace process"; the unilateral disengagement measure emanated from the conception that "the current situation of deadlock is deleterious." The evacuation of settlements and military installations was to take about a year—that is, until the end of 2005.[35] The voting generated high drama—until the actual show of hands it was far from clear that the measure enjoyed majority support or how cabinet ministers would cast their ballots. But the drama wound down. The move was approved by quite a large margin of 67 to 45, with 7 abstentions. Apart from Minister Uzi Landau, the other wavering ministers (headed by Netanyahu) allowed themselves to be guided by political rather than ideological considerations. The disappointment on the right was sharp. More than ever, Sharon was pictured as a "dictator," bending his party's majority decisions to his own needs and pushing through disengagement in the Knesset only through the threat of dismissing ministers. An ad in huge letters at the Judea and Samaria Council read: "Beware dictatorship!" and "Sharon is tearing the people apart." A "torn" Star of David flanked the letters. The prime minister and supporters of disengagement were shown as disconnected from reality and from the people. In contrast to the "disconnected" (who for all practical purposes were implementing the platform of the leftist camp), settlers and their supporters were shown as "connected" with reality and the people, a motif that featured in numerous published New Year greetings. Thus, an ad by the head of the Samaria Regional Council read:[36]

> May
> This year
> Coming upon us
> Be a year of planting
> Not uprooting
> A year of building
> Not dismantling
> A year of engagement
> Not disengagement

On numerous occasions, the right contended that a withdrawal from Gush Katif settlements in the Gaza Strip warned of something much larger: questioning the right of Jews to settle in all areas of the land of Israel. Pinhas Wallerstein, one of the prominent figures on the J&SC, stressed that "not a single resident believed that disengagement would end with the evacuation of the settlements of the [Gaza] Strip and northern Samaria. Any reasonable person, not just the settlers, understood that this was merely the beginning. It was a battle between the Left and the Right over the Zionist character of the state of Israel.[37] Journalist Uri Elitzur voiced another of the right's pet claims, namely that the settlers of Gush Katif were pioneers who had turned barren land into a flourishing garden. They "are not in Gaza nor close to Gaza, nor do they stand in the way of the IDF quitting Gaza. They live on land that was never Palestinian . . . not a single Palestinian ever lived there and for hundreds of years or more, no one has ever used it. It has been a Jewish area for 35 years. If the Jewish people did not have the right to settle there, because the place belongs to Arabs, this means that the Jewish people did not have the right to build Tel Aviv or Hadera or the state."[38]

The internal discussions of mainstream settlers and their supporters filled more and more pages of *Nekuda*, the chief organ of the settlers and the J&SC. A whole range of national, security-related, and even *halakhic*-Jewish arguments were invoked to condemn disengagement and present it as a sure recipe for "civil war" of the kind that had brought down disaster on the Jewish people in the past. Opposition to the plan, it must be noted, was not the sole preserve of settlers. In a polemic appearing in *Nekuda* (September 2004), Yoav

Gelber of the Department of Land of Israel Studies at Haifa University maintained that the purpose of the plan was not to solve the problem of Gaza but to be rid of it. The initiative was based on assumptions that had no realistic basis; it was a reflection of Sharon's surrender to an atmosphere created by a minority of "noble-minded bleeding hearts." Disengagement would not bring Israel security or ease.[39] One illuminating discussion in *Nekuda* wondered how it was that most of the Jewish public supported withdrawing from Gaza and northern Samaria? Apart from the common claim made by settlers ("we did not succeed in settling in the hearts of most of the Jewish people"), the responses were enlightening. One example may be found in the article by journalist Uri Orbach, who is well known for his right-wing views. As he put it:

> Even though most of the public is ready to agree with the statement that "the land of Israel belongs to us," in practical terms there is broad accord across the board that "we'd like to see few Arab maidservants around us." The desire to be rid of, to separate, not to see the Palestinians is so rooted in Jewish society that we are prepared to pay a heavy price to avoid rubbing against them. . . . the entire right and most of the left are not interested in Palestinian "justice." They are not interested in the right of Palestinians to a state, nor do the "wrongs" of occupation really bother them. The solutions gaining a following across the board are not solutions of peace but solutions of separation: quitting Lebanon, a separation fence, quitting Gaza.[40]

Rabbi Yaacov Madan, a settler at Alon Shvut, spoke of the need to be receptive to the voice of the Israeli public rather than to hole up within the right's own four walls. He suggested that the right show wisdom rather than self-righteousness. "The considerations for and against [disengagement] are many and varied," he said, and it is thus better to campaign "against a specific portion of the plan, rather than against the entire plan."[41]

Differing positions on the right about the disengagement plan and the ways to thwart it broke down into four chief groups: a mainstream, represented by the J&SC; a not insignificant minority that called for physical opposition to any evacuation (including the Hilltop Youth)—all nationalists, the offspring of settlement residents; and a more militant group including Israelis who did not dismiss the possibility of armed confrontation with the security forces (prominent among them, Kach and Kahanah Hai activists). Alongside these three, there were reports about another group of indeterminate size, its members resigned to the government decision and even prepared to be evacuated in exchange for appropriate compensation. The dividing line between the different groups revolved around the sort of action to be taken. As the air of emergency thickened, the different right-wing groups seemed to nourish one another. The stance of the Hilltop Youth and the militants challenged not only the rule of law and the military but right-wing groups as well, notably the J&SC. Intractably, militant settlers called for struggle by all and any means to scotch disengagement. In their eyes, the evacuation of any settlement, or even any outpost, undermined the Jewish right to settle everywhere in the land of Israel. The Israeli media increasingly leaked reports from security sources that the settler "hard core" intended to torpedo the government plan and the IDF by various means, which included threats on the life of the prime minister and the head of the Disengagement Authority; damage to the Temple Mount mosques; and, of course, a resort to violence, including the use of arms. As a result, more and more J&SC members abandoned the compromising line they had taken at the start of the crisis. At the end of December 2004, Wallerstein published a call to sharpen the opposition to disengagement, even at the risk of breaking the law and imprisonment. The J&SC website carried previous assertions made by state leaders, including Sharon's proclamation that "the status of the Netzarim [settlement] was equivalent to the status of [Kibbutz] Negba and Tel Aviv. Netzarim's evacuation would only encourage terror and step up the pressure on us."[42] Given the disparity between his election promise and his current policy, the prime minister was featured as an opportunist and a liar. In the religious-nationalist rhetoric of some settler spokespeople, he was described as a leader taking advantage of his authority to do wrong. J&SC leader Shaul Goldstein declared: "Major crimes too have been committed in the past under the cover of democracy."[43]

Disengagement—Reactions from Abroad

The chances of any significant Israeli or Palestinian initiative succeeding had from the start of the Oslo process depended to a large degree on US support and to a lesser degree on the positions of leading Arab states (primarily Egypt). Well aware of this, Sharon's initiative was closely coordinated with Bush's top brass in steady contacts behind the scenes (especially between Dov Weisglass and Condoleezza Rice). These efforts climaxed in the Bush-Sharon White House summit, with the US president depositing a valuable letter in the hands of the Israeli prime minister (14 April 2004).[44] As in the meeting between them, so in the letter Bush showered praised on Sharon's bold leadership, describing the content of his blueprint as "historic and courageous actions. . . . These steps can open the door to progress toward a peaceful, democratic, viable Palestinian state."[45] As for the move's unilateral nature, Israeli and US leaders and their aides were wary of the very word, referring instead to "gradual disengagement." The word *unilateral* did not appear at all in the letter exchanged or in the subsequent press conference, a "laundering" that obviously could not take care of the actual problems involved in a far-reaching, one-sided measure. Bush's support was aimed at helping Sharon against his serious opposition at home. Thus, at the press conference, Bush twice stressed US commitment to Israel "as a vibrant Jewish state." And his letter stated that the

United States supported the disengagement plan, which might spell "real progress" toward realizing the vision proclaimed by President Bush in June 2002 and toward peace.

A close look at the president's words shows that he chose "to adjust" his vision to the priorities the two men shared. At the summit's conclusion, Bush related to the vision of peace in the Middle East thus: "The heart of this vision is the responsibility of all parties—of Israel, of the Palestinian people, of the Arab states—to fight terror, to embrace democracy and reform, and to take the necessary steps for peace."[46] The phrasing of the Bush memorandum was an attempt—not particularly successful—to combine support for the Israeli prime minister's initiative with adherence to the principles of US policy. But no special interpretation was required for Sharon to conclude that many would see the memorandum as a basic departure from the US position, namely, that the United States—as patron and chief intermediary in the Israeli-Palestinian conflict—should avoid taking a stand on issues to be discussed in final-status negotiations. Indeed, Bush sounded as if he had decided to move away from the traditional position on such complex questions as the future of the settlements, the problem of refugees, and permanent borders. In order to ensure Israel's continued existence as a Jewish state, he called for settling the refugees in the Palestinian-state-to-be, "rather than in Israel." On the question of borders, he seemed to be echoing Israel's traditional interpretation of Security Council Resolution 242, which demanded that major settlement blocs remain under Israeli sovereignty: "Israel must have secure and recognized borders which should emerge from negotiations between the parties. . . . In light of new realities on the ground, including already existing major Israeli population centers, it is unrealistic to expect that the outcome of final status negotiations will be a full and complete return to the armistice lines of 1949."[47] At the same time, the memorandum contained a clause that appeared to contradict these declarations. "As you know, the United States supports the establishment of a Palestinian state that is viable, sovereign, and independent." As a result, Sharon could embrace those portions of the letter helpful to him while the Americans could tell their critics that they were sticking to their permanent positions on the Israeli-Palestinian conflict. Letter in hand, Sharon repeatedly underscored the far-reaching significance he found in the US commitments formulated by the presidential letter, particularly in response to domestic critics. A few days after returning from Washington, the prime minister noted in the Knesset (22 April 2004): "The political support we won on my visit to the US is an unprecedented gain for Israel. Political support of the scope and force expressed in the President's letter has not been given us since the establishment of the state of Israel. . . . The Palestinians regard the President's letter as their hardest blow since the War of Independence."[48]

Not only did the Bush administration welcome Sharon's initiative virtually without demur, but it undertook to recruit international support. And these efforts bore fruit. Two days after Sharon's trouncing in the Likud poll, the Quartet representatives declared (4 May 2004) that the withdrawal from the Gaza Strip and part of the West Bank might present a rare opportunity to push ahead with the peace process in conjunction with the Roadmap. The United States and its Quartet partners ignored both the thorniness of unilateralism and the possibility that Sharon's measure was aimed at, among other things, torpedoing the Roadmap.

The reactions of the Palestinian leadership to unilateral disengagement were complicated, evolving over time. The chance of Israeli troops withdrawing and settlements being dismantled was welcomed by many. Any Israeli withdrawal—the writers of the PLO website maintained—marked victory for Palestinian resistance and a step forward in the struggle to end the occupation. The ayes in Knesset and cabinet were a firm indication that the idea of a Greater Israel was bankrupt.[49] However, vigorous opposition to unilateral Israeli moves was strongly voiced. Yasser Abd Rabbo and Hanan Ashrawi noted that unilateralism would return the two sides to the days when Israel had tried to ignore the Palestinians. Those attempts did not work in the past, and they would not work in the future.[50] According to Muhammad Dahlan, state minister of security affairs in the Abbas government of 2003, unilateral disengagement would achieve one undesirable result: it would strengthen the hands of opponents to the peace process. Gradually, it became evident that more and more Palestinian leaders, headed by Abbas, sought to transform the unilateral measure of limited withdrawal into a program to be implemented and coordinated both with them and in conjunction with the Roadmap. Such a measure would enable the Palestinian national leadership to emerge from the corner it had been backed into by Israel and the United States. "We are the partner," key PA leaders claimed, adding that they would be happy to coordinate the withdrawal with Israel, to accept responsibility for the areas evacuated, to enter into serious negotiations on cease-fire, and to resume the political process on the basis of the Roadmap.[51]

Regarding US policy, the PA leadership were very cautious, not wishing to exacerbate their already difficult plight. They saw the unreserved US support for disengagement as freeing Israel of all its commitments under the Roadmap.[52] In contrast, the Arab media—especially satellite TV and the Internet—were heavily critical of the plan, its initiators, and international support. Spokespeople for Palestinian oppositionists described the withdrawal as a victory for their armed struggle. Hamas and the Islamic Jihad claimed that Israel was being chased out of Gaza just as it had fled from Lebanon, that Israel understood only the language of force. Withdrawal should thus be applauded and the armed struggle continued in order to liberate additional occupied Palestinian territories. However, the road to freedom was still long and paved with troubles. Withdrawal would not ease, but rather worsen, the predicament of Gaza's population. In its wake, Gazans would find themselves "in one large prison," the Gaza Strip being utterly under the control of Israeli forces. Israel would remove its forces and civilians from the strip, only to continue to control Gaza's land, sea, and airspace from the outside.[53] Sharon was depicted as striving to exploit the current conjuncture to promote a unilateral plan that in any case could have no Palestinian partner. Arab commentators covering Israeli politics claimed rather convincingly that his purpose was to advance a long-term interim agreement whereby Israel would withdraw from the Gaza Strip and 42 percent of the West Bank (which itself would be broken up into cantons) and thereby dispense with the need to deal with final-status questions. From his point of view, the areas newly evacuated by Israel and ruled by a Palestinian political entity could be called a "state."[54] US support for the plan, especially the commitments in Bush's memorandum, were censured. The plan was couched in the context of the US occupation of Iraq. Various Arab spokespeople contended that the policy of the Bush administration was the chief factor in continuing regional instability and the main obstacle to peace, an act of aggression against Arabs in general and Palestinians in particular. On the website of the Syrian Broadcast Authority, the PA was urged not to cooperate with the unilateral plan since it was an "Israeli trap."

The Egyptian Initiative

Most Arab heads of state rejected the popular cry to stand up to US support for disengagement. They preferred communication to confrontation, fearing that a contest could be to their detriment. Instead, they clutched at the statements and commitments of administration leaders that the Roadmap remained the only agreed-upon plan for resuming the political process. Egypt adopted this tricky stance in mid-2004 with real consequences for both Israeli and Palestinian positions, which makes it significant. Egyptian involvement took shape against Israel's internal political wrestling and the resentment voiced by Arab spokespeople at Egypt's intervention, which was described as meddling in internal Palestinian affairs.[55] The impression created by leaks to the media was that in the eyes of Egyptian leaders, the Bush administration's handling of crises in the Middle East was misguided and might well compound the situation. In view of the delicate relationship between the two countries, however, Mubarak's government was doubly careful to avoid a real upset in relations with Washington. Cairo was well aware that Egyptian-US ties were also being put to the test in the Middle Eastern rumpus. In this respect, its promotion of an Israeli-Palestinian settlement was an integral part of Egypt's overall policy vis-à-vis the sole superpower.

Israel's consenting to a significant role for Egypt in the disengagement plan was unprecedented, and President Mubarak and his aides were quick to see its latent potential. At this stage, from the point of view of Egyptian interests, involvement was far preferable to sitting on the fence. In common with certain US and European counterparts, Egypt's decisionmakers believed that the moment was ripe to embrace Sharon—that is, to put the squeeze on him. At the Bush-Mubarak summit on Bush's ranch (in Crawford, Texas, 12 April 2004), it was agreed, among other things, that the disengagement plan was not a substitute for the Roadmap published the previous year but a phase in its promotion, a spark that might well rekindle the political process.

Official Egyptian spokespeople welcomed Israel's decision to withdraw from the Gaza Strip and a small portion of the West Bank and to evacuate its settlements and armed forces from these areas. Yet they did not conceal their fears that the unilateral measure would end in chaos in the Gaza Strip, on Egypt's very doorstep. Egypt may have thought too that its involvement could dent the sweeping support of Bush's administration for Sharon's policy. Mubarak's government consequently took a step that amounted to accepting disengagement, but along with other measures that targeted three goals: to thwart Israel's intention to unilaterally carry out the plan, to rehabilitate the PA leadership, and to link disengagement with the Roadmap, in effect resuming the political process. Israel had long wished to see Egypt, as the sovereign authority in Sinai, take responsibility for the security of the Egypt-Gaza border area (the "Philadelphi Route" in Israeli parlance or the "Salah al-Din Route," as the Arabs call it). Over the years, the region had become a hotbed for smuggling goods and weapons, and in Israel's appraisal, once it itself retreated, the strip would be inundated with arms. Egypt grappled with the dilemma: if it acquiesced in Israel's request, it would not only have to redeploy in Sinai (its current forces near the border were very thin, in accordance with the peace treaty with Israel), but it also ran the risk of skirmishes with one Palestinian group or another. A more serious fear was that, should violence resume between Israel and the Palestinians, Egypt's forces could be caught in the middle and incur casualties. Finally, voices in Egypt had long clamored for a dispatch of forces to Gaza to protect Palestinians. Egypt had no interest in encouraging these advocates to think that a dispatch of limited forces was a mere vanguard; it had long steered clear of a full-blown crisis with Israel and had every intention of continuing to do so. Yet there was no escaping the fact that Egyptian involvement would bolster Mubarak's regime as a moderating and stabilizing factor in a dangerously restive Middle East, an image Egypt had been deftly nurturing for a long time. Apart from coordinated involvement along the Philadelphi Route, Egypt (with the agreement of the other main players) assumed two more tasks, training Palestinian security and police forces and reopening "dialogue" between Palestinian factions. The goal of the dialogue was for the PA and the oppositionist groups to reach an agreement on highly charged issues, among them the conditions for ceasefire with Israel, the keeping of law and order, and regime reforms. Everyone was well aware that such an agreement could change or even end the al-Aqsa intifada.

Official Egypt's explicit support for disengagement was not aimed at helping Israel's government and certainly not the man at its head. Most of the Egyptian public and leaders found Sharon loathsome. Moreover, Cairo knew too well that if Sharon had been able to promote his plan without Egyptian help, he would have done so with alacrity. The mutual suspicion and antipathy between Sharon and Mubarak had a long history and was shared by some of their ministers and aides. These feelings, however, gave way before the weighty interests on both sides. The Israeli-Palestinian conflict had turned brutal, and the longer it went on, the more it threatened the vital national interests of Arab states, especially Jordan and Egypt, which bordered the arena of conflict. Daily reports on the blows Palestinians suffered had a cumulative effect on local public opinion. Rage against Israel, as at US measures in Iraq, was sometimes reflected in the censure of Egyptian impotence. Although the censure came largely from oppositionist groups, Egypt's public discourse revealed displeasure also among mainstream spokespeople.

Egypt thus opted for stepped-up involvement as part of its reassessment of the dramatic developments in the Middle East and their threat to Egyptian interests. It viewed the Israeli-Palestinian conflict as tightly interwoven with both the US-led global war on terror (part of which was the struggle for control in Iraq) and the diverse initiatives for political reform in Arab states. Important interests hung in the balance, and developments in any one of these spheres could crucially affect the polity and stability of the government of Egypt. Another factor, of course, was the identification of Egyptian society with the Palestinian people, whom they saw as a victim being crushed under a long and hard occupation.

At the end of 2004, the PA leadership again weighed the pros and cons of Israel's disengagement plan, US and international support for it, and Egypt's involvement. But as befits a great drama, fate soon took a hand forcing all the parties to reexamine their positions and policies. On 11 November 2004, Arafat died. The Palestinian leader, who for decades had embodied his people's national struggle, was gone. Some breathed a sigh of relief; others expressed concern. Commentators had a heyday, holding forth on the possible consequences of his demise on the Israeli-Palestinian conflict, including on disengagement. Clearly, Arafat's death again reshuffled the cards of the conflict. What would the new leadership look like? What would policy be on crucial questions on the agenda? How would the Palestinian public, Israel, and the United States receive the new leadership and its policy? For more than four years, Israel and the United States had claimed that there was "no partner." Eyes looked to Jerusalem and Washington, D.C., in an effort to detect the reaction of decisionmakers at a stage when "the obstacle to peace," as they referred to Arafat, was gone. Israel soon adopted the familiar formula that "the test lay in the results." Alongside delight at Arafat's passing, many Israelis claimed that the burden of proof was on the shoulders of the Palestinian leadership. Israel's reaction would be determined by the practical steps taken by the new leadership. The US government welcomed the "window of opportunity" that had opened. All were soon to learn that to take over the reins of government in the post-Arafat era was no mean feat. It demanded intensive effort not only from the Palestinian leadership but from Israel, the United States, and countries both inside the Middle East (primarily Egypt) and beyond. Those who had wrongly depicted Arafat as solely responsible for the failure of the peace process and the acceleration of violence now had to confront their misconceptions in the light of day. Many parties and factors were responsible for the "peace in tatters," a debacle that was the outcome from some of the Oslo Accords and, from the first, created the deception of a "peace process" even as the harsh realities of occupation proceeded undisturbed. What was true in the past remains true now too. Only by courageously and truly facing up to the basic questions of the Israeli-Palestinian conflict—especially the full withdrawal from Palestinian territories and an end to occupation—can the rival societies mend the peace in tatters.

Notes

1. *Dokh mevaker ha-medina mispar 48*, p. 1023. Also, some years later in an interview, Prime Minister Sharon presented documents showing Rabin's support for the construction of a separation fence. *Maariv*, 15 September 2004.

2. Broad public support for the construction of a fence was seen in polls conducted by the Tami Steinmetz Center for Peace Research (Tel Aviv University). In July 2003, some 80 percent of the Jewish population were found to be in favor of a separation fence. For details of the poll, see *Haaretz*, 5 August 2003.

3. Haim Ramon (Labor) was actually the first Israeli politician to advocate a unilateral separation plan. In 2001, he formulated a program whereby Israel would retreat from some 85 percent of the West Bank, evacuate settlements, and relocate the population to "settlement blocs" near the Green Line. The IDF was to redeploy along the new line, where Israel was to build "an obstacle" based on a fence.

4. *Maariv*, 3 August 2004. Margalit is also the political commentator of Israeli Television's Channel 10. As such, he noted (7 January 2005) that before construction of the fence began, "hundreds of Israelis were killed in vain." Barak relentlessly iterates this argument during 2005. See the interview he gave to *Haaretz Friday Magazine*, 20 May 2005.

5. Israel Security Fence—Ministry of Defense, www.securityfence.mod.gov.il/Pages/Heb/default.htm.

6. *Haaretz*, 7 January 2005. According to another *Haaretz* write-up (31 December 2004), "the 'eastern fence,' meant to divide Palestinian population centers from the Jordan Valley, has been put on ice." For B'Tselem website about the fence, see http://www.btselem.org/English/Separation_Barrier/.

7. The document [in Hebrew] was featured on the website of the Intelligence Heritage Center—The Unit for Information on Intelligence and Terrorism. See www.intelligence.org.il/sp/c_t/sec/sec_f9_04.htm. Arnon Sofer, a geographer at Haifa University, also stressed the necessity of a security fence, which, according to him is aimed at "instituting fair, ethnic separation out of an understanding that the only alternative is civil war." See www.demographyproblem.com/page35.asp. In an interview, Sofer noted that Sharon's disengagement plan was in fact "exactly my map." *Yedioth Ahronoth*, Weekly Supplement, 23 May 2003. On academe's contribution, it is worth mentioning bodies that supported peace measures, such as the Jerusalem Institute for Israel Studies (est. 1978), which prepared papers, "the chief aim of which is to provide assistance to and influence decision-makers. . . . From time to time, as per the request of policy-makers, the Institute undertakes to study special problems." In our context, there is a study on the institute website on: "'Jerusalem, a Fence Surrounds Her': The Construction of a Security Fence (the "Separation Fence") Around Jerusalem (2004)" (in Hebrew), http://www.jiis.org.il/fence-abstract.pdf.

8. Biger, "Fences and Borders Around the World," on the website of the "Intelligence Heritage Center—The Unit for Information on Intelligence and Terrorism." See http://www.intelligence.org.il/sp/c_t/sec/sec_f9_04.htm. Similar claims were voiced by nongovernmental organizations, many of them of a security nature, such as "A Security Fence for Israel," "The Council for Peace and Security," and "A Fence for Life."

9. Folman, *Sippura shel gader ha-hafrada*, p. 240. General support for separation had been discussed earlier. See Schueftan, *Korach ha-hafrada*. Makovsky, *A Defensible Fence*.

10. "Politika" [Politics], Israel Television (Channel One, Public TV), 19 February 2002.

11. See the statement by forum chairman Ron Breiman, *Maariv*, 6 September 2004.

12. See www.hagada.org.il/hagada/html/modules.php?name=News&file=article&sid=1844.

13. High Court of Justice Petition 2056/04 (30 June 2004), Clause 86 [in Hebrew]. See http://62.90.71.124/heb/verdict/search/verdict_by_case_rslt.asp?case_year=04&case_nbr. For English, see http://62.90.71.124/eng/verdict/framesetSrch.html.

14. See High Court of Justice Ruling 2056/04, and the similar reaction of the State Prosecution in High Court of Justice Petition 9961/03 (Hamoked Center for the Defence of the Individual versus the State of Israel, 1 January 2004).

15. Ibid.

16. Judge Aharon Barak's ruling (30 June 2004), High Court of Justice Petition 2056/04, Clause 40. For the ruling in English, see http://62.90.71.124/eng/verdict/framesetSrch.html.

17. The full verdict appears on the court's website, www.icj-cij.org/icjwww/idocket/imwp/imwpframe.htm.

18. For a summation of these positions in the media, see Kremnitzer, *"Hashe'elot she-ein meorerim 'al gader ha-hafrada."*

19. "A Fence to Prevent Terror or a Racist Separation Fence," *Al-Hayat*, 18 February 2004 [in Arabic]; and the article, "The Racist Separation Fence in the Jenin Area" (24 November 2004), at www.aldaar.com. On the fence as instituting apartheid, see the statement by Abd-Rabbo, published at the website Searching Jenin, http://www.searchingjenin.com/wire.php?articleid=20031204134308224. For numerous statements against the fence, see Palestine Media Center, www.palestine-pmc.com. For an extensive discussion of the fence's blow to human rights, see the Arabic Network for

Human Rights Information, www.hrinfo.org. The personal and collective blow it dealt Palestinians can be seen in the initiative taken by the heads of the Jayyous township near Tulkarem. "Residents of Jayyous Face Another Nakba," it said on the opening page of the Local Council website, and this was followed by a painstaking elaboration of the infringements on the lands and daily life of the residents. See www.jayyous online.org.

20. *Yedioth Ahronoth*, 7 January 2005.

21. From the introduction to a discussion of the fence on al-Jazeera's website, www.aljazeera.net. An identical claim was made by the Palestinian prime minister, Ahmed Qureia (Abu 'Ala) in the article, "The Racist Separation Fence: Israel's Disengagement Program" [in Arabic], www.pmo.gov.ps.

22. Belal al-Hassan, *Al-sharq al-Awsat*, 21 March 2004. On the fence as a means to prevent the establishment of a Palestinian state of territorial contiguity, see the position of the Adalah organization: www.adalah.org/eng/index.php.

23. Adalah website, www.adalah.org. See also "The separation fence: The racism of occupation and the ruining of Palestinian lives" [in Arabic] (24 November 2004), www.palestine-info.com/arabic/palestoday/reports/report2004/zedar1.htm.

24. "A separation fence or the Berlin Wall—an insulation fence against peace" (30 July 2003) [in Arabic] in the PA website: www.ipc.ps. See also the statement by the Palestinian prime minister (12 November 2003): www.pmo.gov.ps/wall/wall.asp.

25. Khalil Shikaki, "Palestinian Public Opinion and the Peace Process: Changes Before and After the Second Intifada," Symposium at Ben-Gurion University, 11 May 2004. For a thorough discussion on the Hamas strengthening on behalf of the Fatah, see Agha and Malley, "The Lost Palestinians," *The New York Review of Books*, 9 June 2005, pp. 20–24. Agha and Malley present an alternative reading to the common assumption (introduced painstakingly by Shikaki) that differences between generations ("old" vs. "young" guards) have been the main process within Palestinian society since 1993.

26. In this context, Dov Weisglass, Sharon's close adviser, noted that "in the fall of 2003 we understood that everything is stuck. . . . Time was not on our side. There was international erosion, internal erosion. Domestically, in the meantime, everything was collapsing. The economy was stagnant, and the Geneva Initiative garnered broad support. And then we were hit with letters of officers and letters of pilots and letters of commandos [letters of refusal to serve in the territories]." *Haaretz*, 8 October 2004.

27. For Sharon's Herzliya Conference address, see http://www.mfa.gov.il/MFA/Government/Speeches+by+Israeli+leaders/2003/Address+by+PM+Ariel+Sharon+at+the+Fourth+Herzliya.htm.

28. *Maariv*, 15 September 2004.

29. "The Big Freeze," *Haaretz*, 8 October 2004. Weisglass likened the disengagement to formaldehyde, preserving Bush's vision and yet stymieing a political process in which Israel was not interested: "The disengagement is actually formaldehyde. It supplies the necessary amount of formaldehyde so that there will be no political process with the Palestinians."

30. "Disengagement from Gaza is disengagement from the chief threat to the existence of the State of Israel as a Jewish, democratic state," MK Haim Ramon summed up Labor's position during political deliberations in the Knesset. Labor's only reservations, it emerged from his words, concerned the timetable; Labor wanted to see it brought forward and coordinated with the Palestinian and European partners. *Knesset Proceedings* (22 April 2004), Session 124; see the Knesset website (text in Hebrew): http://www.knesset.gov.il/Tql//mark01/h0017517.html#TQL. Subsequently, Shimon Peres, too, called on Knesset members to support the disengagement plan. The Yahad

Party website carried articles spelling out the political necessity to support disengagement.

31. "The Peace Index: December 2004," *Haaretz*, 5 January 2005.

32. Clause 1 of the cabinet decision. For the wording of the decision and disengagement plan, see the prime minister's website, www.pmo.gov.il/PMO/Government/Desicions/2004/06/des1996.htm.

33. *Haaretz*, 10 September 2004. For a report on the demonstration, see *Haaretz*, 13 September 2004.

34. *Haaretz*, 17 December 2004.

35. "Tochnit ha-hitnatkut shel rosh ha-memshala Ariel Sharon" [Prime Minister Ariel Sharon's disengagement plan], Prime Minister's Office website, www.pmo.gov.il/PMO/Hitnatkut.

36. For the ad of the Judea and Samaria Council, see *Maariv*, 3 November 2004. For the greetings of the Samaria Regional Council, see *Nekuda* 274 (September 2004): 45.

37. *Yedioth Ahronoth*, 24 December 2004.

38. Ibid.

39. Yoav Gelber, "Ha-im ha-hitnatkut ma'asit?" [Is disengagement realistic?] *Nekuda* 274 (September 2004): 42–45.

40. Uri Orbach, "Zeh lo biglaleinu" [It's not because of us], *Nekuda* (May 2004):28.

41. *Nekuda* (June 2004), p. 19. Rabbi Yuval Charlo claimed that in addition to furthering settlements, the rightist public should review its earlier positions on "compromise," "peace," democracy, and human rights, which pose significant challenges that need to be faced. *Nekuda* (May 2004): 12–17.

42. Sharon's remarks were made at an AIPAC conference (24 April 2002). See www.yesha.org.il.

43. *Haaretz*, 12 September 2004. On Sharon as a liar, see the article by Moshe Leshem, "Ha-hitnatkut—khomer le-mahshava" [Disengagement: Food for thought] (24 October 2004), www.gamla.org.il/article/2004/oct/11.htm.

44. For the official version of the Bush letter, see the White House website: http://www.whitehouse.gov/news/releases/2004/04/20040414-3.html. The Israeli-US understandings were set forth in letters exchanged by the director of the Prime Minister's Office (Dov Weisglass) and the national security adviser (Condoleezza Rice). These documents were presented by Sharon "as an integral part" of the disengagement plan he initiated.

45. From Bush's statement at the press conference after the summit with Sharon. See www.whitehouse.gov/news/releases/2004/04/20040414-4.html.

46. Ibid.

47. www.pmo.gov.il/NR/rdonlyres/31982575-BC8D-4271-B2DB-03BCDFF765EB/0/7211202025.ppt. One should recall that in the talks between Israel and Syria (in Shepherdstown), it transpired that at certain spots it is very difficult to ascertain where the exact border was on the eve of the Six Day War. The armistice line (1949), however, is very clear. The Bush administration perhaps used this confusion to create a new starting point to move negotiations along, skipping over what till then had proved a stumbling block.

48. *Knesset Proceedings* (22 April 2004), Session 124; see the Knesset website (text in Hebrew): http://www.knesset.gov.il/Tql//mark01/h0017517.html#TQL.

49. See the Fatah website, www.alkrama.com/alkrama/alkrama76.htm.

50. Abd Rabbo's statement on the Palestine Media Center website: "Yasser Abd Rabbo's Speech at Herzliya Conference" (18 December 2004), http://www.palestine-pmc

.com/details.asp?cat=2&id=776&search=1&key1=unilateralism; Pat McDonnell Twair, "Hanan Ashrawi Assures Californians That Palestinians Won't Emigrate or Evaporate" (November 2003) on Washington Report on Middle East Affairs website: http://www.wrmea.com/archives/November_2003/0311030.html.

51. www.aad-online.org/2004/ArabicSite/Arabiclinks/23-9ar/aad8/3.htm. These positions found sporadic support in the Arab media. See www.an-nour.com/old/160/home.htm. Against the barrage of Arab criticism of disengagement, there were also voices advising the Palestinians not to be overly hasty in rejecting the possibilities latent in Israel's initiative.

52. See Arafat's and Erekat's interviews on al-Jazeera TV, 20 December 2003.

53. Nidal Hamad, "The Withdrawal Plan Is the Conquest of Gaza from the Outside," http://www.falasteen.com/auteur.php3?id_auteur=7.

54. "The Retreat from Gaza and the Palestinian Position," www.aljazeera.net, 22 December 2004; Hussein Ma'alum, "The Retreat from Gaza and the Aims of Disengagement," al-Khalig, 9 December 2004.

55. On a series of key topics, Egypt's position differed from the PA's. Nevertheless, they were disagreements between sides subscribing to a similar conception of a permanent settlement. The differences did and do concern the steps to be taken. The overall objective is a two-state solution based on the 4 June 1967 borders and an agreed-upon resolution of final-status questions. At the same time, Mubarak and his envoys supported the call for significant regime reforms in the PA, including decentralization of the authorities and spheres of responsibility held by President Arafat.

12

Conclusion

As noted in Chapter 11, at the end of November 2004, fate took a hand in the Israeli-Palestinian conflict. Arafat's health deteriorated, and he died in a hospital outside Paris. To Palestinians, he had been the symbol of their struggle for liberation. To non-Arabs, Israel and the United States in particular, he was the prime factor in the failure of the peace process; the leader who had failed his people at the moment of truth. To me, the palaver about the consequences of his death and the significance of Abbas's appointment as his successor brought on a sense of déjà vu. All at once, political commentators saw a rare "window of opportunity" to stop the violence and resume the political process. Once more, the "peace process" starred in the media, in both the Middle East and beyond. No longer did Israeli and US spokespeople repeat the mantra that "there is no one to talk to and nothing to talk about," an assertion that had been common since the summer of 2000. As if by magic, it was increasingly claimed that "there is someone to talk to and something to talk about."

Not that Sharon's initiative to withdraw from Palestinian Occupied Territories and evacuate settlements should be underestimated. Nor should one belittle the fact that the new Palestinian leadership seeks to change national priorities. Statements by leaders, primarily by Abbas, convey a real commitment to ending the acts of hostility and pursuing the political process. Israeli and Palestinian leaders are promoting these changes with resolve, as demonstrated by the understandings formulated at the Sharm al-Sheikh summit (8 February 2005). In practical terms, they spell out a mutual suspension of armed actions, the adoption of measures to coordinate Israel's withdrawal from the Gaza Strip and West Bank Palestinian cities, and an easing of daily life for millions of people in the Occupied Territories. Although these moves are highly significant, there is still a great gap between the national goals and expectations of Israeli and Palestinian leaders. Disturbing questions must be addressed, notably as to the suitability of both Israel's disengagement plan and the Roadmap as the framework to settle the Israeli-Palestinian conflict. Another concern is that in Israel and beyond there tends to be a focus on personalities, Abbas's and Sharon's, while the conflict's wider contexts—particularly, the ongoing state of occupation—are minimized. A similar approach colored the entire Oslo process, embedding simplistic conceptions about the clash between the two peoples, devising a distorted narrative about the "peace process," and cultivating vain hopes over the chances of achieving a final-status settlement. Now, too, both in Israel and beyond, there is little critical examination of the causes leading to the collapse of the political process and hardly any discussion of the problematic aspects of the separation fence and disengagement plan. There is conspicuous disregard for the direct connection between the continued occupation and its effects on the daily lives of millions of Arabs and Jews in the disputed land.

The year 2005 began with internal struggles topping the agendas of both Israeli and Palestinian society. Domestic developments could well exert a crucial influence on the promotion of disengagement and the resumption of the political process and on the survival of Sharon's government and the chances of the new Palestinian leadership succeeding. Both leaders face serious opposition. As shown elsewhere in this book, from the start of the Oslo process, internal political divisions on both sides decisively affected decisionmakers and the policies adopted. The protests of Israel's right against Sharon's government are gaining momentum. Opposition to disengagement is evident in the ranks of Likud and in the Knesset and even among a number of ministers in Sharon's cabinet. In mid-February 2005, a large majority of Israel's Knesset and government voted in favor of disengagement, enabling the evacuation of settlements. Nevertheless, the campaign between Sharon and his opponents is far from over. One cannot dismiss the possibility that Israel will begin the arduous process of withdrawal from the Gaza Strip but will be hard put to complete the disengagement plan. The struggle over dismantling settlements could pit the government and security forces against a significant portion of the public. The ensuing schisms in Israeli society could become irreversible.

On the Palestinian side, although Abbas won the presidential elections with a substantial majority, internal Palestinian divisions still weigh heavily on the new leadership. It is no secret that the Fatah, the movement Abbas heads, is more divided than ever and support for it has slumped, as evinced by the struggles within the Fatah and the results of the recent municipal elections. Palestinian political commentators estimate that the Fatah will find it difficult to win a majority in the elections for the National Council scheduled for the autumn of 2005. Should this scenario come to pass, domestic political tensions will intensify. Thus, the struggle over the reins of Palestinian government is also far from over. Arafat's death and Abbas's election were only the opening shot in this internal struggle, which, to a large extent, will be decided not only by the new president's policy on the political process but also by domestic political developments. The forecasts of possible civil war, should the new leadership forcibly attempt to promote a controversial political process, have not escaped the attention of Abbas and his close aides. The heavy price Palestinians paid for bitter rivalries and internal divisions at the critical stage of the conflict with the Zionists in the first half of the twentieth century is a common theme in the public discussion. In itself, of course, this awareness is no safeguard against clashes and escalation. Palestinian spokespeople also emphasize the wide gulf between predictions of armed internal-factional conflict and the actual likelihood of this pessimistic scenario. They note that, despite the divisiveness of Palestinian society, there are also attenuating influences against armed flare-up, namely the sociopolitical situation that finds members of the same families belonging to different factions. In Gaza, for example, where Hamas enjoys the widest support, many of the movement's activists are close kin of members of the PA's regular security forces. This is the dam against Palestinian civil war.

The discussion of how Abbas and his aides will negotiate both the internal Palestinian maze and the political tightrope is full of question marks. Arafat managed to dodge bullets to rally the different factions around him and consolidate broad consensus about Palestinian national objectives. To him, this national consensus and his continued rule were one tight, symbiotic knot, a supreme goal to be carefully guarded. Throughout the long years that he led his people, he generally succeeded in averting interfactional clashes. He ensured support for and loyalty to himself and his associates in varied ways, combining a time-honored policy of "divide and rule" with the exploitation of a soiled, corrupt, and inefficient government apparatus. To warrant loyalty, he did not hesitate to hand out favors, jobs, and monopolies. Nor did he hesitate to harshly punish critics of his policy and style of government.

Palestinian society and beyond does not regard Abbas as sharing Arafat's leadership traits. There is quite a gap between the policies he seeks to promote and those of opposition groups. The attempt to institute regime reforms and resume the political process based on the disengagement plan and the Roadmap may well end in open confrontation, not only with the traditional opposition (Hamas, Islamic Jihad, and the PDFLP and PFLP), but within the Fatah itself. Moreover, Israeli and US expectations of the new Palestinian leadership have remained unchanged: to campaign uncompromisingly against the groups championing armed struggle. The efforts of the PA to enforce the rule of "one weapon," meaning that only the security forces would be allowed to carry arms, could degenerate into violent clashes between the different Palestinian forces with unforeseeable consequences. The prevalent contention in both the traditional opposition and the ranks of the PLO is that the armed struggle forced Israel to opt for disengagement. Both also declare that they will not hand over their weapons until the occupation ends. On the national level, many—not only oppositionists—expect the new leadership to fight relentlessly against the erection of the separation fence and to actively block Israel's intention to impose a long-term interim arrangement on the Palestinians. Internally, most of the population longs for amelioration of everyday life, mainly freedom of movement—that is, the removal of checkpoints, permission for Palestinian workers to enter Israel, Israel's release of Palestinian prisoners, and an improvement in personal safety and law and order.

The intensive public discussions in Israeli and Palestinian societies since 2000 make it clear that the basic internal differences are not limited to disputes with settlers or armed groups, respectively. Consensus positions are no less complicated. One of the larger implications of this book is that the conception of "no partner"—shared by most Israelis and Palestinians over the past four years—molded a state of mind receptive to unilateral measures. This mentality found one expression in the widespread Israeli support for a separation fence and disengagement (in its unilateral form as well). Furthermore, the Zionist left parties proved to be the most faithful supporters of Sharon's government: if Labor had not joined the government and Yahad (under Yossi Beilin) had not voted for disengagement in the Knesset, that legislation could not have passed. Without this support, Sharon's government might have fallen, resulting in Israeli general elections at the start of 2005.

Israel's adoption of unilateral measures was also an indirect result of US policy. At the end of his term of office, President Clinton placed full blame for the failure of Camp David on the Palestinians (especially on Arafat). In so doing, he contributed significantly to the formulation of the flawed narrative as to who was responsible for the collapse of the "peace process." Under the Bush administration, this narrative continued to be promoted, and when the Bush vision was publicized as a two-state solution to the conflict, its implementation was made conditional on a change of Palestinian leadership. Moreover, the Bush administration made the promotion of reform and democratization the chief aim of US policy in the Middle East. In the past four years, the US government took hardly any steps to break the cycle of violence, even when the sides, especially Israel, embarked on clear-cut unilateral measures.

As I write these lines, many people are searching for answers to a number of critical questions: will Israel manage to complete the withdrawal of its forces and settlers from the Gaza Strip and northern Samaria? Do the disengagement plan and the steps taken by the new Palestinian leadership augur the start of the Roadmap's implementation, in all its components and stages? Are we on the threshold of a political process that may lead towards the hoped-for peace, or is this merely another respite to be followed by a resumption of hostilities? In my opinion, even if the most optimistic forecast about disengagement is borne out and the political process is resumed on the basis of the Roadmap, the chances are still very slim that this blueprint will lead to an overall, durable settlement between Israel and the Palestinians. In Chapter 11,

I pointed out that the disengagement plan was devised as a unilateral measure based on the assumption that there is "no [Palestinian] partner" for peace and therefore, in the visible future, there is no reason to discuss final-status issues. I also noted that although the Roadmap relates to the contingency of final-status negotiations, the mechanism it proposes is too general and rests on the establishment of a Palestinian state with "provisional borders." Advocates of separation and disengagement in Israel are not opposed to such a blueprint, for they believe an interim stage to be inevitable in light of past experience and of their evaluation that there is little likelihood of reaching a final-status agreement.

Like the Oslo blueprint, the disengagement plan and Roadmap, too, aim at political formulations that would make it possible to circumvent, rather than deal with, the basic problems of the Israeli-Palestinian national conflict. Thus the dearth of public discussion on final-status issues is hardly surprising, with most of the "peace camp" in both societies continuing to cling to simplistic assumptions about the "peace process" and its potential failure. Furthermore, the widening of the discussion of the "peace process" even as unilateral measures are being taken that undermine it—primarily the continued construction of the separation fence and the implementation of disengagement—is not a good omen for peace-seekers. The chief fear of the new Palestinian leadership is that Israel will succeed in forcing a protracted interim agreement on them, using the Roadmap and the support of the United States to do so. In a recent interview in the *New York Times* ("Abbas Declares War with Israel Effectively Over," 14 February 2005), Abbas noted that he would prefer to begin talks on final status with Sharon as soon as possible. The new Palestinian leader voiced his opposition to the format of a "state with provisional borders" (which is the Roadmap's second phase). Like many Palestinians, he too—as it emerged from his words—sees an interim agreement as a "trap" aimed at avoiding a settlement of final status. The attempt to enforce interim arrangements will not lead to regional peace, he summed up, putting his finger on the major bone of contention. It is precisely on the question of interim arrangements, likely to be part of the political process in the foreseeable future, that Sharon and Abbas diverge.

It is difficult to point to the blueprint favored by the new Palestinian leadership. Statements by leaders contain no few contradictions. All welcome Israel's withdrawal from the Gaza Strip and northern Samaria and call for a speedy resumption of the political process on the basis of the Roadmap. At the same time, they fear the establishment of a Palestinian state with "provisional borders" as spelled out in the Roadmap. They may be critical of the blueprint of the political process taking shape, but at this stage, they themselves have not managed to crystallize and present a clear, agreed-upon alternative. As the discussion in this book attempted to show, the two sides might have benefited from imaginative ideas about settling conflict rather than have allowed themselves to be boxed in by the Oslo blueprint. Creative thinking is vital because in both societies, the majority supports a "two-state solution" yet simultaneously is entrenched in hackneyed positions on such questions as refugees, Jerusalem (including sovereignty over the Temple Mount/al-Haram al-Sharif), and permanent borders. It is worth noting that Israelis and Palestinians interested in stepping "out of the box" usually explore new ideas in unofficial ("track two") channels. Only a handful of people participate in them, and, on the whole, their ideas receive no publicity and do not make it into the public and political discourse.

To date, the most significant attempt to think outside of the Oslo "box" has been Sharon's disengagement plan, in other words, to adopt a unilateral measure based on the assumption that a final-status settlement could not be achieved in negotiations. Thus far there have been two main variations on the prime minister's plan: (1) unilateral withdrawal from the Gaza Strip and northern Samaria as part of an interim situation to last many years ("freezing the political process," in the words of Sharon and Weisglass, his aide) and (2) disengagement in coordination with the new Palestinian leadership and expression of support for the establishment of a Palestinian state with provisional borders (according to the second phase of the Roadmap). It goes without saying that both these variations are much more modest than the proposals made to the Palestinians in the latter half of 2000. The Palestinians considered those proposals inadequate, and there is no reason to believe that they will accept the more limited ones today.

Although the conclusions arising from this book are not overly encouraging, I believe that they contain an important insight: the Israeli-Palestinian conflict can be settled by peaceful means. But that can happen only if there will be a Palestinian state based on the borders of 4 June 1967, as well as resolution of both the refugee problem and Palestinian sovereignty. For this fitting resolution to the Israeli-Palestinian conflict to come about, it must be preceded by critical Israeli and Arab public discussion of the contentious issues. It is difficult to believe that any Palestinian leadership would accept any other solution. Yet as these lines are being written, this sort of solution is unacceptable to Israel's leadership and most of its public. The opposition, as the analysis in this book has attempted to show, stems primarily from the entrenchment of the hegemonic narrative about the Camp David summit, about exclusive Palestinian responsibility for the failure of the "peace process," and about the exposure of the Palestinians' ostensibly "real" intentions vis-à-vis Israel. This simplistic narrative must be subjected to critical discussion as a basic condition for change that might one day lead to the mending of the "peace in tatters." Unfortunately, large publics in Israel and beyond are pinning exaggerated hopes on the disengagement plan and the Roadmap. A political process based on these plans is doomed to failure because they are merely additional attempts at "conflict management" of one form or another. As in the past, these vain attempts will lead to interim arrangements and unilateral measures that will not shrink the basic differences between the two sides. At best, interim solutions may offer a temporary respite, not a permanent solution.

* * *

"These are the times of chaos; opinions are a scramble; parties are a jumble; the language of new ideas has not been created," wrote French poet Alphonse de Lamartine on the eve of the collapse of the July Monarchy (1830–1848), adding: "It is the problem of the times to classify things and men." I set out to write this book with similar feelings, and they have remained with me through its conclusion.

Appendix 1:
Chronology of
Key Events, 1947–2005

29 November 1947	UN General Assembly Resolution 181
14 May 1948	Establishment of the state of Israel and outbreak of the 1948 war
11 December 1948	UN General Assembly Resolution 194
30 October 1956	Outbreak of the 1956 war
1 January 1964	Establishment of the Palestine Liberation Organization (PLO)
5 June 1967	Outbreak of the 1967 war
1 September 1967	Arab summit conference (Khartoum's resolutions)
22 November 1967	UN Security Council Resolution 242
6 October 1973	Outbreak of the 1973 War
22 October 1973	UN Security Council Resolution 338 calls for cease fire and implementation of Resolution 242
21 December 1973	Geneva peace conference
4 September 1975	Israeli-Egyptian Interim Agreement
9 November 1977	Declaration of president Sadat's peace initiative
19–20 November 1977	Sadat's visit to Israel and his Knesset speech
17 September 1978	Signing of the Camp David Accords
26 March 1979	Signing of the Israeli-Egyptian peace treaty
30 July 1980	Basic Law: Jerusalem is the capital of Israel
7 August 1981	King Fahd's plan for a comprehensive peace in the Middle East
6 October 1981	President Sadat's assassination and the beginning of Mubarak's term
30 November 1981	Memorandum of understanding concerning a strategic cooperation between the United States and Israel
14 December 1981	Golan Heights Law approved by the Knesset
6 June 1982	Outbreak of the Lebanon war
1 September 1982	US president Reagan's plan for a comprehensive peace in the Middle East
8 September 1982	Arab summit proposal for a comprehensive peace in the Middle East (Fez's plan)

17 May 1983	A peace agreement between Israel and Lebanon (annulled on 5 March 1984)
11 April 1987	London Document (Peres-Hussein Document)
8 December 1987	Outbreak of the first intifada
31 July 1988	King Hussein's declaration concerning the separation of the West Bank from the Kingdom of Jordan
17 November 1988	Palestinian National Council accepts Resolution 242
14 May 1989	Peace initiative of Israel's national unity government
19 September 1989	President Mubarak's Ten-Point Plan
6 December 1989	Secretary of State James Baker's Five-Point Plan
2 August 1990	Iraq's invasion of Kuwait
17 January 1991	Outbreak of war for the liberation of Kuwait
30 October 1991	Madrid Conference
13 September 1993	Signing of Declaration of Principles between Israel and the PLO
4 May 1994	Gaza-Jericho Agreement
25 July 1994	Washington Declaration (Israel-Jordan)
26 October 1994	Israeli-Jordanian peace accord
30 October 1994	Casablanca summit for economic cooperation in the Middle East
28 September 1995	Interim Agreement between Israel and the PLO
31 October 1995	Beilin–Abu Mazen (Abbas) document
4 November 1995	Assassination of Israeli prime minister Yitzhak Rabin
13 March 1996	Peacemaker's summit in Sharm al-Sheikh
26 April 1996	Israeli-Lebanese cease-fire understandings
29 May 1996	Benjamin Netanyahu elected Israeli prime minister
21–23 June 1996	Arab summit (Cairo)
17 January 1997	Hebron redeployment protocol
21 January 1997	An agreement concerning a temporary international presence in Hebron
23 October 1998	Wye River Memorandum
17 May 1999	Ehud Barak elected Israeli prime minister
4 September 1999	Sharm al-Sheikh Memorandum
5 October 1999	Protocol concerning "safe passage" between the West Bank and the Gaza Strip
4 May 2000	Opening of Israeli-Palestinian secret channel talks in Stockholm
11–25 July 2000	Camp David summit
28 September 2000	Outbreak of the second intifada
21–22 October 2000	Emergency Arab summit (Cairo)
23 December 2000	US president Clinton suggests his ideas concerning the permanent agreement
22–27 January 2001	Taba talks
27 January 2001	Joint Israeli-Palestinian declaration at the end of the Taba talks
6 February 2001	Ariel Sharon elected Israeli prime minister
27–28 March 2001	Arab summit ('Aman)
30 April 2001	Mitchell report
14 June 2001	US CIA director George Tenet's plan for an Israeli-Palestinian cease-fire

12 March 2002	UN Security Council Resolution 1397
27–28 March 2002	Arab summit (Beirut) and the adaptation of an Arab peace plan based on the Saudi initiative
24 June 2002	US President Bush's vision of an Israeli-Palestinian peace
4 December 2002	Prime Minister Sharon's Herzliya speech
20 March 2003	Initiation of war against Iraq by United States and Great Britain
25 March 2003	Third draft of Palestinian State Constitution
30 April 2003	Presentation of the Roadmap
30 April 2003	Formation of Prime Minister Mahmoud Abbas's (Abu Mazen's) government
1 May 2003	Bush's declaration: Major fighting activities in Iraq are over
23 May 2003	Israel's government agrees to implement the Roadmap, while presenting fourteen reservations
3 June 2003	Arab leaders' summit with President Bush in Sharm al-Sheikh
4 June 2003	'Aqaba Summit (Bush, Sharon, and Abbas)
8 June 2003	Sharon introduces the Roadmap at the Likud Central Committee while using the term *occupation*
25 June 2003	Ami Ayalon and Sari Nusseibeh's "Declaration of Principles" is presented
29 June 2003	A *hudna* (temporary cease-fire) is declared
8 September 2003	Ahmad Qureia (Abu 'Ala) appointed Palestinian Prime Minister
9 September 2003	Terror attacks in Jerusalem and Tzrifin end the *hudna*
1 December 2003	Geneva Initiative is officially signed
13 December 2003	Saddam Hussein captured by American forces
18 December 2003	Sharon presents his Unilateral Disengagement Plan at the Herzliya Conference
12 April 2004	Bush-Mubarak summit at Crawford, Texas
14 April 2004	Bush's letter to Sharon supporting "gradual disengagement"
2 May 2004	Likud Central Committee rejects the Unilateral Disengagement Plan
4 May 2004	Quartet officials declare they see the Unilateral Disengagement Plan as a positive step
6 June 2004	Israeli government approves the Unilateral Disengagement Plan
9 July 2004	International Court of Justice in The Hague calls to immediately cease the construction of the separation "wall"
11 November 2004	Arafat dies in Paris
9 January 2005	Abbas wins the Palestinian elections

Appendix 2:
President George W. Bush
Calls for New Palestinian
Leadership, June 2002

For too long, the citizens of the Middle East have lived in the midst of death and fear. The hatred of a few holds the hopes of many hostage. The forces of extremism and terror are attempting to kill progress and peace by killing the innocent. And this casts a dark shadow over an entire region. For the sake of all humanity, things must change in the Middle East.

It is untenable for Israeli citizens to live in terror. It is untenable for Palestinians to live in squalor and occupation. And the current situation offers no prospect that life will improve. Israeli citizens will continue to be victimized by terrorists, and so Israel will continue to defend herself.

In the situation the Palestinian people will grow more and more miserable. My vision is two states, living side by side in peace and security. There is simply no way to achieve that peace until all parties fight terror. Yet, at this critical moment, if all parties will break with the past and set out on a new path, we can overcome the darkness with the light of hope. Peace requires a new and different Palestinian leadership, so that a Palestinian state can be born.

I call on the Palestinian people to elect new leaders, leaders not compromised by terror. I call upon them to build a practicing democracy, based on tolerance and liberty. If the Palestinian people actively pursue these goals, America and the world will actively support their efforts. If the Palestinian people meet these goals, they will be able to reach agreement with Israel and Egypt and Jordan on security and other arrangements for independence.

And when the Palestinian people have new leaders, new institutions and new security arrangements with their neighbors, the United States of America will support the creation of a Palestinian state whose borders and certain aspects of its sovereignty will be provisional until resolved as part of a final settlement in the Middle East.

In the work ahead, we all have responsibilities. The Palestinian people are gifted and capable, and I am confident they can achieve a new birth for their nation. A Pales-

Source: White House, Office of the Press Secretary, 24 June 2002, www.whitehouse.gov/news/releases/2002/06/print/20020624-3.html.

tinian state will never be created by terror—it will be built through reform. And reform must be more than cosmetic change, or veiled attempt to preserve the status quo. True reform will require entirely new political and economic institutions, based on democracy, market economics and action against terrorism.

Today, the elected Palestinian legislature has no authority, and power is concentrated in the hands of an unaccountable few. A Palestinian state can only serve its citizens with a new constitution which separates the powers of government. The Palestinian parliament should have the full authority of a legislative body. Local officials and government ministers need authority of their own and the independence to govern effectively.

The United States, along with the European Union and Arab states, will work with Palestinian leaders to create a new constitutional framework, and a working democracy for the Palestinian people. And the United States, along with others in the international community will help the Palestinians organize and monitor fair, multi-party local elections by the end of the year, with national elections to follow.

Today, the Palestinian people live in economic stagnation, made worse by official corruption. A Palestinian state will require a vibrant economy, where honest enterprise is encouraged by honest government. The United States, the international donor community and the World Bank stand ready to work with Palestinians on a major project of economic reform and development. The United States, the EU, the World Bank, the International Monetary Fund are willing to oversee reforms in Palestinian finances, encouraging transparency and independent auditing.

And the United States, along with our partners in the developed world, will increase our humanitarian assistance to relieve Palestinian suffering. Today, the Palestinian people lack effective courts of law and have no means to defend and vindicate their rights. A Palestinian state will require a system of reliable justice to punish those who prey on the innocent. The United States and members of the international community stand ready to work with Palestinian leaders to establish finance—establish finance and monitor a truly independent judiciary.

Today, Palestinian authorities are encouraging, not opposing, terrorism. This is unacceptable. And the United States will not support the establishment of a Palestinian state until its leaders engage in a sustained fight against the terrorists and dismantle their infrastructure. This will require an externally supervised effort to rebuild and reform the Palestinian security services. The security system must have clear lines of authority and accountability and a unified chain of command.

America is pursuing this reform along with key regional states. The world is prepared to help, yet ultimately these steps toward statehood depend on the Palestinian people and their leaders. If they energetically take the path of reform, the rewards can come quickly. If Palestinians embrace democracy, confront corruption and firmly reject terror, they can count on American support for the creation of a provisional state of Palestine.

With a dedicated effort, this state could rise rapidly, as it comes to terms with Israel, Egypt and Jordan on practical issues, such as security. The final borders, the capital and other aspects of this state's sovereignty will be negotiated between the parties, as part of a final settlement. Arab states have offered their help in this process, and their help is needed.

I've said in the past that nations are either with us or against us in the war on terror. To be counted on the side of peace, nations must act. Every leader actually committed to peace will end incitement to violence in official media, and publicly denounce homicide bombings. Every nation actually committed to peace will stop the flow of money, equipment and recruits to terrorist groups seeking the destruction of Israel—including Hamas, Islamic Jihad, and Hezbollah. Every nation actually committed to peace must block the shipment of Iranian supplies to these groups, and oppose regimes that promote terror, like Iraq. And Syria must choose the right side in the war on terror by closing terrorist camps and expelling terrorist organizations.

Leaders who want to be included in the peace process must show by their deeds an undivided support for peace. And as we move toward a peaceful solution, Arab states will be expected to build closer ties of diplomacy and commerce with Israel, leading to full normalization of relations between Israel and the entire Arab world.

Israel also has a large stake in the success of a democratic Palestine. Permanent occupation threatens Israel's identity and democracy. A stable, peaceful Palestinian state is necessary to achieve the security that Israel longs for. So I challenge Israel to take concrete steps to support the emergence of a viable, credible Palestinian state.

As we make progress toward security, Israel forces need to withdraw fully to positions they held prior to September 28, 2000. And consistent with the recommendations of the Mitchell Committee, Israeli settlement activity in the occupied territories must stop.

The Palestinian economy must be allowed to develop. As violence subsides, freedom of movement should be restored, permitting innocent Palestinians to resume work and normal life. Palestinian legislators and officials, humanitarian and international workers, must be allowed to go about the business of building a better future. And Israel should release frozen Palestinian revenues into honest, accountable hands.

I've asked Secretary Powell to work intensively with Middle Eastern and international leaders to realize the vision of a Palestinian state, focusing them on a comprehensive plan to support Palestinian reform and institution-building.

Ultimately, Israelis and Palestinians must address the core issues that divide them if there is to be a real peace, resolving all claims and ending the conflict between them. This means that the Israeli occupation that began in 1967 will be ended through a settlement negotiated between the parties, based on U.N. Resolutions 242 and 338, with Israeli withdrawal to secure and recognize borders.

We must also resolve questions concerning Jerusalem, the plight and future of Palestinian refugees, and a final peace between Israel and Lebanon, and Israel and a Syria that supports peace and fights terror.

All who are familiar with the history of the Middle East realize that there may be setbacks in this process. Trained and determined killers, as we have seen, want to stop it. Yet the Egyptian and Jordanian peace treaties with Israel remind us that with determined and responsible leadership progress can come quickly.

As new Palestinian institutions and new leaders emerge, demonstrating real performance on security and reform, I expect Israel to respond and work toward a final status agreement. With intensive effort by all, this agreement could be reached within three years from now. And I and my country will actively lead toward that goal.

I can understand the deep anger and anguish of the Israeli people. You've lived too long with fear and funerals, having to avoid markets and public transportation, and forced to put armed guards in kindergarten classrooms. The Palestinian Authority has rejected your offer at hand, and trafficked with terrorists. You have a right to a normal life; you have a right to security; and I deeply believe that you need a reformed, responsible Palestinian partner to achieve that security.

I can understand the deep anger and despair of the Palestinian people. For decades you've been treated as pawns in the Middle East conflict. Your interests have been held hostage to a comprehensive peace agreement that never seems to come, as your lives get worse year by year. You deserve democracy and the rule of law. You deserve an open society and a thriving economy. You deserve a life of hope for your children. An end to occupation and a peaceful democratic Palestinian state may seem distant, but

America and our partners throughout the world stand ready to help, help you make them possible as soon as possible.

If liberty can blossom in the rocky soil of the West Bank and Gaza, it will inspire millions of men and women around the globe who are equally weary of poverty and oppression, equally entitled to the benefits of democratic government.

I have a hope for the people of Muslim countries. Your commitments to morality, and learning, and tolerance led to great historical achievements. And those values are alive in the Islamic world today. You have a rich culture, and you share the aspirations of men and women in every culture. Prosperity and freedom and dignity are not just American hopes, or Western hopes. They are universal, human hopes. And even in the violence and turmoil of the Middle East, America believes those hopes have the power to transform lives and nations.

This moment is both an opportunity and a test for all parties in the Middle East: an opportunity to lay the foundations for future peace; a test to show who is serious about peace and who is not. The choice here is stark and simple. The Bible says, "I have set before you life and death; therefore, choose life." The time has arrived for everyone in this conflict to choose peace, and hope, and life.

Thank you very much.

Appendix 3:
Prime Minister Ariel Sharon's Speech at the Herzliya Conference, December 2002

Twenty-seven months ago the Palestinian Authority commenced a campaign of terror against the State of Israel. Since then, we have been confronting a ferocious battle against a culture of bloodshed and murder, which has targeted Jews and Israelis everywhere. This campaign of terror was not coincidental; it was meticulously planned and prepared by the Chairman of the Palestinian Authority who misconstrued the high regard for human life in Israeli society as a way to compel us to capitulate to terrorism and coerce us into additional political concessions, concessions with nothing in return.

The past two years have been a difficult and painful test for Israel's national strength. The callousness and brutality of the terrorists was aimed—first and foremost—at undermining the sense of justness of the people of Zion. This is not the place to ask what led the PA Chairman to question the inner strength and determination which has always characterized the citizens of Israel, but it is clear that the terror has not defeated and will never defeat the State of Israel. They tried to break our spirit—and failed. This failure has resulted in scathing Palestinian criticism of Arafat, his path of terrorism and ongoing strategy of violence against Israel.

Today, most of the weight of the global leadership is in the United States. From the first days of the establishment of the State of Israel, our bond with the United States has been a supreme strategic asset. My Government has further consolidated our relations with the United States and formed a special closeness with the U.S. Administration and Congress. These special relations, the understanding of Israel's needs, and the cooperation with President Bush and his administration are unprecedented. Israel has in the United States true friends who genuinely and honestly care for our security.

Source: State of Israel, Prime Minister's Office, 4 December 2002, http://www.pmo.gov.il/ english/ts.exe?tsurl=0.41.6842.0.0.

Our political understandings with the United States and the Administration's understanding of our security needs have provided us with the required leeway in our ongoing war on terrorism. The war on terror has been accompanied by exorbitant costs and harsh financial damage, and I hope and believe that in the coming months we will receive special aid, to support us in our economic campaign.

On June 24th this year, President Bush presented his plan for a true solution to our conflict with the Palestinians [see Appendix 2]. The peace plan outlined in the President's speech is a reasonable, pragmatic and practicable one, which offers a real opportunity to achieve an agreement. We have accepted in principle the President's plan and the sequence presented therein. Our agreements with the Palestinians are based on the lessons the Americans learned from the Clinton-Barak plan, and my experience as one who has, for many years, participated in the security and political campaign in the Palestinian arena.

After concerted efforts, the U.S. Administration has understood and agreed that the only way to achieve a true peace agreement with the Palestinians is progress in phases, with the first phase being a complete cessation of terror. President Bush's speech is a fatal blow to Arafat's policy of terrorism and serves as proof of the failure of his attempt to achieve political gains by means of violence and terrorism. Only after a cessation of terror—and this is already agreed by most world leaders—will the commencement of peace negotiations between the parties be possible.

The American plan defines the parties' progress according to phases. The transition from one phase to the next will not be on the basis of a pre-determined timetable—which would have resulted in a buildup of heavy pressure on Israel towards the end of one phase and approaching the next phase. Rather, progress is determined on the basis of performance—only once a specific phase has been implemented, will progress into the next phase be possible.

On the basis of lessons learned from past agreements, it is clear to all that Israel can no longer be expected to make political concessions until there is proven calm and Palestinian governmental reforms.

In this context, it is important to remember that political concessions which will be made in the future—as those made in the past—are irreversible.

Even the current security reality, with the IDF operating freely inside Palestinian cities, arises from security needs and has not changed the political situation of two years ago. Israel will not re-control territories from which it withdrew as a result of political agreements. Therefore, the achievement of true and genuine coexistence must be a pre-condition to any discussion on political arrangements.

The Jewish people seek peace. Israel's desire is to live in security and in true and genuine coexistence, based, first and foremost, on the recognition of our natural and historic right to exist as a Jewish state in the land of Israel, while maintaining genuine peace.

The achievement of true coexistence must be carried out, first and foremost, by the replacement of the Palestinian leadership which has lied and disappointed, with different leadership which can—and more importantly—is willing to achieve real peace with the State of Israel. Unfortunately, there remain a few in Israel who believe that Arafat is still relevant. However, the U.S. Administration—with the world following in its footsteps—has already accepted our unequivocal position that no progress will be possible with Arafat as the Chairman of the Palestinian Authority. This man is not—and never will be—a partner to peace. He does not want peace.

The reconstruction of a Palestinian government should commence with governmental reforms which will ultimately lead to the establishment of a new, honest and peace-seeking administration, the removal of Arafat from his command of power and sources of financing, and from the decision-making process, and his relegation to a symbolic role.

In concordance with the sequence presented by President Bush, a Chief Executive Officer for Reforms will be appointed to the Palestinian Authority, and will constitute the head of the executive authority and the source of administrative authority. The provisional Palestinian government will administer a more efficient governmental system, fight the prevailing corruption in the PA and adhere to regulations of proper management. That government will lead a comprehensive process of reforms, maintain coexistence and prepare the general elections.

The elections in the Palestinian Authority should be held only at the conclusion of the reform process and after proper governmental regulations have been internalized. The goal is that these will be true elections—free, liberated and democratic.

Parallel with, and perhaps even prior to the governmental reforms, a security reform will be carried out, consisting of three principle parts:

1. Dismantling all existing security (terrorist) bodies, the majority of which are, in fact, involved in terror; these organizations, which are directly subordinate to Arafat, are essentially corrupt, and responsible for the deaths of hundreds of Israelis. These bodies will be replaced by two or three new organizations which will consist of a police force and security services; these new organizations will have a uniform command, which will be responsible for dismantling the current complex web of militias and armed gangs.
2. A Minister of the Interior will be appointed, and will be responsible for collecting illegal weapons and transferring them to a third party which will remove them from the PA territories and destroy them, and outlawing terrorist organizations.
3. In addition, cooperation on security issues between the PA and Israel will be renewed immediately.

The security reform must accompany a sincere and real effort to stop terrorism, while applying the "chain of preventive measures" outlined by the Americans: intelligence gathering, arrest, interrogation, prosecution and punishment.

Another important matter is the international demand for honest, effective, non-corrupt and transparent administration of the PA financial system; it is of great importance that the PA manage its financial affairs in concordance with the rules of proper government which will obligate the Palestinian Authority, inter alia, to produce a detailed budget, under a budgetary control system. This budgetary auditing system will ensure a balance between income and expenditure, and will verify that budget spending only serves appropriate economic purposes for the benefit and welfare of the Palestinian people. Such a supervising mechanism will also prevent the transfer of money for the financing of organizations or individuals involved in terror.

Taking the financial system out of Arafat's hands, and appointing a strong Minister of Finance with authority, constitutes an important factor for stopping the terrorist system operated by the Palestinian Authority. We are hopeful that the newly appointed PA Minister of Finance will operate a body to oversee and handle foreign aid funds received by the PA, and channel those funds to clearly defined projects which will benefit the Palestinian people and which are not contaminated by terror and corruption.

Peace and coexistence cannot be achieved without reform in the fields of education, media and information; the virulent incitement mechanism instigated by the PA against Israel must be stopped immediately; there can be no peace while the Palestinian education system instills in their young generation a culture of hatred, violence and terror.

Today, there is an increasing understanding in the world that stopping the phenomenon of suicide terrorism is dependent on: the cessation of incitement, ending the religious ratification of terrorism by radical elements in the Muslim world—with the encouragement and support of various Arab states.

The Palestinian justice system and law-enforcement must also undergo significant reforms. It is unheard of that in a law-abiding country, one hour after being arrested for theft, a suspect is sentenced and hanged, while on the other hand those involved in terror enter and leave prison in the "revolving door" principle. As long as those who commit crimes against the State of Israel are not severely punished, no progress will be made in President Bush's sequence.

The two sides will advance to the next phase of President Bush's sequence when a new, different, responsible and non-corrupt Palestinian leadership emerges. Terror will cease, and the Palestinian leadership will not allow it to be renewed. Civil and economic cooperation will be established. Incitement will be stopped and education towards peace will be fostered. At the same time, Israel will act to lift military pressure, create territorial continuity between Palestinian population centers, and ease daily life for the Palestinian population.

The second phase of President Bush's sequence proposes the establishment of a Palestinian state with borders yet to be finalized, and which will overlap with territories A and B, except for essential security zones. This Palestinian state will be completely demilitarized. It will be allowed to maintain lightly armed police and interior forces to ensure civil order. Israel will continue to control all entries and exits to the Palestinian state, will command its airspace, and not allow it to form alliances with Israel's enemies.

As I have promised in the past, President Bush's sequence will be discussed and approved by the National Unity Government which I intend to establish after the elections, and I will do my utmost to establish as broad a National Unity Government as possible.

In the final phase of President Bush's sequence negotiations will be opened to determine the final status of the Palestinian state and fix its permanent borders. As I emphasized, no progress will be made from one phase to the next until such time as quiet has been restored, Palestinian rule has undergone fundamental changes, and coexistence is ensured.

We all want peace. It is not a competition over who wants peace more. We also know that entering into political negotiations for peace is the true path which will bring about acceleration of economic growth and prosperity. I have said it before, and will say it again today: Israel is prepared to make painful concessions for a true peace. However, the government under my leadership will not be seduced into believing false promises which will endanger the security of the State of Israel.

My ideological and political path is well-known to you from the many functions I was privileged to fill during my decades of public service. These decisions are not easy for me, and I cannot deny that I have doubts, reservations and fears; however, I have come to the conclusion that in the present regional and international reality Israel must act with courage to accept the political plan which I described. There are risks involved, but also enormous opportunities.

I know that there are many who will attack the political outline I have just detailed. During the last few years many of us were tempted to believe in lightning-quick solutions which would lead to the security and peace we have longed for, and that this long-lasting conflict between our two peoples could be solved by the "blade of a sword"—I am familiar with these voices from both sides of the political spectrum.

Regrettably, this is not the way things are. These methods have failed—the solution to the conflict must be gradual and controlled. We must, in all stages, act with prudence and determination, exercise judgment, and make very sure that all commitments and agreements are implemented by both sides.

It is true that this is not a shining path which will lead us to instant, magical solutions, but I am certain that only by going forward in this direction, step by step, will we be able to achieve security for the Israeli people, and reach the peace we all yearn for.

Thank you, and happy holiday.

Appendix 4:
A Performance-Based Roadmap to a Permanent Two-State Solution to the Israeli-Palestinian Conflict, April 2003

The following is a performance-based and goal-driven roadmap, with clear phases, timelines, target dates, and benchmarks aiming at progress through reciprocal steps by the two parties in the political, security, economic, humanitarian, and institution-building fields, under the auspices of the Quartet [the United States, European Union, UN, and Russia]. The destination is a final and comprehensive settlement of the Israel-Palestinian conflict by 2005, as presented in President Bush's speech of 24 June, and welcomed by the EU, Russia and the UN in the 16 July and 17 September Quartet Ministerial statements.

A two-state solution to the Israeli-Palestinian conflict will only be achieved through an end to violence and terrorism, when the Palestinian people have a leadership acting decisively against terror and willing and able to build a practicing democracy based on tolerance and liberty, and through Israel's readiness to do what is necessary for a democratic Palestinian state to be established, and a clear, unambiguous acceptance by both parties of the goal of a negotiated settlement as described below. The Quartet will assist and facilitate implementation of the plan, starting in Phase I, including direct discussions between the parties as required. The plan establishes a realistic timeline for implementation. However, as a performance-based plan, progress will require and depend upon the good faith efforts of the parties, and their compliance with each of the obligations outlined below. Should the parties perform their obligations rapidly, progress within and through the phases may come sooner than indicated in the plan. Non-compliance with obligations will impede progress.

A settlement, negotiated between the parties, will result in the emergence of an independent, democratic, and viable Palestinian state living side by side in peace and security with Israel and its other neighbors. The settlement will resolve the Israel-Palestinian conflict, and end the occupation that began in 1967, based on the foundations of the Madrid Conference, the principle of land for peace, UNSCRs 242, 338, and 1397, agreements previously reached by the parties, and the initiative of Saudi

Source: U.S. State Department, 30 April 2003, usinfo.state.gov/regional/nea/summit/roadmaptexts.htm.

Crown Prince Abdullah—endorsed by the Beirut Arab League Summit—calling for acceptance of Israel as a neighbor living in peace and security, in the context of a comprehensive settlement. This initiative is a vital element of international efforts to promote a comprehensive peace on all tracks, including the Syrian-Israeli and Lebanese-Israeli tracks.

The Quartet will meet regularly at senior levels to evaluate the parties' performance on implementation of the plan. In each phase, the parties are expected to perform their obligations in parallel, unless otherwise indicated.

Phase I: Ending Terror and Violence, Normalizing Palestinian Life, and Building Palestinian Institutions—Present to May 2003

In Phase I, the Palestinians immediately undertake an unconditional cessation of violence according to the steps outlined below; such action should be accompanied by supportive measures undertaken by Israel. Palestinians and Israelis resume security cooperation based on the Tenet work plan to end violence, terrorism, and incitement through restructured and effective Palestinian security services. Palestinians undertake comprehensive political reform in preparation for statehood, including drafting a Palestinian constitution, and free, fair, and open elections upon the basis of those measures. Israel takes all necessary steps to help normalize Palestinian life. Israel withdraws from Palestinian areas occupied from September 28, 2000 and the two sides restore the status quo that existed at that time, as security performance and cooperation progress. Israel also freezes all settlement activity, consistent with the Mitchell report.

At the outset of Phase I:

- Palestinian leadership issues unequivocal statement reiterating Israel's right to exist in peace and security and calling for an immediate and unconditional ceasefire to end armed activity and all acts of violence against Israelis anywhere. All official Palestinian institutions end incitement against Israel.
- Israeli leadership issues unequivocal statement affirming its commitment to the two-state vision of an independent, viable, sovereign Palestinian state living in peace and security alongside Israel, as expressed by President Bush, and calling for an immediate end to violence against Palestinians everywhere. All official Israeli institutions end incitement against Palestinians.

Security

- Palestinians declare an unequivocal end to violence and terrorism and undertake visible efforts on the ground to arrest, disrupt, and restrain individuals and groups conducting and planning violent attacks on Israelis anywhere.
- Rebuilt and refocused Palestinian Authority security apparatus begins sustained, targeted, and effective operations aimed at confronting all those engaged in terror and dismantlement of terrorist capabilities and infrastructure. This includes commencing confiscation of illegal weapons and consolidation of security authority, free of association with terror and corruption.
- GOI [government of Israel] takes no actions undermining trust, including deportations, attacks on civilians; confiscation and/or demolition of Palestinian homes and property, as a punitive measure or to facilitate Israeli construction;

destruction of Palestinian institutions and infrastructure; and other measures specified in the Tenet work plan.

- Relying on existing mechanisms and on-the-ground resources, Quartet representatives begin informal monitoring and consult with the parties on establishment of a formal monitoring mechanism and its implementation.
- Implementation, as previously agreed, of U.S. rebuilding, training, and resumed security cooperation plan in collaboration with outside oversight board (U.S.-Egypt-Jordan). Quartet support for efforts to achieve a lasting, comprehensive cease-fire.
- All Palestinian security organizations are consolidated into three services reporting to an empowered Interior Minister.
- Restructured/retrained Palestinian security forces and IDF counterparts progressively resume security cooperation and other undertakings in implementation of the Tenet work plan, including regular senior-level meetings, with the participation of U.S. security officials.
- Arab states cut off public and private funding and all other forms of support for groups supporting and engaging in violence and terror.
- All donors providing budgetary support for the Palestinians channel these funds through the Palestinian Ministry of Finance's Single Treasury Account.
- As comprehensive security performance moves forward, IDF withdraws progressively from areas occupied since September 28, 2000 and the two sides restore the status quo that existed prior to September 28, 2000. Palestinian security forces redeploy to areas vacated by IDF.

Palestinian Institution-Building

- Immediate action on credible process to produce draft constitution for Palestinian statehood. As rapidly as possible, constitutional committee circulates draft Palestinian constitution, based on strong parliamentary democracy and cabinet with empowered prime minister, for public comment/debate. Constitutional committee proposes draft document for submission after elections for approval by appropriate Palestinian institutions.
- Appointment of interim prime minister or cabinet with empowered executive authority/decision-making body.
- GOI fully facilitates travel of Palestinian officials for PLC [Palestinian Legislative Council] and Cabinet sessions, internationally supervised security retraining, electoral and other reform activity, and other supportive measures related to the reform efforts.
- Continued appointment of Palestinian ministers empowered to undertake fundamental reform. Completion of further steps to achieve genuine separation of powers, including any necessary Palestinian legal reforms for this purpose.
- Establishment of independent Palestinian election commission. PLC reviews and revises election law.
- Palestinian performance on judicial, administrative, and economic benchmarks, as established by the International Task Force on Palestinian Reform.
- As early as possible, and based upon the above measures and in the context of open debate and transparent candidate selection/electoral campaign based on a free, multi-party process, Palestinians hold free, open, and fair elections.
- GOI facilitates Task Force election assistance, registration of voters, movement of candidates and voting officials. Support for NGOs [nongovernmental organizations] involved in the election process.

- GOI reopens Palestinian Chamber of Commerce and other closed Palestinian institutions in East Jerusalem based on a commitment that these institutions operate strictly in accordance with prior agreements between the parties.

Humanitarian Response

- Israel takes measures to improve the humanitarian situation. Israel and Palestinians implement in full all recommendations of the Bertini report to improve humanitarian conditions, lifting curfews and easing restrictions on movement of persons and goods, and allowing full, safe, and unfettered access of international and humanitarian personnel.
- AHLC [Ad Hoc Liaison Committee for the West Bank and Gaza] reviews the humanitarian situation and prospects for economic development in the West Bank and Gaza and launches a major donor assistance effort, including to the reform effort.
- GOI and PA continue revenue clearance process and transfer of funds, including arrears, in accordance with agreed, transparent monitoring mechanism.

Civil Society

- Continued donor support, including increased funding through [private voluntary organization] PVOs/NGOs, for people to people programs, private sector development and civil society initiatives.

Settlements

- GOI immediately dismantles settlement outposts erected since March 2001.
- Consistent with the Mitchell Report, GOI freezes all settlement activity (including natural growth of settlements).

Phase II: Transition—June 2003–December 2003

In the second phase, efforts are focused on the option of creating an independent Palestinian state with provisional borders and attributes of sovereignty, based on the new constitution, as a way station to a permanent status settlement. As has been noted, this goal can be achieved when the Palestinian people have a leadership acting decisively against terror, willing and able to build a practicing democracy based on tolerance and liberty. With such a leadership, reformed civil institutions and security structures, the Palestinians will have the active support of the Quartet and the broader international community in establishing an independent, viable state.

Progress into Phase II will be based upon the consensus judgment of the Quartet of whether conditions are appropriate to proceed, taking into account performance of both parties. Furthering and sustaining efforts to normalize Palestinian lives and build Palestinian institutions, Phase II starts after Palestinian elections and ends with possible creation of an independent Palestinian state with provisional borders in 2003. Its primary goals are continued comprehensive security performance and effective security cooperation, continued normalization of Palestinian life and institution-building, further building on and sustaining of the goals outlined in Phase I, ratification of a democratic Palestinian constitution, formal establishment of office of prime minister, consolidation of political reform, and the creation of a Palestinian state with provisional borders.

- International Conference: Convened by the Quartet, in consultation with the parties, immediately after the successful conclusion of Palestinian elections, to support Palestinian economic recovery and launch a process leading to establishment of an independent Palestinian state with provisional borders.
- Such a meeting would be inclusive, based on the goal of a comprehensive Middle East peace (including between Israel and Syria, and Israel and Lebanon), and based on the principles described in the preamble to this document.
- Arab states restore pre-intifada links to Israel (trade offices, etc.).
- Revival of multilateral engagement on issues including regional water resources, environment, economic development, refugees, and arms control issues.
- New constitution for democratic, independent Palestinian state is finalized and approved by appropriate Palestinian institutions. Further elections, if required, should follow approval of the new constitution.
- Empowered reform cabinet with office of prime minister formally established, consistent with draft constitution.
- Continued comprehensive security performance, including effective security cooperation on the bases laid out in Phase I.
- Creation of an independent Palestinian state with provisional borders through a process of Israeli-Palestinian engagement, launched by the international conference. As part of this process, implementation of prior agreements, to enhance maximum territorial contiguity, including further action on settlements in conjunction with establishment of a Palestinian state with provisional borders.
- Enhanced international role in monitoring transition, with the active, sustained, and operational support of the Quartet.
- Quartet members promote international recognition of Palestinian state, including possible UN membership.

Phase III: Permanent Status Agreement and End of the Israeli-Palestinian Conflict—2004–2005

Progress into Phase III, based on consensus judgment of Quartet, and taking into account actions of both parties and Quartet monitoring. Phase III objectives are consolidation of reform and stabilization of Palestinian institutions, sustained, effective Palestinian security performance, and Israeli-Palestinian negotiations aimed at a permanent status agreement in 2005.

- Second International Conference: Convened by Quartet, in consultation with the parties, at beginning of 2004 to endorse agreement reached on an independent Palestinian state with provisional borders and formally to launch a process with the active, sustained, and operational support of the Quartet, leading to a final, permanent status resolution in 2005, including on borders, Jerusalem, refugees, settlements; and, to support progress toward a comprehensive Middle East settlement between Israel and Lebanon and Israel and Syria, to be achieved as soon as possible.
- Continued comprehensive, effective progress on the reform agenda laid out by the Task Force in preparation for final status agreement.
- Continued sustained and effective security performance, and sustained, effective security cooperation on the bases laid out in Phase I.
- International efforts to facilitate reform and stabilize Palestinian institutions and the Palestinian economy, in preparation for final status agreement.

- Parties reach final and comprehensive permanent status agreement that ends the Israel-Palestinian conflict in 2005, through a settlement negotiated between the parties based on UNSCRs 242, 338, and 1397, that ends the occupation that began in 1967, and includes an agreed, just, fair, and realistic solution to the refugee issue, and a negotiated resolution on the status of Jerusalem that takes into account the political and religious concerns of both sides, and protects the religious interests of Jews, Christians, and Muslims worldwide, and fulfills the vision of two states, Israel and sovereign, independent, democratic, and viable Palestine, living side-by-side in peace and security.
- Arab state acceptance of full normal relations with Israel and security for all the states of the region in the context of a comprehensive Arab-Israeli peace.

Bibliography

Abbas, Mahmoud (Abu Mazen). "An Interview Held in the First Anniversary of Camp David Negotiations." *Al-Ayam*, 28–29 July 2001.

———. *Through Secret Channels*. Reading, UK: Garnet, 1995.

Abu Lughod, Lila. *Dramas of Nationhood: The Politics of Television in Egypt.* Chicago: University of Chicago Press, 2005.

Agha, Hussein, and Robert Malley. "The Last Negotiation: How to End the Middle East Peace Process." *Foreign Affairs* 81, no. 3 (May 2002): 10–18.

Ajami, Fouad. *The Dream Palace of the Arabs*. New York: Pantheon, 1998.

Albright, Madeleine. *Madam Secretary: A Memoir*. New York: Miramax, 2003.

Ali Kamel, Hassan. *Muharibun wa—mufawidun* [Warriors and peacemakers]. Cairo: Markaz al-Ahram lil-Targima wal-Nashr, 1986.

Alpher, Yossi. *V'gar ze'ev 'im ze'ev: ha-'Mitnahalim v'ha-Falastinim* [And the wolf shall dwell with the wolf: The settlers and the Palestinians]. Tel Aviv: Hakibbutz Hameuchad, 2001.

Amirav, Moshe. *Ha-ma'vak ha-Falastini 'al Yerushalayim* [The Palestinian struggle for Jerusalem]. Jerusalem: Jerusalem Institute for Israel Studies, 2002.

Arab Republic of Egypt. *White Paper on the Peace Initiatives Undertaken by President Anwar al-Sadat, 1971–1977*. Cairo: Ministry of Foreign Affairs, 1978.

Arafat, Yasir. "The Palestinian Vision of Peace." *New York Times*, 3 February 2002.

Aronson, Geoffrey. *Settlements and the Israel-Palestinian Negotiations: An Overview.* Washington, D.C.: Institute for Palestine Studies, 1996.

Artz, Lee, and Yahya Kamalipour, eds. *Bring 'em on: Media and Politics in the Iraq War*. Lanham, Md.: Rowman and Littlefield, 2004.

Aruri, Naseer. *Dishonest Broker: America's Role in Israel and Palestine*. Cambridge: South End Press, 2003.

'Asfur, Hasan. "Shlomo Ben-Ami's Occupation Complex." *Haaretz Friday Magazine,* 19 October 2001. In Hebrew.

"Ayalon-Nusseibeh Statement of Principles." *Haaretz*, 3 September 2002.

Azulai, Ariela, and Ophir Adi, eds. *Yamim ra'im: Bein ason l'utopya* [Bad days: Between disaster and utopia]. Tel Aviv: Patish, 2002.

Barghouti, Mustafa. "Generous to Whom?" *al-Ahram Weekly*, 10 May 2001.

Begin, Ze'ev Binyamin. *Sipur atsuv* [A sad story]. Tel Aviv: Yedioth Ahronoth, 2000.

Beilin, Yossi. *Laga'at bashalom* [To touch the peace]. Tel Aviv: Yedioth Ahronoth, 1997.

―――. *Madrikh le-yona petzu'ah* [Guide for a wounded dove]. Tel Aviv: Yedioth Ahronoth, 2001.

―――. *The Path to Geneva: The Quest for Permanent Agreement, 1996–2004.* New York: RDV Books, 2004.

Ben-Ami, Shlomo. *Chazit lelu oref: Mas'a el gevulot tahalich ha-shalom* [A front without a rearguard: A voyage to the boundaries of the peace process]. Tel Aviv: Yedioth Ahronoth, 2004.

―――. *Makom lekulam* [A place for all]. Tel Aviv: Hakibbutz Hameuchad, 1998.

Ben-Eliezer, Uri. *The Making of Israeli Militarism.* Bloomington: Indiana University Press, 1998.

Bentsur, Eytan. *Ha-derech lashalom overet b'Madrid* [The road to peace crosses Madrid]. Tel Aviv: Yedioth Ahronoth, 1997.

Benvenisti, Meron, ed. *Ha-boker l'maharat: 'Idan ha-shalom—lo utopia* [The morning after: The era of peace—not utopia]. Jerusalem: Carmel, 2002.

Blix, Hans. *Disarming Iraq: The Search for Weapons of Mass Destruction.* New York: Pantheon, 2004.

Boutros-Ghali, Boutros. *Egypt's Road to Jerusalem: A Diplomat's Story of the Struggle for Peace in the Middle East.* New York: Random House, 1997.

Carter, Jimmy. *Keeping Faith: Memoirs of a President.* New York: Bantam, 1982.

Clarke, Richard. *Against All Enemies: Inside America's War on Terror.* New York: Free Press, 2004.

Clinton, Bill. *My Life.* New York: Alfred A. Knopf, 2004.

Cohen, Akiba, and Gadi Wolfsfeld, eds. *Framing the Intifada: People and the Media.* Norwood, NJ: Albex, 1993.

Confino, Michael, ed. *Koach ha-milim v'khulshat hade'ah: Ta'amula, hasata v'hofesh ha-dibur* [The power of words and the frailty of reason: Propaganda, incitement, and freedom of speech]. Tel Aviv: Itzhak Rabin Center for Israel Studies, 2002.

Darwish, Mahmoud. *Halat hisar* [A state of siege]. Beirut: Riyad al-Rayyis lil-Kutub wa-al-Nashr, 2002.

Darwish, Mahmoud, and Samih al-Qasim. *Bein shnei hatsa'ei ha-tapuz* [Between the orange's two halves]. Translated by Hannah Amit-Kochavi. Jerusalem: Mifras Books, 1991.

Dayan, Moshe. *Breakthrough: A Personal Account of the Egypt-Israel Peace Negotiations.* London: Weidenfeld and Nicolson, 1981.

Dokh mevaker ha-medina mispar 48 [Annual Comptroller's Report no. 48]. Jerusalem: Mevaker ha-Medina, April 1998.

Dor, Daniel. *'Itonut tachat hashpa'ah* [Newspapers under the influence]. Tel Aviv: Babel, 2001.

―――. *M'ahorei homat magen* [Behind Operation Defensive Shield]. Tel Aviv: Babel, 2003.

"Draft of [the] Peace Agreement Between the State of Israel and the Arab Republic of Syria—Full Version." *Haaretz*, 13 January 2000. In Hebrew.

Drucker, Raviv. *Harakiri: Ehud Barak b'mivhan ha-totsa'ah* [Harakiri: Ehud Barak facing the results]. Tel Aviv: Yedioth Ahronoth, 2002.

Drummond, Philip, and Richard Patterson, eds. *Television in Transition.* London: British Film Institute, 1985.

Efrat, Elisha. *Jeojrafya shel kibush: Yehuda, shomron v'hevel 'aza* [Geography of occupation: Judea, Samaria, and the Gaza Strip]. Jerusalem: Carmel, 2002.

Eldar, Akiva, and Idit Zartal. *Adunei Ha'aretz: Hamitnahalim u-medinat Israel 1967–2004* [Lords of the Land: The Settlers and the State of Israel, 1967–2004]. Or Yehuda: Dvir, 2004.

Eldar, Akiva, and Nimrod Goren. *Ma'arav yerushalmi: ha-mahalachim l'ha'avarat shagrirut Artzot ha-brit labira* [The Jerusalem capital ambush: The political maneuvers to relocate the US embassy in Israel]. Jerusalem: Jerusalem Institute for Israel Studies, 2002.

Enderlin, Charles. *Shattered Dreams: The Failure of the Peace Process in the Middle East, 1995–2002.* Translated by Susan Fairfield. New York: Other Press, 2003.

Esposito, John. *Unholy War: Terror in the Name of Islam.* New York: Oxford University Press, 2002.

Feige, Michael. *Shtey mapot la'gada: Gush Emunim, Shalom Achshav v'itsuv ha-merhav ha-Yisraeli* [One space, two places: Gush Emunim, Peace Now, and the construction of Israeli space]. Jerusalem: Hebrew University Magnes Press, 2003.

Flamhaft, Ziva. *Israel on the Road to Peace.* Boulder, Colo.: Westview, 1996.

Folman, Yeshayahu. *Sippura shel gader ha-hafrada: Ha'omnam hafkarat hayim?* [The story of the separation fence: Life repudiation indeed?]. Jerusalem: Carmel, 2004.

Frum, David, and Richard Perle. *An End to Evil: How to Win the War on Terror.* New York: Random House, 2003.

Gavison, Ruth. *Yisrael k'hevra yehudit v'democratit* [Israel as both Jewish and democratic: Tensions and prospects]. Tel Aviv: Hakibbutz Hameuchad, 1999.

"Geneva Initiative: A Model for an Israeli-Palestinian Permanent Agreement." Tel Aviv: Geneva Initiative Headquarters, November 2003. In Hebrew.

Giacaman, George, and Dag Jorund Lonning, eds. *After Oslo: New Realities, Old Problems.* London: Pluto, 1998.

Gil, Eyal. "Dangerous Liaisons: The Relations Between Military Intelligence and Middle Eastern Studies in Israel." *Theory and Society* 20 (Spring 2002): 137–164.

Gowers, Andrew, and Tony Walker. *Arafat: The Biography.* London: Virgin, 1994.

Grossman, David. *Hiyuch ha-g'di* [The smile of the lamb]. Tel Aviv: Hakibbutz Hameuchad, 1983.

———. *Nochahim nifkadim* [Present though absent]. Tel Aviv: Hakibbutz Hameuchad, 1992.

———. *The Yellow Wind.* Translated by Haim Watzman. New York: Delta, 1989.

al-Hakim, Tawfiq. *The Return of Consciousness.* Translated by Bayly Winder. London: Macmillan, 1985.

Hall, Stuart. "Encoding and Decoding in Television Discourse." In Simon During, ed., *The Cultural Studies Reader.* London: Routledge, 1993, pp. 90–103.

Hammami, Rema, and Salim Tamari. "The Second Uprising: End or New Beginning?" *Journal of Palestine Studies* 30 (Winter 2001): 5–25.

Hanieh, Akram. "The Camp David Papers." *Journal of Palestine Studies* 30 (Winter 2001): 75–97.

Har'el, Yisrael. "On Three Oslo Crimes." *Haaretz,* 17 May 2001. In Hebrew.

Hass, Amira. *Drinking the Sea at Gaza: Days and Nights in a Land Under Siege.* New York: Metropolitan Books, 1999.

Hasson, Shlomo. *ha-Irgun ha-munitsipali shel metropolin Yerushalayim: Halufut ra'ayoniyot* [The municipal organization of the Jerusalem metropolitan area: Conceptual alternatives]. Jerusalem: Jerusalem Institute for Israel Studies, 1997.

Heikal, Muhammad. *Secret Channels: The Inside Story of Arab-Israeli Peace Negotiations.* London: HarperCollins, 1996.

———. *Sphinx and Commissar.* London: Collins, 1978.

Heller, Mark. *A Palestinian State: The Implications for Israel*. Cambridge: Harvard University Press, 1983.

Hirschfeld, Yair. *Oslo, Nuscha l'shalom: Ha-masa u-matan 'al heskem Oslo—ha-astrategya u-mimusha'* [Oslo, a formula for peace: From negotiation to implementation]. Tel Aviv: Am Oved, 2002.

Huntington, Samuel. *The Clash of Civilizations and the Remaking of World Order*. New York: Simon and Schuster, 1996.

Israel/Palestine Center for Research and Information [IPCRI]. "Analysis and Evaluation of the New Palestinian Curriculum: Reviewing Palestinian Textbooks and Tolerance Education Program." Jerusalem, Report 1, March 2003; Report 2, June 2004.

———. "Examination of Israeli Textbooks in Elementary Schools of the State Educational System." Jerusalem, April 2004.

"Israeli-Palestinian Interim Agreement on the Subject of the West Bank and Gaza Strip: Signed in Washington, D.C., September 28th 1995." Jerusalem: Information Center, Publication Service, 1996. In Hebrew.

Jamal, Amal. "The Palestinian Media: An Obedient Servant or a Vanguard of Democracy?" *Journal of Palestine Studies* 29 (Spring 2000): 45–59.

Kaspit, Ben, and Kfir Ilan. *Ehud Barak: Hayal mispar 1* [Ehud Barak: Israel's number 1 soldier]. Tel Aviv: Alpha Tikshoreth, 1998.

Katz, Elihu, and Tamar Liebes. "Mutual Aid in the Decoding of Dallas." In Philip Drummond and Richard Patterson, eds., *Television in Transition*. London: British Film Institute, 1985.

Kepel, Gilles. *Jihad: The Trail of Political Islam*. Cambridge: Harvard University Press, 2002.

Kerr, Malcolm. *The Arab Cold War, 1958–1967: Gamal 'Abd al-Nasir and His Rivals, 1958–1970*. London: Oxford University Press, 1971.

Khashan, Hilal. "Arab Attitudes Towards Israel and Peace." Washington, D.C.: Washington Institute, 2000.

al-Khuli, Lutfi, ed. *al-Ma'ziq al-'Arabi* [The Arab predicament]. Cairo: Markaz al-Ahram lil-Targima wal-Nashr, 1986.

Kimmerling, Baruch. *Politicide: Ariel Sharon's War Against the Palestinians*. London: Verso, 2003.

Kimmerling, Baruch, and Joel Migdal. *The Palestinian People: A History*. Cambridge: Harvard University Press, 2003.

Klein, Menachem. *Jerusalem: The Contested City*. New York: New York University Press, 2001.

———. *The Jerusalem Problem: The Struggle for Permanent Status*. Gainesville: University Press of Florida, 2003.

———. *Shovrim taboo: Ha-maga'im l'hesder keva b'yerushalayim, 1994–2001* [Shattering a taboo: The contacts toward a permanent status agreement in Jerusalem, 1994–2001]. Jerusalem: Jerusalem Institute for Israel Studies, 2001.

———. *Yonim beshmey yerushalayim: Tahalich ha-shalom v'ha'ir, 1977–1999* [Doves over Jerusalem's sky: The peace process and the city, 1977–1999]. Jerusalem: Jerusalem Institute for Israel Studies, 1999.

Kremnitzer, Yuval. "Ha-she'elot she-ein meorerim 'al gader ha-hafrada" [The questions not asked about the separation fence]. Israeli Democracy Institute, http://www.idi.org.il/hebrew/seventheye/article.asp?id=2162. In Hebrew.

Lewis, Bernard. *What Went Wrong? Western Impact and Middle Eastern Response*. New York: Oxford University Press, 2002.

Liebes, Tamar. *Reporting the Arab-Israeli Conflict: How Hegemony Works.* London: Routledge, 1997.

Lord, Amnon. *Ibadnu kol asher yakar haya: 'Al shorshav shel ha-smol ha-post-yehudi* [We have lost all that was dear: On the roots of the Israeli post-Jewish left]. Tel Aviv: Tamuz, 1988.

al-Madfai, Madiha Rashid. *Jordan, the United States, and the Middle East Peace Process, 1974–1991.* Cambridge, UK: Cambridge University Press, 1993.

al-Mahdi, Amin. *al-Sira'a al-'Arabi al-Yisra'ili: Azmat al-dimuqratiyya wal-salam* [The Arab-Israeli conflict: The crisis of democracy and peace]. Cairo: al-Dar al-Arabiyya lil-Nashr, 1999.

"Mahmud Abbas's Call for a Halt to the Militarization of the Intifada." *Journal of Palestine Studies* 32 (Winter 2003): 74–78.

Makovsky, David. "A Defensible Fence: Fighting Terror and Enabling a Two-State Solution." Washington, D.C.: Washington Institute for Near East Policy, Strategy Paper April 2004.

———. *Making Peace with the PLO: The Rabin Government's Road to the Oslo Accord.* Boulder, Colo.: Westview Press and the Washington Institute for Near East Policy, 1996.

Malley, Robert, "Fictions About the Failure at Camp David." *New York Times,* 8 July 2001.

———. "Mideast Prism Changed." *Los Angeles Times,* 20 September 2001.

Malley, Robert, and Hussein Agha. "A Reply to Ehud Barak." *New York Review of Books,* 13 June 2002.

———. "Camp David: The Tragedy of Errors." *New York Review of Books,* 9 August 2001.

———. "A Reply." *New York Review of Books,* 27 June 2002.

———. "Why Barak Is Wrong." *Guardian,* 27 May 2002.

Ma'oz, Moshe. *Syria and Israel: From War to Peacemaking.* Oxford: Clarendon Press, 1995.

Massad, Joseph Andoni. *Colonial Effects: The Making of National Identity in Jordan.* New York: Columbia University Press, 2001.

Meital, Yoram. "An Angry Ya'ari Is Not a Right Ya'ari." *Haaretz Friday Magazine,* 8 February 2002. In Hebrew.

———. *Egypt's Struggle for Peace: Continuity and Change, 1967–1977.* Gainesville: University Press of Florida, 1997.

———. "The Khartoum Conference and Egyptian Policy After the 1967 War: A Reexamination." *Middle East Journal* 54, no. 1 (Winter 2000): 64–82.

———. "The Lighthouse: On the Quality of the Israeli Commentators of Arab affairs." *The Seventh Eye,* 41 November 2002, pp. 38–39. In Hebrew.

Morris, Benny. "Arafat Didn't Negotiate—He Just Kept Saying No." *Guardian,* 23 May 2002.

———. *The Birth of the Palestinian Refugee Problem Revisited.* 2nd ed. New York: Cambridge University Press, 2004.

———. "I Do Not Support [Expulsion]." *Haaretz Friday Magazine,* 23 January 2004.

———. "For the Record." *Guardian,* 14 January 2004.

———. "An Interview with Ehud Barak." *New York Review of Books,* 13 June 2002.

———. "A New Exodus for the Middle East?" *Guardian,* 3 October 2002.

———. "Peace? No Chance." *Guardian,* 21 February 2002.

———. "The Rejection: Bleak Conclusions from the History of a People." *New Republic,* 21 and 28 April 2003.

————. *Righteous Victims: A History of the Zionist-Arab Conflict, 1881–1999*. London: John Murray, 2000.

Morris, Benny, and Ehud Barak. "Camp David and After—Continued." *New York Review of Books*, 27 June 2002.

el-Nawawy, Mohammed, and Adel Iskandar. *Al-Jazeera: The Story of the Network That Is Rattling Governments and Redefining Modern Journalism*. Cambridge: Westview, 2003.

Netanyahu, Benjamin. *A Place Among the Nations: Israel and the World*. New York: Bantam Books, 1993.

————. *Fighting Terrorism: How Democracies Can Defeat Domestic and International Terrorists*. New York: Noonday Press, 1997.

Nevo, Joseph. "Jordan, the Palestinians and the al-Aqsa Intifada." *Civil Wars* 6, no. 3 (2003): 70–85.

Newman, David. *The Impact of Gush Emunim: Politics and Settlement in the West Bank*. London: Croom Helm, 1985.

————. *A Durable Peace: Israel and Its Place Among the Nations*. New York: Warner Books, 2000.

————. *Population, Settlements, and Conflict: Israel and the West Bank*. Cambridge: Cambridge University Press, 1991.

Ophir, Adi, ed. *Zman emet: Intifadat al-Aqsa v'ha-smol ha-Yisraeli* [Real time—al-Aqsa intifada and the Israeli left]. Jerusalem: Keter, 2001.

Oren, Michael. *Six Days of War: June 1967 and the Making of the Modern Middle East*. New York: Oxford University Press, 2002.

Ortner, Sherry, ed. *The Fate of "Culture" and Beyond*. Berkeley: University of California Press, 1999.

Oz, Amos. *B'etsem yesh kan shtey milhamot* [But these are two different wars]. Jerusalem: Keter, 2000.

Palestinian National Authority. "Palestinian Vision for the Outcome of Permanent Status Negotiations: Nonpaper, 30 June 2002." http://www.pna.gov.ps/search/TitleDetails.asp?txtDocID=769.

Pearlman, Wendy. *Occupied Voices: Stories of Everyday Life from the Second Intifada*. New York: Thunder's Mouth Press, 2003.

Peres, Shimon. *The New Middle East*. New York: Henry Holt, 1993.

Peri, Yoram. *Between Battles and Ballots: Israeli Military in Politics*. Cambridge: Cambridge University Press, 1985.

————. "The Israeli Military and Israel's Palestinian Policy: From Oslo to the al-Aqsa Intifada." Washington, D.C.: U.S. Institute of Peace, Peace Works No. 47, 2002.

Pundak, Ron. *M'Oslo v'ad Taba: Tahalich sh'-shubash* [From Oslo to Taba: A process went wrong]. Jerusalem: Davis Institute for International Relations, 2001.

Quandt, William. *Camp David: Peacemaking and Politics*. Washington, D.C.: Brookings Institution, 1986.

————. *Peace Process: American Diplomacy and the Arab-Israeli Conflict Since 1967*. Washington, D.C.: Brookings Institution Press, 2001.

Reich, Zvi. "Reporters and Sources: Formation Patterns of News in Israel." Ph.D. diss., Hebrew University, September 2003.

Ross, Dennis. *The Missing Peace: The Inside Story of the Fight for Middle East Peace*. New York: Farrar, Straus and Giroux, 2004.

Rubenberg, Cheryl. *The Palestinians: In Search of a Just Peace*. Boulder: Lynne Rienner, 2003.

Rubinstein, Elyakim. *Drachey shalom* [Paths of peace]. Tel Aviv: Ministry of Defense, 1992.

Sadat, Anwar. *In Search of Identity: An Autobiography.* New York: Harper and Row, 1978.

Said, Edward. *The End of the Peace Process.* London: Granta Books, 2002.

———. *Out of Place: A Memoir.* London: Granta Books, 1999.

Savir, Uri. *The Process.* New York: Random House, 1998.

Sayigh, Yezid. "Armed Struggle and State Formation." *Journal of Palestine Studies* 26 (Summer 1997): 17–32.

———. *Armed Struggle and the Search for State: The Palestinian National Movement, 1949–1993.* Oxford: Oxford University Press, 1999.

Schueftan, Dan. *Korach ha-hafrada: Yisrael v'ha-rashut ha-falestinit* [The necessity of separation: Israel and the Palestinian Authority]. Haifa: Haifa University Press, 1999.

Seale, Patrick. "The Syria-Israel Negotiations: Who Is Telling the Truth?" *Journal of Palestine Studies* 29 (Winter 2000): 65–77.

"The Security Fence—Background, Facts, and Arguments from a Defensive Point of View: The Work of a Special Security Team. Updated February 2004." State of Israel, Ministry of Defense, http://www.intelligence.org.il/sp/c_t/sec/sec_f4_04 .htm. In Hebrew.

Sharansky, Natan. *The Case for Democracy: The Power of Freedom to Overcome Tyranny and Terror.* New York: Public Affairs, 2004.

Shavit, Ari. "Survival of the Fittest? An Interview with Benny Morris." *Haaretz Friday Magazine,* 9 January 2004.

Shehadeh, Raja. *Strangers in the House: Coming of Age in Occupied Palestine.* South Royalton, VT: Steerforth Press, 2002.

———. *When the Bulbul Stopped Singing: A Diary of Ramallah Under Siege.* London: Profile Books, 2003.

Sher, Gilead. *Be-merhak neggi'ah: 'Adut* [Within hand's reach: A testimony]. Tel Aviv: Yedioth Ahronoth, 2001.

Shikaki, Khalil. "Palestinian Public Opinion and the Peace Process: Changes Before and After the Second Intifada." Symposium at Ben-Gurion University, 11 May 2004.

Shilhav, Yosseph. *Hamayat yonim o hash'hat 'Avim? Vikuach pnim-yehudi 'al 'atid yerushalayim* [Territorial iconography: Geographical symbols of Jerusalem—A Jewish-Israeli perspective]. Jerusalem: Jerusalem Institute for Israel Studies, 2001.

Shlaim, Avi. *The Iron Wall: Israel and the Arab World.* London: Penguin Press, 2000.

Smith, Charles. *Palestine and the Arab-Israeli Conflict: A History with Documents.* 4th ed. Boston: Bedford/St. Martin's, 2001.

Sofer, Arnon. *Yisrael—demografya, 2003–2020: Sikunim v'efshruyot* [Israel's demography, 2003–2020: Risks and opportunities]. Haifa: Haifa University Press, 2003. In Hebrew.

Sontag, Deborah. "Quest for Mideast Peace: How and Why It Failed." *New York Times,* 26 July 2001.

Telhami, Shibley. *Power and Leadership in International Bargaining: The Path to the Camp David Accords.* New York: Columbia University Press, 1990.

Tessler, Mark. *A History of the Israeli-Palestinian Conflict.* Bloomington: Indiana University Press, 1994.

Teveth, Shabtai. *The Tanks of Tamuz.* New York: Viking, 1969.

Walsh, Elsa. "The Prince." *New Yorker,* 24 March 2003.

Watson, Geoffrey. *The Oslo Accords.* Oxford: Oxford University Press, 2000.

Woodward, Bob. *Bush at War.* New York: Simon and Schuster, 2002.

Ya'ari, Ehud. "I Was Right." *Haaretz Friday Magazine*, 1 February 2002. In Hebrew.

Yuran, Noam. *Arutz 2: Ha-mamlachtiyut ha-hadasha* [Channel 2—The new statehood]. Tel Aviv: Resling, 2001.

Zureiq, Qustantine. *al-A'mal al-fikriyya al-'amma lil-duktur Qustantine Zureik* [The complete works of Qustantine Zureik]. Beirut: Markaz Dirasat al-wahda al-'Arabiyya, 1994.

———. *Ma'na al-nakba* [The meanings of the *Nakba*]. Beirut: Dar al-'Ilm lil-Malayin, 1948.

Index

About the Book

Peace in Tatters was born in a set of questions with which the author, an Israeli scholar, has struggled for some years: What went wrong in the Israeli-Palestinian peace process before the July 2000 Camp David summit and during the crucial negotiations? How have the dominant narratives about the collapse of the peace process been crafted? Does the ongoing crisis mark the end of the road for the idea that the conflict can be settled on the basis of a two-state solution, with Palestinians and Israelis living as peaceful neighbors? Yoram Meital offers a powerful explanation of how and why the peace process developed, evolved, and ultimately fell apart.

Though rich in historical context, *Peace in Tatters* focuses primarily on the critical years of 2000–2004. Meital examines the major developments in the Israeli-Palestinian conflict, the evolving public-political discourse in Israeli and Palestinian societies, and, unflinchingly, US policy in the Middle East. He also explores the dramatic repercussions of the aborted political process for Israelis and Palestinians and for their opinions about the failure of the negotiations and the eruption of violence. His clear-sighted appraisal will help readers not only to understand what went wrong but also to see present events in an essentially different way.

Yoram Meital is senior lecturer in the Department of Middle East Studies and chair of the Chaim Herzog Center for Middle East Studies and Diplomacy at Ben-Gurion University. His previous publications in English include *Egypt's Struggle for Peace: Continuity and Change, 1967–1977.*